THE
WRIGHT
WAY

Reminiscences on 60 years
of coachbuilding in Ballymena

Jack Kernohan

Dedication

This book is dedicated to all those – the employees of The Wright Group, its suppliers, chassis partners and customers – who have made the company what it is today and who have worked together to design and build the highest quality products over the last sixty years.

Of course, none of this would have come about without the enthusiasm and foresight of two men – Bob Wright and his son William. We owe them a debt of gratitude.

Management and staff gather outside the Galgorm factory to mark the company's sixty years in business.

First Edition
First impression

© Jack Kernohan and Colourpoint Books 2010

Designed by April Sky Design, Newtownards
Printed by W&G Baird Ltd, Antrim

ISBN 978 1 906578 50 3

Unless otherwise credited images are from the
company's or author's collections.

Colourpoint Books
Colourpoint House
Jubilee Business Park
21 Jubilee Road
NEWTOWNARDS
County Down
Northern Ireland
BT23 4YH

Tel: 028 9182 6339
Fax: 028 9182 1900

E-mail: info@colourpoint.co.uk
Web site: www.colourpoint.co.uk

Jack Kernohan was born in 1937 on a farm on the outskirts of Ballymena, approximately two miles from where The Wright Group is based today. He's the oldest in a family of six – four boys and two girls.

He attended the Fourtowns Primary School, in the local village of Ahoghill, before completing his education at Ballymena Technical College.

Jack's father was a carpenter and he wanted to follow in his father's footsteps so he began an apprenticeship with McLaughlin and Harvey, then one of the largest engineering and building contractors in Northern Ireland, in 1951.

He was attracted to coachbuilding and joined Robert Wright and Son Limited, as the company was then known, in 1955 and accepted every opportunity to aid his progression through the company.

Appointed Workshop Foreman in 1961, Jack became Production Manager two years later. This latter position was a challenging role in that he was entirely responsible for the operations of the company during a period when many technological changes were taking place within the industry.

By 1967, the company needed to provide an after sales service support for its range of products and Jack saw this as a major opportunity. Supporting the customer in their time of need would ensure that the company sales team had a better chance of securing that customer's next order.

In February 1970 Jack was appointed Sales Manager, initially for Ireland; this territory was increased to also cover all of the United Kingdom. He was promoted to Sales Director in 1988, a position he held up until his retirement on 31 August 2005.

During his long service with the company, Jack made numerous friends. Many, like him, have since retired but they all still retain an interest in the latest range of products which the company now builds.

Kowloon Motor Bus AVW64 (LR 7009) is a Volvo Super Olympian. It is seen on the busy Nathan Road, Kowloon.

The Wright Group is proud of its partnerships with local, national and international suppliers. We are pleased that several of our partners have supported Jack with generous contributions to help bring his reminiscences of our proud history to a wider audience.

TECHNOLOGY WITH INTEGRITY

Although this volume sets out to record the reminiscences of author Jack Kernohan, in reality it achieves this and a great deal more. Jack has, from his personal viewpoint, effectively written the history of Wrightbus. Few are better qualified to undertake this task as he was one of the very small, tightly knit team who helped transform a small bespoke coachbuilder into a world leader in bus manufacturing.

As an author, as in real life, Jack never loses sight of the human aspects of the enterprise and this provides additional interest even beyond his excellent chronicles of business change through the decades. He writes with an obvious fondness for his subject and I am grateful that the story of Wrightbus has been so assiduously documented for present and future generations to enjoy.

History and nostalgia are to be enjoyed, but we can also learn some lessons. Wrights is a family firm and as a successful business we have attracted offers to be taken over by companies from outside Northern Ireland. Instead we have put our faith in the people of Ballymena and the surrounding districts, and they have not let us down. In recent years we attracted many workers from other countries, especially from Eastern Europe and they, too, played an important role. A great many people, past and present, have contributed to the success of Wrightbus and for all their efforts I am very grateful.

This book is not intended to be an academic study, neither does it require specialist knowledge to enjoy. It is a good read and I have pleasure commending it to you.

Dr William Wright, OBE

Peter Hendy CBE
Commissioner of Transport
for London

Transport
for London

I first came across Wrights in 1987-8. At the time London Buses was moving from a monolithic, monopoly organisation to one subject to competitive tendering and having to innovate to survive. We had recently experimented successfully with the first (for London) generation of minibuses, and I was pursuing a project to convert two Routemaster routes to high-frequency midibus operation. Trevor Erskine brought me a bold design of body on a mid-engined Leyland small coach chassis – it was a great design, but couldn't compare with the Mercedes 811. So although Wrights didn't get that order, it was noticed at London Buses. A little later the 11 companies were formed, and I became MD of CentreWest. We pursued a bold policy of converting services to midibus at high frequency, and generating patronage. Experience with Mercedes 811s, conventionally coachbuilt, convinced me that we would do better to find a stronger body construction, but with parts that could be unscrewed for repair rather than bonded, welded, or rivetted. So we looked at Wrights for the bodies for 90 Renault S75s. I remember going to the (old) factory, a collection of several sheds, it seemed to me, and being both amazed at the relatively primitive working environment but also by the sophisticated nature of the Alusuisse body frame and the ingenuity with which our ideas had been turned into a very sturdy, but simply repaired, body. John Whitworth (the CentreWest Engineering Director) and I were both delighted by the bodies on the 90 buses (maybe it was Wrights largest bus order at that time?) – and it helped us through our disappointment at the lack of stamina of the chassis ... those bodies, of course, would have lasted twice the life of the chassis, and we subsequently used the buses at Beeline, when we bought that company in 1996, and then in FirstGroup at Leicester and other places. We registered all the buses in Ballymena, too, the first ever London buses with Northern Ireland numberplates!

We found that conventional van chassis were not good enough for mainstream operation in London. Dennis just then brought out the Dart, firstly only bodied by Duple. We thought the body ugly, badly designed, and didn't buy any. Then William managed to get the first of the chassis to be released for alternative bodywork, and Trevor designed the Handybus, which CentreWest bought, in the end, about 140 or so of. That design will stand as one of the best modern bus designs since the war – a tribute to attending to customer needs and 'fitness for purpose' – robust, easy to repair, comfortable, and handsome. I think that design really put Wrights on the map. It wasn't the cheapest to buy, but I'm sure the whole life costs amply repaid the initial investment.

Andrew Braddock at the time was advancing the cause of low-floor, wheelchair access vehicles. London Buses were persuaded by him to fund the development of single-deck designs, and two chassis were ordered - Scania and Dennis. Wrights, of course, first off the mark for innovation, built the bodies, and they paved the way for the low-floor bus of today, and subsequently the low-floor midibus and the

low-floor double-decker. CentreWest got the second batch (we couldn't be first all the time!) but we made the most noise about the success of Wrights design!

William had never built a double-decker, and I can remember talking to him about the limitations to his business of not being able to do so . . . so, in due course, came a new factory, with a higher roof and, later, a double-decker, stylish, well built, and with the same repairability as the other products.

One of the hallmarks of Wrights, and William's leadership, is the constant drive to look forward. The bus revolution in London that started after the new mayoralty in 2000, produced the growth in the market that the new factory was poised to supply; together with a fine poster advertising 'Here in greater numbers – more than 300 extra buses in London', with, no accident, a phalanx of Wrights Geminis cresting a hill in a blaze of sunshine! The foyer of the "new" factory has one; and my dining room has another. (See page 175)

And then London got interested in hybrid power, as a means of reducing emissions and economising on fuel. Wrights, in the lead again, with the first single-deck hybrids in London and the first double-decker, not only in London but the world, led all the rest; a tribute to William's foresight and energy, and the product still developing.

The change of Mayor from Ken Livingstone to Boris Johnson in May 2008 did not change the emphisis on progress in London. Hybrid bus development continued, with more vehicles entering service. The new Mayor, however, committed himself to the design and manufacture of a 'New Bus for London', which we at Transport for London took up with enthusiasm. Whilst the enthusiast world (and general public) were entering into a competition to see what the shape of such a vehicle would look like, Wrights was busy taking an old Routemaster to bits to learn the lessons of the past in a bid to be part of the future. That proved to be successful, when Wrights won the contract to design and build the New Bus for London in December 2009. All of the resourcefulness shown by the company so far will be needed to deliver a brand new, emissions friendly, 21st century bus by the end of 2011, but on my experience, if anyone can do this, Wrights can, utilising the strengths of the company built up over many years.

I salute William and his company for the tremendous strides in growth and innovation; huge contributions to the industry over many years, and good products for operators and passengers. And also, of course, the nicest people one could wish to meet – good to do business with, and now, of course, old friends too.

Peter Hendy CBE

This is a story that had to be told. And note that I say a story, not a history. It's about two men who had a vision, who knew what could be achieved and, ultimately, built what is today one of the United Kingdom's main suppliers of service buses. Those men were Robert Wright and his son, William.

There are two things which are important to me about the development of what is now The Wright Group –

1. It's a successful Northern Ireland company based in a small town in County Antrim; and

2. I was a part of it for over fifty years and I will be eternally grateful to the Wright family for allowing me to be a part of the company's success.

So this book is dedicated in appreciation to the Wright family, but particularly William, who first made the investment and opened the door to me to a career that I have thoroughly enjoyed.

I said that this book was a story, not a history, and that's because much of what is here is written from memory. That's one of the reasons you'll find that people are often to the fore. Historical detail for much of the early years simply doesn't exist, probably because Wrights is a company which is always looking to the future.

The content of this book has been compiled with the assistance of a number of my former colleagues. Like the development and the progress of the company, it was a team effort, and without their input and assistance this story may never have been written. I am enormously indebted to all those who helped not only in the preparation of this record of the company's progress, but also to all those who assisted me in my various management roles, over my fifty years working for the company. The thoughts expressed in this book are entirely mine and may not necessarily be the thoughts of the management of the company.

I must particularly mention:

Mr Robert Wright, his son William and daughter Muriel, William Finlay, Robert Craig, Albert Hanna, Damian McGarry (who succeeded Albert Hanna), Trevor Erskine, Aveline Finlay (a daughter of Muriel), Sam McCartney, Adrian Robinson, Ivan Stewart, Allister Campbell, Paul Blair and last but not least my colleague in sales, Charles Moseby and all the girls in the sales office who assisted the team achieve their objectives in winning new customers. I must pay tribute to William's family: Jeff Wright, Mandy Knowles, Dr Lorraine Rock and their mother Ruby who kindly provided me with a number of old family photographs.

There are others, too many to name, within the company, its customers and the suppliers' teams to whom I will be eternally grateful for their friendship and support; I am indebted to them all. But there are four people who deserve special mention in connection with this project. Ted Hesketh, previously Managing Director of Translink and now a Director of The Wright Group, was the one who encouraged me to place my memories of the Company on record. He has supported the project from start to finish. At Ted's suggestion, Paul Savage was asked to come on board and I'm extremely grateful to him for his advice and expertise that have turned my ramblings into the work you have before you. Paul spent many hours reading and re-writing my text, dividing it into sensible chapters and asking me awkward questions along the way. His comprehensive knowledge of buses and his many contacts in the industry have been invaluable to me in writing this book. He was also

Jack with Louise Macdonald, Company Secretary (left) and Claire Coulter, Marketing Manager.

responsible for enhancing many of the photographs in the following pages. Louise Macdonald, the Company Secretary, used all her organisational skills to provide an invaluable link with the management team. The final person in the team was the Company's Marketing Manager, Claire Coulter. Claire has been most helpful, keeping Paul and I updated with press releases, brochures and photographs and was more than happy to get answers from her contacts when we were stuck. I know both Ted and Paul will join me in saying a big 'Thank You' to Claire; she really is an asset to the Company!

I must put on record, too, my thanks to those who sent me such ringing endorsements of the Company. I found that particularly gratifying. You will note that, in several of those endorsements, memories of Northern Ireland, and the hospitality of its people in what were difficult times, remain strong. That, I believe, comes from the down to earth way the Company worked in its early days as a bus manufacturer.

It would be remiss of me not to put on record my appreciation of the expertise of not only the engineers developing and preparing the engineering drawings but also the dedication and loyalty of the entire workforce. On many occasions they delivered products to customers given a very short lead-time. I should add that, as a result, we were able to build a good rapport with our customers. We must also include the after sales service team, later to be called Wright Customcare, in supporting all of the company's products. Without them we would not have succeeded.

And finally in this long list of thanks, I must also pay tribute to someone who supported me throughout my career at Wrights, my wife, Martha. She put up with me leaving home early in the morning, coming back late at night, away for days on end, missing meals, our children's birthday parties and other family celebrations, all without a bad word. Now that this book is on the shelves she will be much happier, especially when I've tidied up all the papers and photographs which have been spread around our home for the last three years!

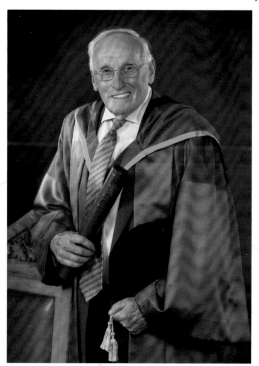

Dr William Wright, OBE

But we are rushing ahead; we need to go back to where it all started, to learn how William Wright, from humble beginnings in his father's business in Warden Street, Ballymena has become one of the most successful industrialists in Northern Ireland. Yes, like everyone else he has made mistakes; he'll willingly tell you the major one was developing the Contour coach. It was an excellent product, just the wrong time, but he saw what was happening in the coach market and quickly got out of it! However, there is a positive side. William decided to mothball the Contour until the market improved, and although times and money were tight the company survived whilst others, such as Duple, went under. In the meantime, a fire had destroyed all the Contour moulds with the consequence that the model was never resurrected.

Wrights not only survived but, with William's dynamic leadership and go-ahead management, went on to develop the company into what today is one of the largest family-owned bus manufacturing businesses in Europe, and one of the most successful commercial businesses in Northern Ireland, something which has been recognised by his being appointed an Officer of the Order of the British Empire by Her Majesty, Queen Elizabeth II, for his business acumen and in 2009, as work on this volume was drawing to a close, William was awarded the honorary degree of Doctor of Science (DSc) by the University of Ulster for his services to manufacturing in Northern Ireland.

Jack Kernohan
Ballymena, May 2010

Humble Beginnings

Travel anywhere in the United Kingdom by public transport today and the chances are high that at some stage you will use the products of a factory in Ballymena, Northern Ireland. That modern, hi-tech factory is at Galgorm and is the home of The Wright Group of companies, but known to most in the industry simply as Wrights of Ballymena. But it wasn't always like this – gleaming and full of hi-tech equipment . . .

Robert Wright and his wife, Mary, on their wedding day in 1926.

The history of Wrightbus goes back to 1900 when Robert Wright was born on a farm at the Doonans, in the headlands of the pretty village of Carnlough, on County Antrim's world famous, scenic coast road. When he was in his mid-teens, Bob (as he was better known) began an apprenticeship as a joiner, working for various building firms in and around Ballymena. It was also while travelling to work in the Ballymena area that he met the girl who would later become his wife. She was Mary Thompson, a young lassie from the village of Broughshane. They were married in 1926.

In the early 1930s, in search of a better life with better job prospects, Bob emigrated to New Zealand and whilst there worked on the construction of the Dunedin Exhibition Centre. The plans were that, when he got established, Mary would join him but this was not to be. Those plans were changed by a death in Mary's family and Bob returned to Ireland, setting up home in Warden Street, close to the Ballymena Show Grounds. He took a job with Brownlee's, a local builder, before setting up his own joinery business behind the house in Warden Street.

Reminiscences on 60 years of coachbuilding in Ballymena

The man with the vision to make it happen – Robert Wright

These were the years following the Second World War; times were hard and work in the building trades was difficult to find unless you went over to London where work was more plentiful rebuilding the bombed city. As Robert and Mary now had two children – William and Muriel – to feed and clothe, that wasn't an option. Initially, the business was founded on house repairs and general building and whatever work was available. Bob was a highly skilled carpenter and his skills with the use of wood working equipment were recognised and he often had calls asking for assistance outside the remit of a general builder.

One such call was from the manager of Ballymena and Harryville Co-op asking for his assistance to repair the wooden framework on several bread delivery vans; in those days most vehicle bodywork was constructed from hardwoods. Bob saw an opportunity and, on being asked by the manager if he could build a van if they were to purchase a chassis scuttle from the chassis manufacturer, the reply was, "I most certainly can and if I cannot build a better van than you are currently receiving I will close the doors."

The rest of the story, as they say, is now history . . .

In 1946, Bob Wright was asked by the manager of Ballymena and Harryville Co-op to repair the wooden framework on a few of their bread delivery vans. Bob saw an opportunity and, on being asked if he could build a van, his reply was, "I most certainly can." Austin RZ 171 was one such van.

Robert Wright Coachworks Limited – The Early Years

The Co-op venture was a success and Bob decided to concentrate on coachbuilding. In 1946, he laid the foundations for the thriving business which exists today by setting up Robert Wright Coachworks Ltd. Even then it was known simply as Wrights of Ballymena!

Bob's son, William, was educated at Ballymena Technical College and subsequently joined his father in the business. The company went from strength to strength and soon additional staff were required to cope with the demand. House repairs had been phased out and high quality coach-built products were now the company's mainstream products. And, as the economy of Northern Ireland was beginning to recover following the war and the transport of goods by road was becoming more important, the decision by Bob to develop a coachbuilding company was proving to have been the right one. The sales potential for the Wright products was increasing and to meet the increased demand, additional workspace and employees were needed.

William Wright at the age of 25. Now in his 80s, he still takes a keen interest in developing the Company's product range.

Although he was extremely busy at work, William still had time to look at the ladies, and made what was to prove another wise decision in the history of the company; in 1953, he married, Ruby, a daughter of David Kernohan who resided in the Moravian village of Gracehill, about three miles from Ballymena, and just a short distance from the present factory. Ruby has been a tower of strength, providing moral support and encouragement when needed. I hasten to add that Ruby, for whom I have the highest regard, is not on my family tree which I have researched, going back to 1730.

In 1951, a large site was purchased in Hugomount, off Ballymena's Cushendall Road. The Wrights initially built a new home on the site and, when that was complete, a new purpose-built factory was also built there. The factory included a machine shop, stores and offices, which ultimately would bring all the company's operations all under one roof.

With the additional space available, and a growing order book, the company set about recruiting additional staff. One of the company's employees in those early days was Bobby Cameron, a native of Gracehill. We were pals attending dances, etc at the weekends. He advised me that the company was employing additional workers and I met with William, had a brief interview and joined the company in September 1955.

To assist in the management of the company, Bob's daughter, Muriel, had joined in 1947. Her role was vitally important to the company at that stage in its development – purchasing, wages, banking, telephones, etc to mention a few of the many duties for which she was responsible. Muriel retired from the company in 1986 to assist her husband run their business, Technical Transport Products.

In those early days William had a dual role. Apart from managing the workshops and interviewing and recruiting staff, his other key task was equally important – meeting with prospective customers, selling the company's products, whilst developing new ones to meet customers' future needs. Action had to be taken to reduce his workload. William turned to a boyhood friend and recruited Robert Craig, who resided locally on the outskirts of the village of Cullybackey. Robert's role in the company was to initially increase production and, by improved manufacturing techniques, to reduce labour costs.

Muriel Wright joined her father's business in 1947 taking responsibility for purchasing, wages, banking, etc. She retired in 1986

William Wright was, certainly up until my retirement, the driving force in the company. However then, like today, it was the flexibility of the workforce and team spirit that motivated the company. When Robert Craig left the company William approached me with an offer to take overall responsibility for product production/services. This was a new challenge which I readily accepted, and have never regretted.

The success of the company owed a lot to the workforce, which had been recruited by both William Wright and Robert Craig. Most of those recruited were locals, living within a ten mile radius of the factory. Individuals who played a significant role in the company in those early years included:

- George Hill from Ballylurgan, Randalstown, who went on to become a schoolteacher specialising in teaching woodwork;
- William Finlay from Kells, now Managing Director of local company, Technical Transport Products;
- Bobby Cameron from Straid, Ahoghill who on leaving the company became a teacher in the College of Technology in Belfast before becoming a civil servant;
- David Robinson from Broughshane went on to be Sales Manager of Marley Div. in Northern Ireland;
- John Wright from Rocavon, Broughshane;
- James Scullion from Ballymena;
- Gordon Frew from Cloughmills;
- Ray Martin from Broughshane;
- Wylie Alexander from Ahoghill; and
- one of his apprentices, Jimmy Smyth, from Kells, who has recently retired from the company having completed fifty years service.

Of course, there were many others who over the years played an equally important role in the progress of the company. In those days there was no drawing office, no draughtsman, no engineers, no structural engineers, and NO computers!; most of the work was not repetitive and therefore all the production decisions were made by the skilled workforce (some of whom I have paid tribute to above) and the production supervisor.

Production facilities had been expanded to meet demand so, to ensure that the company maximised its full potential, additional field sales staff were now required. The company policy was to promote from within its own workforce and William Finlay, who up to then had played an important role in the machine shop, applied for the position in sales, a role in which he was to become very successful.

William Finlay was working in the busy sales office with Bob Wright's daughter, Muriel. Obviously she wasn't always engrossed in her work and she couldn't help but notice the good-looking lad from Kells sitting across the office. It soon became apparent that this partnership was destined to become much more. Their love blossomed and they got married on 21 March 1964. They now have a family of three, all girls, two of them now assisting their father run the successful Technical Transport Products business in Ballymena.

Purchasing and Stores now needed to be upgraded and reorganised and the company recruited a man who was to play a very important role in its future development. Albert Hanna, originally from Harryville in Ballymena, joined Wrights in 1964. Albert had served his apprenticeship in the motor trade in RJ Moore's in the town's Linenhall Street. Initially his tasks were to ensure the raw materials were purchased at a competitive price

William Finlay, from Kells, Co Antrim, worked in the sales office with Bob's daughter, Muriel. They married in 1964.

Albert Hanna, who joined Wrights in 1964 and was played a pivotal role in the Company's development. Albert retired in 2000.

and were available when production called them off. His success in achieving his targets, and motivating the men under his control, led to Albert being promoted to Production Manager then to Production Director before his retirement in 2000, having completed thirty-six years service. Albert was tasked by the company management to assist the sales team penetrate the United Kingdom mainland market and deliver orders to new customers. On many occasions, he was asked to do the (almost) impossible, but with the assistance of the dedicated workforce he always delivered the product on time. Today's management and workforce at The Wright Group owe a lot to the engineering and management expertise of Albert Hanna.

An early version of the Company logo as applied to all products leaving the factory.

The 1950s and 1960s
Shopping with Wrights

A Commer flat bed lorry delivered locally to Mr Burns in Rasharkin, is seen outside the Wright family home/workshop on Warden Street, Ballymena.

In the early 1950s, potential customers had a much greater choice than now when purchasing a new commercial vehicle; it could be a Ford, Commer, Karrier, Austin, Morris, Albion, Leyland, AEC, Dodge, Guy, Foden, ERF or a Bedford. These vehicles were all manufactured in the United Kingdom but over the years, one by one, these manufacturers have all disappeared. The blame for losing these valuable engineering resources lies, in my view, with various Governments who, over the years, allowed these manufacturing skills to disappear. Today, for example, as a result of this, most British buses are built on foreign chassis. No doubt some of the blame lies with the senior management of the companies who failed to respond to the needs of the market by not investing in product research and development. Robert Wright Coachworks Ltd was familiar with all of the aforementioned chassis having built specialist bodywork on all of them over the years.

In the late 1950s/early 1960s, when there were considerably fewer cars on the roads, few women in Northern Ireland had the opportunity to learn to drive. They, therefore, had difficulty in getting to the local shops to purchase the groceries. There were no supermarkets, although the local communities were well provided for by large grocery outlets, all family-owned. William Wright saw a niche in the market. If the housewife had difficulty getting to and from the shops, why not design and build a mobile shop that would

Wrights developed the mobile shop concept. This one is on a Bedford chassis.

Interior of mobile shop showing the different storage and shelving which could be fitted.

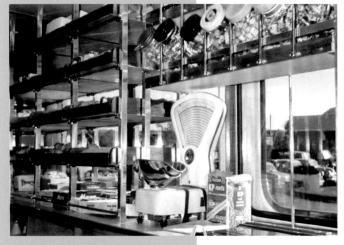

bring the groceries to her door? Within a few weeks the company had developed the project to the pre-production stage.

William discussed the project with TBF Thompson, a local businessman from Garvagh, who saw the many advantages the mobile shop could offer. Thompson's company was the area distributor for Commer Commercials, in whose product range was the Walk Thru, an ideal chassis, competitively priced for the market. A chassis for the initial prototype was delivered to the factory and build commenced, supervised by Robert Craig.

Whilst a regular supply of groceries was important in rural areas, many of the local farmers' wives also sold their surplus farm produce, eg hen eggs, to the company operating the mobile shop and this surplus was collected when the groceries were being delivered. As electrical power supply was not available to many residing in rural areas, the Wrights-built mobile shops were also designed to provide a wider range of services to the customers. For example, a large compartment, with access from the rear, housed the eggs, peat briquettes

The mobile shop was built on chassis other than Bedford. This one, now preserved by Boyd Fenton, is on a Karrier. The gentleman in the picture is Wrights Alastair Campbell.

and bottled gas cylinders, while fitted below floor level was a 200-gallon paraffin oil tank to ensure that homes without electricity, and there were many, had sufficient heat and light during the long winter evenings.

The range of mobile shops soon expanded to cover other segments of the market such as butchers, drapery and hardware, including mobile exhibition/display units. TBF Thompson supplied most of the Commer chassis and such was the demand that they built orders for stock providing 'off-the-shelf' delivery to their customers. This idea of building stock vehicles was an entirely new sales process and benefited both companies; Wrights had continuous production whilst TBF Thompson's sales team could offer immediate delivery. A friendship developed between the management of the two companies that is still enjoyed today, some fifty years later. Mr Thompson, a devout Christian, passed away in December 2008.

The success of this product range and the partnership with the chassis distributor gave Wrights the confidence to examine other potential markets and develop new products.

The workforce c1960, including Bob and William Wright (extreme right)

Darryl Magee

William Wright is, in my mind, not only one of life's true characters in every sense of the word, but he has been one of Northern Ireland's outstanding entrepreneurs, a man of vision and leadership, and a man of innovation, whose legacy will live on for generations to come.

Down through the years Wrightbus has featured strongly and consistently on the pages of *Export & Freight*, the transport magazine of which I was one of the founding joint publishers; today I have a 'consultative role' on the magazine now headed up by publishers Garfield Harrison and Helen Beggs, who trade as 4Square Media.

Export & Freight has tracked the Wrightbus story right from those early days, reporting on the development and successes of virtually all the models to come off the production lines, those that served routes around the streets of Belfast to those making an impact today on the streets of Las Vegas.

Those early models, I recall, included the Wright Handybus, a single-deck bus body built primarily on a Dennis Dart chassis, although it was also built on a small number of Leyland Swift chassis. Today, of course, Wrightbus vehicles are more of an eye catcher, like the StreetCar, and it too has featured prominently in our magazine, and rightly so.

One of my first encounters with William, and I will never forget it, was back in the 1960s. It ended up with me coming away with a bottle of whiskey, and I don't even drink the stuff; mind you, neither did William.

We were drawing up a feature on the company for *Export & Freight* and I was invited, along with other magazine journalists from across the UK, to take part in a driving competition around a set course in Antrim. It was to promote a new bus model – on a Bedford, I believe - and there were more experienced drivers there than me, but as fortune would have it, I won the darn thing and my prize was a big bottle of Irish whiskey; like I said I am not a whiskey drinker, so I handed it to the guy who came second. All in all it was a memorable day, and William was at the centre of it all.

To me, William Wright is in the same league as Harry Ferguson. Why do I say that? Because William could anticipate future trends. He could see long before anybody else what was needed and what would become popular. Indeed, he was the first to come up with the idea of a mobile shop. Back in the 1960s, not everyone had the luxury of a car, and getting to the shops was a challenge for many, so why not bring the shop to the customer. William saw an opportunity to sell groceries from mobile shops, and he was quite successful in that manufacturing venture.

Not so, however, when he moved into trailer making. The trailer industry was far too competitive and complex, so that was a short lived venture, as far as I recall. Then he moved into buses, and that's when he started to make his mark. Like I said earlier, I remember featuring his first models in *Export & Freight*, and there was lots of reader interest in those stories. That interest only grew as Wright buses started to make an impact on the global marketplace.

In many ways, William Wright helped put Northern Ireland on the map for, if you pardon the pun, all the right reasons. Remember, this was at a time when the Troubles were making the headlines all over the world, but here was a man with something more positive to offer, with a good story to tell about the Province, and I am very proud of what he achieved in that regard.

I have watched Wrightbus grow in stature and reputation over almost five decades and no matter where I travel in the world today – and I have visited many places on both business and on holiday – you can almost be virtually assured of seeing a Wrightbus and that is some success story to come from a little place like Northern Ireland. I am honoured to have been, in some small way, instrumental in telling that story.

As for the man himself, well the William Wright of today is still the same William Wright I met all those years ago. He hasn't changed one iota. He is still a driving force in the industry, albeit in these later years of his life, from the back seat! He'll be a hard act to follow.

Darryl Magee

Darryl Magee

Commercial Vehicle Production – Tippers, Trailers and Vans

An early tipper on a Ford Thames Trader chassis.

In the 1960s, at long last, the Government of Northern Ireland was spending money on improving roads and building motorways and again Wrights saw an opportunity. A deal was signed with Telehoist, a hydraulic tipping gear manufacturer and, having agreed terms with that company, Wrights designed tipping bodies, tailored specifically for the needs of contractors building new housing and factories, as well as those working on improving Northern Ireland's roads and the construction of its motorway network. There was (initially) no major competition and this was a sector of the market which Wrights had specifically targeted for sales. This venture was a great success.

Again the company benefited from a friendship, this time with the senior manager of Vauxhall Motors, whose local office was then based at Antrim, less than 10 miles from Wrights factory. Both companies saw an opportunity and signed an agreement to build stock vehicles. This provided Wrights with orders that assisted the production management to maintain a constant flow of product from the factory to the customers. And for Vauxhall, this initiative ensured Bedford commercial vehicle distributors were able to offer immediate delivery to potential customers.

Bedford was represented by several very proactive dealers in Northern Ireland:

Right: This Bedford TK tipper was built in 1989 for Richard Logan of Ahoghill (on a second-hand military-use LHD chassis dating from 1979) and is still in regular use.

General Motor Works, Ballymena;
Bradford Brothers, Cookstown;
Stuart and Company, Coleraine;
Roadside Motors, Lurgan;
Eakin Brothers, Claudy, Londonderry;
Saville Motors, Dunmurry;
David Marshall, Belfast;
Sydney Pentland, Belfast;
Lochside Motors, Enniskillen; and
Charlton's, Omagh.

James McDowell of Charles Hurst (Commercials) Ltd hands over this Leyland to P Coll and Son of Dungiven, Co Londonderry.

All of these companies, which were family-owned, contributed to the success of Robert Wright Coachworks Limited. With the demise of Bedford Commercial Vehicles, all of these companies have ceased trading in commercials vehicles, with the exception of Eakin Brothers who are now Iveco Truck dealers supplying the northwest of the Province.

Telehoist also manufactured a range of skip loaders, known as Load Luggers. Wrights agreed to market this new product and, like the hydraulic tipping gears, was an immediate sales success. Obviously, potential customers would also require skips, so Wrights designed a range of sizes to suit operators' needs. All were manufactured in Ballymena and again increased the range of products the company could supply. One employee who played a vital role in providing after sales support for the Telehoist range of products was Gordon Frew. He had previously trained in hydraulics and was therefore the ideal candidate to provide the customers with field sales support.

Bedford had built up a very strong market for van conversions with Dormobile, a company based in Folkestone, Kent. Dormobile, like Wrights, had a bank stock agreement with Bedford, only theirs was for the van range and was supplied to them in both left and right-hand drive configuration.

This is the Telehoist Load Lugger skip loader on a Ford D series chassis. Readers might be surprised to learn that the skip was also a Wrights-built product!

Dormobile manufactured a range of personnel carriers in various trims. These ranged from the basic Workabus with side facing seats, used mostly by the construction industry to transport workers to various sites, to more luxurious models which were fitted with forward facing seats with a higher trim specification. Bedford introduced Wrights to Dormobile in 1972 and an agreement was reached whereby Wrights would assemble and market Dormobile products for the Bedford dealers in Northern Ireland. These conversions would be carried out using a kit of parts supplied by Dormobile. The Bedford van conversions were undertaken in the original workshop in Warden Street where the company had first set up business in 1946. Although the product was good, Wrights had great difficulty making a profit on the conversions for a number of reasons, such as:

Jack Kernohan hands over a skip lorry and digger trailer to Strabane District Council.

Above and below: Cookstown District Council purchased a Load Lugger skip loader on a Dodge chassis as did the Borough of Carrickfergus.

Left: Local building contractor, FB McKee, took this Ford D series skip lorry. Note the skip is fitted with a drop down end for ease of loading.

Above: William Wright (seated) signs the agreement with John Wade of Dormobile.

- Bedford sales in Northern Ireland never reached volumes which could sustain a production assembly line; and
- the product was being sold at the same price as Dormobile who, with the much larger GB and Europe market, was able to operate continuous production lines.

Dormobile also manufactured a range of motor home conversions and touring caravans. Wrights marketed all of these products through the Northern Ireland Bedford dealers network.

The range of touring caravans designed and built by Dormobile was sold to the general public from the sales office on the factory complex. After a period of time the company, needing all the space and manpower available, decided to stop production and sales of all Dormobile products. With production of these conversions ceasing, the workshop where the company first set up business in Warden Street, closed its doors for the last time in 1972.

Wrights built a range of trailers including boxes, drop frame, flat beds, fridges, grain carriers, tippers and for carrying containers. In this selection we see single and double-axle trailers for containers, a box under construction and a flat bed.

With the ongoing improvements to Northern Ireland's road infrastructure, local industries were rebuilding and expanding their production facilities and consequently a new market was developing in the road freight sector.

Farming was one of the first sectors to recover and with the subsequent expansion in production, there was obviously a need to transport that farm produce. Milk lorries, with their load of creamery cans, were a common sight on the roads, but were replaced by tankers; indeed today those large creamery cans are now a collector's item. The flatbed platform lorry, transporting animal feedstuffs, fertilisers, timber and building materials, potatoes, etc, along with large purpose-built trucks carrying cattle, sheep and pigs to and from markets all over Ireland and the United Kingdom would be seen on roads throughout the land. Wrights expanded to meet this challenge but, with that, the workforce were working overtime to meet demand for its products for that new segment of the market.

There was one product that was becoming ever more popular with operators and Wrights did not have anything to offer its customers. The articulated trailer was very manoeuvrable and offered many advantages to transport operators. Dennison's of Ballyclare had up to then cornered this segment of the market. The decision was made by Wrights management to enter this market; the components were purchased, and the longitudinal beams were cut and shaped ready for assembly. The first of many Wright trailers was assembled, under the expert supervision of Albert Hanna, on a Saturday (when there were no visitors

around). And so, having established that the company could actually build trailers, and make a profit and compete with Dennison's, the sales team wasted no time in approaching potential purchasers and soon articulated trailers were rolling off the assembly lines. The trailers came in all sizes:
- 26'0" to 40'0" flat bed trailers with ISO wristlocks to secure containers;
- drop frame;
- tippers;
- bulk grain carriers
- machinery carriers;
- box vans;
- curtain siders;
- refrigerated transport

And all designed in-house to meet purchasers' specific needs.

Wrights Trailer Division was soon well established, but then Dennison's sold their manufacturing plant to Crane Fruehauf which at that time was the largest trailer manufacturer in Great Britain. With their know-how, coupled with their vast purchasing power in axles, wheels, tyres, landing gear, etc, it soon became apparent to Wrights sales and management teams that the company could no longer compete effectively in the volume market. Having made that decision the product range was reduced and the sales team concentrated its efforts on selected niche markets within this same market segment where Wrights could be more competitive and still achieve a reasonable return on its investment.

One such niche market was trailers for the bakeries, such as Mothers Pride of the Rank Hovis McDougall Group, Ormo and Sunblest, and the large food distributors such as Spar of the John Henderson Group.

Many of the new trailers seen on the roads of the United Kingdom or the Republic of Ireland today are manufactured in Northern Ireland by Montracon, a division of Montgomery Transport, or by SDC (South Derry Coachworks). This was a growth market and with hindsight there is the distinct possibility that Wrights pulled out of the trailer market too soon.

The manufacturing sector was also expanding rapidly in Northern Ireland, especially in the textile industry, with large plants being established by ICI and Courtaulds to produce modern synthetic textiles. With this expansion there was, again, an obvious need for suitable transport for delivering raw materials to the factories and delivering the finished goods.

One of the first men to see and to grasp the opportunity was Charles Vincent Armstrong. In those days, Londonderry was renowned for the quality of the shirts made in the city. Charles Armstrong worked for one of those shirt manufacturers and he saw the need for a transport system to deliver the finished products from the large number of manufacturing plants in Londonderry to the companies' distributors in Great Britain, so he

Above: **This box trailer for Sunblest Bread featured a Zepro tail lift for ease of loading. Charlie Maguire (in white coat) was Transport Manager for Sunblest.**

Above right: **The Milk Marketing Board for Northern Ireland received this refrigerated box for the carriage of dairy products. It was hauled by a Bedford TM tractor. In the picture are Crawford Gourley and Billy Miskelly (Transport Manager, Bangor Dairies).**

set up his own transport business, CVA Roadfreight Limited. The key to this successful enterprise was the need to keep costs down. This was partly achieved by bringing the raw materials for the factories back to Northern Ireland in the same trailers which were delivering the completed goods, hence he had a return load to the same factory where, after unloading, the next load was packed and the cycle began again – no lost time and no additional mileage ensured a profitable business. That keen eye for business was to lead to him building up additional work in the North of the Province.

Wrights supplied large drop frame, box van trailers to Mr Armstrong's business. With imports from low cost manufacturers overseas (where energy and labour costs were/are much lower) ever increasing, shirt manufacturing in the North West of the Province began its terminal decline. Charles Armstrong saw what was happening and moved on, establishing the Everglades Hotel in Londonderry and, with other business interests in County Donegal, he sold his transport business. This is only one example of many transport systems which were designed and manufactured by Wrights to meet the specific operational needs of the management of local factories and transport operators.

The management of Wrights was now focusing its attention on new materials and components which, while reducing labour and material costs, would provide the customers with a more attractive vehicle with greater durability at a competitive price.

An opportunity to purchase a site to the left of Hugomount Road, on land owned by what was then Stewart's Nurseries, arose in 1974. William Wright grasped this once in a lifetime opportunity and purchased the ground. And so, with the assistance of a friendly Bank of Ireland manager, the company set about building additional factory production space, new offices for the management and sales team and additional stores space.

With the general move from wood being the major component in the construction of the framework to aluminium extrusions specifically developed for the coach-building industry, the next move was to play a significant role in the company's progress – one-piece Glass Reinforced Plywood, available in colour impregnated finish, with different thicknesses of plywood core offering immense strength, durability and ease of cleanliness. This product was ideal for the transportation of food, for example bakery produce. The GRP panels were easily assembled and, although expensive, were able to be used in the construction of all sizes of vehicles, ranging from a small bread vans with panel sizes from 12'0" × 6'0" up to 40'0" × 9'0", a size used extensively in the construction of articulated trailers.

Insulated GRP panels were soon developed, these consisting of two plywood panels each with a colour impregnated outer skin and an insulated core of varying thickness, 50mm for a chilled van and 100mm for all vehicles to be used for transporting of deep frozen perishable foodstuffs. Wrights negotiated a deal with TPI (Transport Product Industries) the major suppliers of these panels, to market the panels exclusively in Ireland. Stocking the panels and cutting them to size was no problem. However unloading and loading was difficult, and very time consuming, especially where the insulated panels were concerned and, if not handled carefully, they could easily de-laminate. The benefits though, far outweighed the problems and, very soon after, Wrights introduced the product on a new van, which was supplied to Spar, one of the major food distributors. Demand for these new GRP panels was way above the company's expectations. Wrights also supplied the panelling cut to size to other coachbuilders and trailer manufacturers all over Ireland.

A chance meeting with a manager of a local company, Masstock Ltd, then based in Antrim, provided Wrights with a major export opportunity. Masstock, which had vast farming experience, was working with the Saudi Royal Family to develop farms in what was desert – a very difficult job. They had been successful and were now looking for a temperature-controlled system to transport milk from the farms to the cities. During the discussions Wrights discovered that the Saudi venture had not as yet built cold storage facilities, and suggested a cheaper, more flexible solution – the Wright Demountable Body System, which offered a convenient transport and storage solution.

One of the DAF-based demountable fridge units delivered to Saudi Arabia.

A line of demountable fridge units which avoided the need to build cold storage facilities in the Saudi capital.

Morgan's, a Belfast-based removals company, purchased demountable units on Bedford chassis.

The demountable system supplied to Castrol Limited is shown here on and off the Bedford chassis. While the box was being loaded at the depot, the Bedford unit would be out on the road making deliveries with a second box.

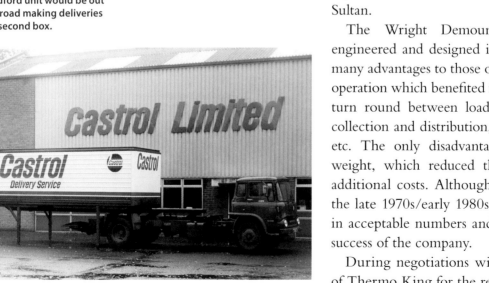

The insulated bodies for the Saudi contract were constructed from GRP sandwich panelling designed for the transportation of bulk goods and fitted with the highly-acclaimed Thermo King refrigeration. They were also fitted with overnight standee facilities. The main advantage of this demountable transport system was that the Saudis did not have to build static cold stores, this then being a major cost saving, and with the fleet of vehicles supplied in 1977 they also purchased additional flat bed demountable bodies which were used to transport other goods. The system proved very successful in operation, with additional fleets subsequently being ordered for two other members of the royal household, Prince Binamar and Prince Sultan.

The Wright Demountable System was engineered and designed in-house and offered many advantages to those operators who had an operation which benefited from the much faster turn round between loads, for example coal collection and distribution, furniture removals, etc. The only disadvantages were the extra weight, which reduced the payload and the additional costs. Although not a big seller, in the late 1970s/early 1980s, the system did sell in acceptable numbers and contributed to the success of the company.

During negotiations with the management of Thermo King for the refrigeration units for the Masstock order, an exclusive agreement was reached for Wrights to become the Thermo King approved dealer for Northern Ireland. Wrights then set up another company, Technical Transport Products, to market and service Thermo King products. The company was a major success in that everyone in refrigerated transport recognised Thermo King as being a quality product, the world best with trained after sales service support all over Europe.

TTP, as the company is now known, is no longer part of The Wright Group, but is owned by William Wright's sister, Muriel and her husband William Finlay. Their two daughters, Tracy and Kathryn, now manage this very successful company with the assistance of their father. Initially based in the same factory complex, they built a new purpose built factory in the Woodside Industrial Estate just off the Broughshane Road on the outskirts of Ballymena.

Having increased the company's sales base in Northern Ireland, Wrights was now looking to expand its customer base to the Irish Republic. So, with a slight relaxation in the import duties, which allowed a manufacturer to import a product as long as it was assembled in the Republic, an agreement was reached in 1979 with Pat Keating, who had set up a coachbuilding operation on the Naas Road in Dublin, to assemble the company's range of van body kits. Business was booming in Dublin and, with the diversity of product, fast delivery and competitive pricing, Pat and his workforce were soon working night and day to meet demand for Wrights products. Unknown to Wrights, however, such was the demand that Pat could not finance the operation and sold a major share of his company to a trailer manufacturing company, Ardagh Trailers. The subsequent changes that took place allowed the new management to have the controlling interest. The goodwill and support built up with Pat Keating was not recognised by the new management and Wrights consequently stopped supplying the new venture.

In the meantime, Wrights, with my assistance, built up a substantial business with Tom Logue, a coachbuilder in County Donegal; his operation was similar to that in Dublin mentioned earlier. Tom had built up an excellent reputation with both the commercial chassis suppliers and with those involved in transport. Donegal was far enough away from Dublin that operators wanted service support from a local manufacturer and they looked more to Northern Ireland than to Dublin for supply. Tom's business soon expanded way above his expectations. Wrights manufactured the body kits and transported them over to County Donegal where Tom assembled and painted the vehicles before delivering them to his (satisfied) customers.

Business continued to expand, so much so that Tom called me one day to advise that he had a major problem – the Income Tax inspectors were investigating his business and he was considering what steps he had to take. I suggested that we both go and meet the Tax Inspectors in Letterkenny and explain the circumstances. A meeting was arranged and when I explained how the company had increased its turnover substantially without needing to increase its labour force, the inspectors accepted his explanation. What I did not explain was the fact that Tom (himself teetotal) also owned a bar and he planned his workload carefully and cleverly; when he needed a lift up with the sides or the roof of a large van, the offer of a free round of drinks brought forth a band of willing workers! Tom Logue was a gentleman in every sense of the word and had the support of his family, especially his wife Peggy. Sadly his life was cut short after he was diagnosed with cancer. The treatment in those days was not as advanced as today and, sadly, Tom passed away. Wrights had lost a valued customer and I had lost a business colleague and a very good friend. The Logue family ceased building van bodies and concentrated on its hotel business, which is based in a beautiful location in Donegal, overlooking Milford Bay.

While Wrights was continually developing new products, its customers were focusing their attention on reducing manual labour costs, and providing faster and faster turn around times and so improving their delivery times and reducing costs. These improvements came about with the greater use of pallets and forklifts. The larger grocery supply chains initially tried this system but ultimately moved to roll on/off pallets, which allowed them to provide the shopkeeper with a system that transported the groceries from the distribution centre direct to the shelves. This reduced handling costs while also reducing breakages.

Market research and product innovation were equally as important in the 1980s as they are today and the company's vehicle designers and engineers had now to come up with a new range of products to take into consideration the customers' operational requirements of palletisation. Sliding doors, roller shutters and curtain-sided vehicles were all designed and developed to meet the specific needs of individual operators.

Roll on/off pallets were a totally different proposition, though. The sidewall of the vehicles had to be specially reinforced, load security systems fitted, floors reinforced and hydraulically-powered tail-lifts fitted. The reliability of the tail-lifts then available from United Kingdom manufacturers was a major problem and when they stopped working obviously the customer would not be particularly happy! Wrights solution to this technical difficulty was negotiated during a visit to the Frankfurt Commercial Vehicle Show, when a deal was struck with a Swedish manufacturer, Zepro Tail-lifts. Although this company's products were considerably more expensive, Wrights customers readily paid the extra costs to have the reliability for which they had become known. Within twelve months all the company's major customers specified the Zepro product. Wrights also benefited from after sales services and from the sale of Zepro products to other coachbuilders.

William Wright, his wife Ruby and family moved from their home beside the factory on Hugomount Drive to a new house, close to the village of Gracehill, in 1968. Robert Wright and his wife, Mary, then moved from their home in Warden Street, Ballymena to the house just vacated by William. Bob still took a great interest in the family firm. Looking back I suppose that Bob, who was a skilled tradesman, took over the role of Quality Controller as, living close to the factory, he had more time to inspect the vehicles before they were dispatched! That was no bad thing as, just like today, the Boss was the final arbiter.

William Wright is a man of high Christian principles and social responsibility, who takes a great interest in all issues that affect the local community. One Sunday morning, on leaving my church in Cullybackey, a local man approached me advising that he had received a phone call from a Mr Cowden of Annalong, County Down asking me to contact him urgently. I called him and was informed that he urgently required a wire rope for a tail-lift. Could I assist?

We all had been instructed that no-one was to be in the factory on Sunday. We could work Saturdays until late evening, but not Sunday. My customers always came first, and I could see no harm in getting him two wire ropes.

On my arrival at the factory, I saw Mrs Mary Wright at the window of their bungalow and I was well aware that William would soon be advised by his mother that I had committed a cardinal sin! The customer was delighted to receive the two ropes but I knew that I would be carpeted on Monday morning. Sure enough, first thing on Monday morning, I received a call to go to Mr Wright's office. Knowing that the meeting was not to thank me for assisting a customer in need, I planned to listen and then provide William with a solution that would solve the problem. This would have had other ramifications, for example who would open up the factory every morning and secure it every evening? The offer of my keys was rejected and common sense prevailed. Over the years I respected Mr Wright's views and only in emergencies did I visit the factory. How times, and attitudes, have changed; we now have Sunday shopping, with all the major stores open for business.

The final word on this humorous little story must go to William. With major societal changes all around us, he still refuses to open the manufacturing plant on a Sunday and I have to say I totally agree with him; no matter how busy the company is, the staff still need a day of rest. I might add that, were I still an employee, I would still open the factory in a case of dire emergency!

Wrights Armoured Division

A new venture that the reader might find strange followed a request from Short's Armoured Division. The company agreed to develop, engineer and manufacture the range of Shorland vehicles! The Shorland, based on a Land Rover, was developed with the assistance of Shorts engineering personnel for use by defence forces using Shorts ground to air missiles.

Albert Hanna was the key to the success of this project. He worked with a hand-picked team to engineer and design, with the assistance of the engineers from Shorts, a range of products for security forces in many overseas countries where Shorts sold their missiles. (I should also add that in the case of the orders from Shorts, Albert was also the sales contact, having built up a special relationship with Eric Tuckey of Shorts.) Albert processed the orders and also prepared the invoices. Considering the complexity of the products being developed, the team assisting him was small, but very effective. The development costs were kept to a minimum whilst both labour and material costs were well within the budgets. Looking back now, Albert never received the recognition, nor would he have wanted it, for the success of these products. I also wonder with all the expertise in the company today how many engineers, product managers, etc would it take to manage a similar project and what the development costs would be. Albert had the ability to manage projects within given time scales and within budget, and to manage and motivate staff under his control, while carrying on with his everyday duties.

The Shorland, built on a Land Rover chassis, was a collaboration with the Armoured Division of Shorts, the well-known aircraft manufacturer. This one was built to a police specification.

For military use, the Shorland could be equipped for various roles, including armoured car and missile launcher.

A Shorland armoured car in
the hills above Ballymena.

Shorlands under construction

Passenger Vehicles – The Beginning

Above: An early personnel carrier built on a Bedford commercial chassis. These early 'buses' bear no resemblance to the products leaving the factory today!

Above right: The County Education Committees in Northern Ireland were early customers for Wright buses. This Commer was delivered to the Tyrone County Education Committee.

In the 1950s and 1960s, fewer people had cars, so good passenger transport was important to the general public; in Northern Ireland, outside Belfast, the buses, and what was left of the rail network, were run by the Ulster Transport Authority (UTA). Most of the Authority's buses were built in-house, at its workshops in Belfast. As we shall see later, Wrights did not enter the PSV market until the mid-1980s when the company did, however, make the strategic decision to enter this market. By the mid-1990s it had moved its total production facilities to the manufacture of buses.

However, Wrights first foray into the passenger vehicle market came in the mid 1950s when it began the manufacture of buses, mostly on commercial chassis, for the County Education Committees in Northern Ireland. These buses were supplied on a range of chassis depending on the seating capacity. The 33-seater bus was built on Bedford, Commer or Leyland chassis – Bedford J2 or Leyland FG chassis in the earlier years and latterly on the

This Austin FG model was delivered to the Armagh County Education Committee.

Commer Walk Thru (which was an ideal low cost chassis). These commercial-based chassis were subsequently replaced by more modern chassis specifically designed for bus manufacturers. Bedford offered three models which were suitable – the VAS for the 33-seat model, the SB for the 42-seat and the YRT for the 53-seater product.

For many years Wrights had great difficulty getting into this market simply because the chassis were distributed by dealers Charles Hurst and AS Baird. Both were based in Belfast and wanted to control the market and, consequently, the price. To solve the problem Wrights purchased chassis from distributors on the United Kingdom mainland. I remember Billy Hempton, Purchasing Manager at the Western Education and Library Board, calling me and asking me to check my figures on a recent tender, the reason being that our price was substantially below that of other local suppliers. From that day on the Education and Library Boards realised that much better value was now available from Wrights! The company had gained their respect, although we never could underestimate our competitors when tendering for the business.

Northern Ireland was a wonderful place for a teenager to grow up in the late 1960s/early 1970s. There were numerous dance halls and other venues, such as Orange, Parochial or Town Halls, where one could go for an evening's entertainment; many a couple met at one of these dances! In those days there was no alcoholic drink (and certainly no drugs) in most of the venues – how times have changed!

Venues like the Flamingo in Ballymena, the Arcadia in Portrush and the Floral Hall on the outskirts of Belfast all wanted the best bands, to attract the biggest crowds and, due to this demand, showbands, which I believe were a particularly Irish phenomenon, emerged all over Ireland. Business was good, the artists now had money and they wanted the very best and that included the best transport to and from the various venues.

By this time William Wright was married and had family commitments. Therefore, other than a few occasions such as the works Christmas dinner, he was seldom, to my knowledge (that's my story and I am sticking to it!) seen on the dance floor. However, this did not stop him seeing another opportunity – to design and build a special coach for the showbands.

Built on a Commer Walk Thru chassis, the rear of the vehicle was designed to transport all of the band's equipment, etc. Access to this storage area was through two large doors fitted in the rear and fitted with heavy duty

A particularly Irish phenomenon in the 1960s was the showband and Wrights saw an opportunity. A vehicle was developed to meet the needs of such bands travelling round the country – comfortable seating, a wardrobe area, secure lockers, high-quality sound systems, etc. This Commer was constructed for *The Freshmen*.

security locks to ensure that the equipment was stored in a relatively safe area. The front passenger saloon accommodated between nine and twelve high quality, reclining seats to allow the band members to get some sleep on the long journey to and from home. To the rear of the seating area, and divided off from the saloon, was a wardrobe area where the band members could store their suits and special outfits. Many of the bands had female lead singers and special provision was made on a number of orders for them to change in privacy.

The Dave Glover Showband, one of the top dance bands in Ireland, placed an early order. This was soon followed by orders from bands such as The Freshmen, The Capitol Showband, The Johnnie Quigley Showband and Derek and the Sounds. Their vehicles were built to the highest standards and incorporated the very best in radio and recording systems that were available in the 1960s. Nothing but the best was good enough and Wrights provided it!

There were problems with this form of transport over which Wrights had no control. Often, in winter, having finished their performance in the early hours of the morning, the band, and especially the driver, had to contend with roads covered with ice and snow. Due to the state of the roads (there were no gritters in those days), these vehicles had more than their fair share of accidents. Insurance premiums went up and the ever-increasing costs to the bands forced them to go back to the car as the preferred method of transport with a van to transport the equipment.

These midibuses were constructed on Ford A series chassis cowls, although Wrights fitted its own style of windscreen.

For those interested in gaining knowledge about the Irish Showbands, it is all available on the internet, all you have to do is type in 'Irish Showbands' and the history of that era is all available to you

Changes have taken place in construction methods and materials over the years. Early Wrights passenger bodies were built using hardwood mahogany for the framing but as the years progressed a change was made to first steel and later aluminium. The limited range of componentry available to the manufacturers in those early years, plus the fact that Wrights were using the chassis of what were commercial vehicles, greatly reduced the company's ability to provide stylish vehicles. It was only in later years that the company could influence the style and design of the products but, again, more of that later.

I have used the foregoing chapters to illustrate the many changes that were taking place within this industry. Wrights could no longer continue to develop products to serve the diverse requirements of the transport industry and it was now time to examine which products it, as a major coachbuilder in Northern Ireland, could manufacture using the company's skilled workforce. New materials were becoming available and current (and impending) legislation now coming in ever increasing volumes from Europe was forcing Wrights, like all other manufacturers, into rethinking which market it could best service.

Michelin has a large production facility in Ballymena and purchased three Wright-bodied Bedfords for staff transport. Geoff Amos (third from the right) shakes hands with William Wright as he takes delivery of them; the author is standing between them.

The County Education Committees became Education Boards but continued to purchase buses from Wrights. This Leyland (Albion) Viking was delivered to the Western Education and Library board in 1978. *(Will Hughes)*

Moving Forward

In 1976, the company carried out extensive market research into the effects European Common Market policies would have on traditional coachbuilders in Europe. The management team then examined the current operations and the alternatives the company had to safeguard its long-term future, and that of its employees. Realising that its long-term prosperity depended on penetrating markets beyond the shores of Ireland, the management team made two major decisions that were fundamental to the firm's later success. The first was to employ a professional design engineer. The second was expand the bus building activities of the company and to design, engineer and develop a range of user-friendly buses for both the schools and welfare markets, but most importantly the PSV market, an area that, up to now, the company had not targeted.

Having made the decision to concentrate the company's management and financial resources in the development of a range of futuristic buses, it was imperative that the company increased the management team by recruiting an engineer with experience in product design/styling. However, Wrights could not change its customer base overnight, so it had no alternative but to continue to manufacture and market the current range whilst developing the products for the future.

An advertisement for a Design Engineer placed in the trade press emphasised the need for all applicants to have experience in the motor industry, particularly in design and styling. From the applicants one young man's experience ticked the right boxes. That man was Trevor Erskine, who at that point in time worked for the Ford Motor Company. Trevor was in the process of completing the initial design study for a new cab for a new range of trucks that Ford would introduce two years later. Trevor visited the plant, liked what he saw and joined the company shortly after his initial interview. Trevor was born in Bushmills, on the North Antrim coast, close by the world famous Giant's Causeway, although he will tell you that it is better known for the production of an excellent whiskey, the Bushmills Distillery's Black Bush!

Trevor had worked for Short Brothers and Harland, then a major aircraft manufacturing concern based in Belfast, before moving into the car industry. Having worked for a number of companies, including Ford, Trevor and his family wanted to return to his native Northern Ireland but Wrights had two reservations about appointing him: all of his working life had been spent with large companies; and would Trevor and his family settle in Northern Ireland when, because of terrorist activity, others were leaving?

Thankfully the family settled well and Trevor adapted easily to operating in an entirely different environment, one where if a decision was needed, you went next door to William Wright's office and got a immediate decision, something that would not have happened at Ford!

The reworking of the design and manufacturing processes began with an in-depth review of the current processes. New materials were examined and selected, processes rewritten and then began the real work of designing and engineering a quality product on a range of bus chassis acceptable to potential customers.

The team which took the company to a new level in the 1980s and 1990s – Trevor Erskine (left) with Dr William Wright (centre), Stephen Hewitt, Jack Kernohan and Albert Hanna.

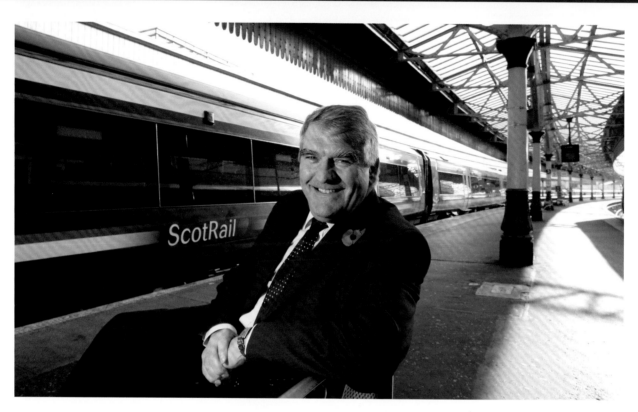

Sir Moir Lockhead, OBE
Chief Executive and
Deputy Chariman

I first met William Wright in the 1980s when I was the Chief Engineer at Strathclyde. William had come to Scotland to demonstrate a new coach the company had developed. The Contour, as it was known, was built using an all aluminium framework and offering very modern styling. Unfortunately for Wrights, it was the right product at the wrong time, as the market for coaches in the UK went through the floor around that time. Nevertheless, even then I recognised in William a formidable and talented individual who in later years was to play such a prominent part in the bus industry.

Along with William I met Jack Kernohan, who was William's right hand man on the sales side of what was then a relatively small business. My daughter was developing a love of horses and was interested in making a purchase. Jack mentioned an up and coming Northern Irish show jumper called Jessica Chesney; introductions were made by Jack and a horse acquired. Thus began a friendship which continues to this day and Jessica, now better known under her married name of Kurten, has achieved international success. This was typical of Jack, nothing was ever too much trouble and, better still, he didn't wait to be asked.

The real breakthrough for Wrights came in the early nineties. William was the first person in the British bus industry to spot the full potential for low floor buses. He also combined his engineering and commercial talents to minimise the cost

premium. More than that, he had the courage of his convictions to press ahead with low floor buses, when many senior industry figures were cynical and hostile to the concept. Looking back now it is hard to understand the opposition, but William never waivered in his belief. I greatly admire his single minded determination and his enthusiasm has benefited all our bus passengers.

Despite his great achievements William has remained a believer in simple solutions. I recall at one time there were minor quality issues with buses leaving the factory in transit to customers. The quality control systems were not working as they should but William had the answer. He gave the gatemen on security the final authority and sign-off rights on all vehicles leaving the plant. One of those men, whose hobby was restoring and maintaining vintage cars, always looked for perfection, so who better to ensure that the products were to the highest quality. No buses were allowed to leave the premises unless and until the gatemen were fully satisfied. William explained it to me stating that no production personnel liked the thought of a security man picking up and recording any quality issues on their workmanship. The problems soon disappeared! The solution was simple, low cost and effective and that epitomises William.

There is no doubt the entire bus industry benefited from his leadership in engineering; and developing and introducing low floor buses in the UK. That achievement alone would have ensured his place in the history of the bus industry. William has never been content to rest on his laurels and, at a time when many would have been enjoying a well earned retirement, he has spearheaded another industry revolution.

William, in his younger days, suffered from asthma that made him particularly sensitive to air quality. Buses enjoy privileged access to most of our city centres and he realised that if this is to continue in the future we need to reduce the pollution that buses create. At the same time the volatility of fuel costs has been a problem for our industry. And the simple solution – buses that burn less fuel and create fewer harmful emissions. That William has been the industry leader in developing these hybrid buses, should surprise no-one, and future generations will benefit from his pioneering work.

First Bus has benefited from the close working relationship between the two companies. From our engineers Wrights learn about the problems in operating buses, they listen and where possible take immediate action to eliminate the problem and improve the product. They were the first manufacturer to take on board the problem of downtime when a bus is involved in an accident. William got his engineers to examine the problems and come up with solutions that would significantly reduce that time. Now when developing a new product, all these benefits are included as standard.

It has been my privilege over many years to have partnered with Wrights in many projects. We shared a vision in the creation of the **ftr** Streetcar, translating the vision into reality in just over twelve months and I was not in the least surprised when Transport for London announced that Wrightbus had been selected as the preferred manufacturer to design, engineer and develop the New Bus for London.

I might add that this prestigious contract was ground breaking for the company, in that it was won against intense international competition. The Wrightbus product will is being designed to reduce air pollution by 30%, but the really good news for the operator is that the new buses will be 40% more fuel efficient in comparison with current diesel buses.

And lest we forget, William Wright pioneered easily accessible city buses in the United Kingdom, and more recently diesel-electric hybrid buses in the United Kingdom – no mean achievement for a relatively small family owned company.

William and his wife, Ruby, have maintained a very close family home life, with strong family values that flow from their simple but deeply held religious faith, At the same time, the family have created a bus building business of international standing. I know that the company is now well recognised not only in the United Kingdom but also in Hong Kong, the United States and more recently Singapore. When I witnessed the 'Streetcar Hybrid' destined for Las Vegas at the mass transit show in San Diego, and the way in which it relegated all its competition to second class status, I realised that Wrightbus is now truly global – **well done!**

Sir Moir Lockhead, OBE

On 28 May 2010, FirstGroup's global headquarters at King Street, Aberdeen was the setting for an historic Scottish military occasion when around 130 Highlanders from 4th Battalion, The Royal Regiment of Scotland (4 SCOTS) and its pipes and drums performed a special ceremony as they paid tribute to their former home. The site was home to the Royal Aberdeenshire Highlanders (which became the Third Battalion of the Gordon Highlanders) between 1862 and 1914, when it was purchased by Aberdeen Corporation Tramways (although the Army re-occupied the premises for another five years due to the outbreak of World War One). Of course, we're pleased to see two of First Aberdeen's Volvo B7RLE/Eclipse Urban taking part in the parade. (FirstGroup)

The Changes Begin

W e now had to look at the manufacturing processes available that would meet both the company's, and our customers', future needs and expectations.

Buses operating in an urban environment have a very tough life, operating long days, seven days a week and with heavy passenger loadings. With the inclement weather in the United Kingdom, often combined with the frost and snow, local authorities use a mixture of salt and sand to assist drivers. This may prevent accidents but it also creates a major problem for bus operators – corrosion and rust. Many vehicles built from mild steel suffered from framework failure due to corrosion. Therefore, if Wrights was to succeed it had to offer a stylish, lightweight, durable, long life bus body, with added benefits which our competitors were not offering and would prove difficult to design into their product range. Many European manufacturers continued to use steel construction, but they do not have the corrosion problems encountered in the United Kingdom.

Whilst visiting the Frankfurt Truck and Bus Show, which in those early days consisted mainly of commercial vehicles, I discovered, quite by accident, a company that was to play a vital role in the success of Wrights. They offered a bus building system that incorporated those important corrosion-resistant components and the associated technical know-how. These components would set the pattern for Wrights future bus and coach developments.

I was examining a trailer, which had the entire subframe manufactured and assembled from large alloy extrusions. The quality of the aluminium welding was extremely good, so good in fact that the company exhibiting the product had simply polished the alloy. A very tall man, who was on the exhibitor's stand, approached me and asked if he could assist. I initially said no, explaining who I was, the company that I worked for and that we were looking for a bus building system, preferably an all alloy system. That tall gentleman was Mr Didier Fiess and he explained that he did not represent the company who manufactured the trailer; he represented the company that supplied the alloy profiles/extrusions. He further advised that his company also supplied alloy extrusions for the bus building industry in Europe, but as this was a commercial show he had no samples or product information available with him. He informed me that a representative from the parent company would be coming to the show that evening and if we could come the following morning he would have both samples and product information leaflets available. We arranged to meet the following morning to discuss potential business opportunities. That evening, I advised both William and Trevor that I had had a very interesting meeting that afternoon with a representative from a company called Alusuisse detailing what they could offer and informing them that I had arranged a meeting for the following morning, which I hoped they would attend.

The following morning we all met and, having examined the information available, it was agreed to visit a number of European coachbuilders who were using the Alusuisse M5438 bus building system. William Wright travelled to Italy and there visited a number of companies. After an in-depth study of the product, the projected costings, including the assembly times and the labour costings, Wrights signed a licensing agreement with Alusuisse a few weeks later. I was then tasked with developing sales for this new product, a task that was initially more difficult than I had anticipated; no-one had heard of the system, as none of our competitors were using it! The key advantage we had with our customers was the fact that many of the local customers trusted both the company and myself.

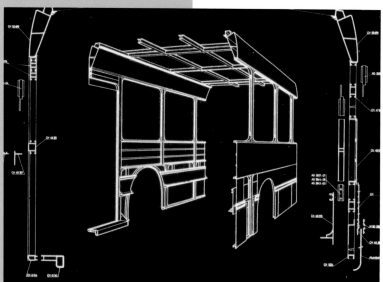

The Alusuisse M5438 system

Wrights had received a substantial order from the Southern Education and Library Board, for 11 metre school buses on Bedford bus chassis, based on traditional build. Wrights needed a fairly substantial order to initially get production of the new product flowing from the factory and, equally as important, to reduce the transport costs, so I visited Joe Rogers, the SELB's Transport Manager, to sell the new system to him. Having explained the new system to him I will always remember his comments, "Go ahead, use the new Alusuisse bus building system. I trust you. And the advice Wrights has given me in the past has been proven to be in the interest of providing the Education Boards with a better product." Trevor Erskine now had to design and engineer a totally new bus using the Alusuisse M5438 bus

Wrights supplied TT bodies on Bedford YMT and VAS chassis to the local Education and Library Boards. TT bodies were also supplied for use as mobile libraries. *(Will Hughes, both)*

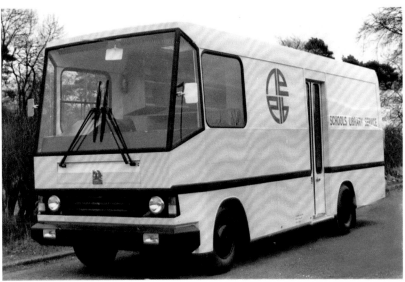

For the lighter-loaded school runs, Wrights supplied bodies built on the Dodge 50-series chassis. In this picture, a Wright-bodied Leyland Viking can be seen on the left and a mobile library on the right. *(Will Hughes)*

building system. (Wrights was the first manufacturer in the UK to use this system.) The buses were used daily on the roads of County Armagh until replacement Bedford componentry was difficult to obtain due to the fact that company had ceased production.

Regional Authorities, Health Boards and Community Transport Associations were major customers for midi- and minibuses. Wrights offered a range of buses with special adaptations to facilitate the transport of passengers on wheelchairs and, having saturated the market in Northern Ireland, it was agreed that the company would begin marketing this product range on the United Kingdom mainland. The gamble worked, with sales increasingly coming from Scotland and England.

The first major success was in 1978 with Strathclyde Regional Council, the largest Regional Council in the United Kingdom. The Transport Team there consisted of Dick Housley, John Lindsay and Harry Douglas, all of whom became very close friends over the years. Unfortunately, a reorganisation of local government meant that Strathclyde's internal transport division was ultimately amalgamated with the Roads Division. In the reorganisation, all of the then current management took early retirement.

For several years Strathclyde Regional Council placed substantial orders with Wrights for buses initially on the Leyland Cub, a derivative of the Leyland Terrier commercial chassis and later on the Bedford VAS chassis, specially adapted to meet their operational requirements. At one point they had over 150 Wright-bodied buses in operation. Enquiries were now coming from other regions, Dumfries and Galloway, Cumbria and Durham to name but a few. London and the Home Counties should have provided considerably more orders, but were much more difficult areas in which to sell the Wright range. The operators in this area had local suppliers who, because they were based fairly close by, could offer a better support service than Wrights, or so we thought!

A line up of Wrights buses outside Wrights factory at Coatbridge, Scotland, en route to Strathclyde Regional Council.

However, one major customer that Wrights was able to capture was the London Borough of Havering, out on the northeast side of the city, on the border with Essex. Havering Borough was a major user of this type of adapted vehicle. George Monroe was the Transport Manager there in those days. Mr Monroe was an engineer as well as a Transport Manager and shortly after we supplied the first bus, on a Bedford VAS chassis, I was invited to London to discuss future business. George saw the many advantages of the Alusuisse system and was delighted with not only the products but also the after sales service.

On many occasions, on being asked by prospective customers about after sales service support, I referred them to George Monroe. Actually, on one occasion I was phoned back by an engineer and asked how much we were paying Mr Monroe as he had given him a very positive report in that he could have spares with him from our factory in Ballymena faster than from the other side of London.

Having purchased his first bus from Wrights in 1981, and having compared it with what he had been buying previously, it was no contest as far as George was concerned. Wrights then supplied every bus to Havering until the borough contracted out its transport services and George retired. On a lighter note, I was asked by George to build a small bus with all the special facilities on a Bedford CF, a lightweight chassis, with a gross weight of only 3.86 tons. This I suspected would be a one-off, but the company agreed to build it because of the volumes of orders we had received from George.

The Bedford CF minibus that's mentioned in the text as being delivered to the London Borough of Havering.

One of the TX200-bodied Iveco welfare buses built for Liverpool Social Services.

Jeff Wright, son of William Wright, had joined the company in 1981 and was just beginning his career. He was given the task of developing this project. The two key objectives were costs and weight and to give Jeff credit he achieved both. George was delighted with the vehicle and a few years later he asked me to accompany him to see the bus. It was still as new; the two ladies who operated the bus had carpeted the floor and had kept their bus as if it was their own car. The interesting part of this story has yet to come.

Jeff and his team had achieved such a lightweight low-cost minibus, that when Iveco introduced the 49.10 chassis Wrights developed the concept that Jeff had pioneered and introduced the TX range in two models – the 200 as a welfare vehicle and the 400 as a 17-seater coach. The sales of the TX200 model penetrated new markets for the company. One of the largest orders received for this type of bus was from Liverpool City Council and was won against stiff competition from other United Kingdom manufacturers. The TX200 was much lighter and it

Similar TX200s were built for the welfare sector in Northern Ireland.
(Will Hughes)

was competitively priced, thanks to George Monroe's initial order.

George has long since retired, but he still keeps in touch with old friends in Ballymena, like the first time he saw one of the new Gemini double-decks operating in his area or, more recently, when the new StreetCar was featured on his local TV network, he called me to ask about the new product.

In 1981, Ulsterbus sent Wrights two 11m Leyland Leopard chassis. One, No 258 in the Ulsterbus fleet, was bodied with a 53-seat TT body and put to work on a mix of express and local service work. The other, No 259, was built to a more luxurious specification for use on Ulsterbus Tours, although it was rather let down by the choice of seats. This vehicle was fitted with additional luggage space and bonded glazing. To distinguish it from the standard TT body, on which it was based, it was christened the Royal. This historic vehicle is now preserved by the members of the Irish Transport Trust.

Brochure for the Royal body

Wrights had opened a small satellite factory in Scotland at Wishaw in 1981 to provide support to its customers both in Scotland and in England. In the event of a major accident buses could be repaired more easily. Space was at a premium. Therefore a relocation was arranged, to Coatbridge on the outskirts of Glasgow, and not too far from Wishaw, as the company wanted to retain the workforce. The factory was staffed by local people with Mr Bill Jenkins (Manager) and Mr Ronnie Forsythe (Sales) providing the management skills. The move to Coatbridge was not a success, and if the management had been aware of the potential problems before the move then it would not have relocated to that area. After being burgled on a number of occasions, when substantial equipment and tooling was stolen, Wrights closed the factory in 1986, after just five years.

In 1981, Ulsterbus sent two 11m Leyland Leopard chassis to Ballymena. One was bodied with a 53-seat TT body and given fleet number 258. It was then used on a mixture of express and local duties. *(Paul Savage)*

The second Ulsterbus Leopard was bodied with an enhanced version of the TT body. Christened Royal, this was built to a luxurious specification featuring bonded glazing. *(Paul Savage)*

Steve Dewhurst
Managing Director, Volvo Bus

My first dealings with Wrights go back to the mid-1980s. Whilst I can't remember the exact year, though probably 1986, I remember the meeting very vividly. I was working for Leyland Bus and visited Ballymena where I met William Wright and George Richards to advise them on their submission of a London Transport quotation – with its hundred pages of legal terms – a frightening document to us all, but in particular to this two per week small bodybuilder, based 'overseas' in Northern Ireland!

I remember William proudly introducing me to his young son who had just joined the business and was learning his trade in the factory – no special treatment, he would have to learn about the business from grass roots. A shy, gangly Jeff arrived in blue overalls with his father pointing at him saying, "One day this lad will run the business". At that stage, I doubted that even William, a true visionary, would have believed where the Company would be today!

With the Volvo acquisition of Leyland in 1988 came the real opportunities for working closely with Wrights and the rest is history – a history well documented in this book.

Why it worked so well is not easy to explain, but work it did, for both companies. I guess that we developed a trust in each other and we could rely with confidence on each other – very important traits. The drive, quality and innovation worked well for both parties.

Mind, we didn't always get it right and we often argued on many issues! From my point, I have to admit to advising Wrights on many occasions not to enter the double-deck market as they would never get a foothold!! This was much to Jack Kernohan and William's frustration – well you can't always get it right!

We have also had fun times over the years – too many to mention. My favourite story involved Jack, Thomson Baxter and myself back in the early days. After a hard day's work we found ourselves in Bushmills – my first visit. Desperate for a beer – well it was 5.00 pm – we visited the only pub in town and it was closed. No problem to Jack, who knocked on the door. The landlord's comment lives with me to this day, "I'm sorry we're not open 'til 5.30, but come in and have a drink while you wait." The pub was full of locals who had been there all afternoon and the singing began. I guess this is another of Wrights' strengths. They can open doors that seem impossible to open.

I am grateful to be given this opportunity to write a few words. Well done to Jack for his enthusiasm and dedication in bringing this book to print.

It tells a truly amazing story of the growth of a small Ballymena company which is now an internationally respected player in the bus industry.

Thanks for allowing me along for the ride!

Steve Dewhurst

Steve Dewhurst

Brian King
Chairman, Wellglade Limited –
owners of Trent Barton

Wellglade

Wrights first came onto my radar when I was talking to a fellow operator many years ago. He had bought some Handybus bodies on early Darts. He said that Wrights were lovely people to deal with but you could never be quite sure when the vehicles would arrive! That was then and now is now. What a difference!

Some time after that I had a phone call, out of the blue, from a chap called Jack Kernohan. He was convinced that low floor buses were going to be the future and he had some early thoughts to share with us. Ian Morgan and I arranged to meet him and took a look at an early prototype. It took no time at all to confirm the description "lovely people" as we progressively met Jack, William, Jeff and the Wright team. The buses, though, were 'shoe boxes on wheels' – very functional and lacking in style. We told them of our desire to soften the look of buses, to turn the front into a friendly face and to get rid of harsh, aggressive interiors. They introduced us to Trevor Erskine, another lovely man, who as a former designer of cars was intended to do just that.

We stayed in touch over many years and exchanged ideas but despite the best efforts of Volvo nothing really clicked until we saw the marriage of Scania's L94 with Wrights Solar body. Suitably impressed we bought 92 of them! Volvo came back with the B7 married to a Wrights Eclipse body and we bought 51 of those. It is pretty good going from a standing start to have 143 Wrightbus vehicles in a front line fleet of 280 over seven years. Such has been the strength of the relationship with these lovely people. The quality has been very good, the delivery reliable, the factory totally transformed from my early visits – some irony then that an operator which regards itself as a retailer and its buses as mobile shops should be buying them from a company that once specialised in building mobile shops!

Brian King

The Bedford connection –
The Contour coach and orders from overseas

Over the years, whilst working with Bedford (Bus Division), we had built a strong relationship with the management of Scottish Motor Traction (SMT) in Glasgow and particularly with Bob Flockhart (Bus and Coach Sales Manager) who had many years experience of selling and marketing buses and coaches in Scotland. When I first met Bob (in 1979), he was selling Dormobile bus products in the same market segment in which we were interested. That soon changed, and with Bob's expertise on Bedford chassis, his customer base, who were well known to him personally, coupled with my knowledge of what Wrights could offer, ensured that both companies increased their sales both in Scotland and further afield. Bob Flockhart played a major role, increasing sales especially in Scotland and in the northern counties of England.

Once Bedford decided to close its manufacturing operations in the United Kingdom one of the first casualties was SMT. When the news broke, Bob was en route delivering a bus to Cumbria. On his return to base that evening he was informed that he was being made redundant. This was a major blow to a man who had given years of excellent service, enjoyed excellent health and was now 63 years of age. Bob had been looking forward to retirement in another two years when his wife retired from teaching. I had called his office for an update on his visit to our customer, to be informed that on

Bob Flockhart, Bus and Coach Sales Manager at SMT in Glasgow, examines the tail lift before the vehicle is delivered to the customer.

receiving the news Bob had gone home. Later that evening, after consulting with William Wright, I called Bob at home. He advised me of his current position and how he felt SMT had treated him after many years of service. I then gave him the good news that he could commence work for Wrights on Monday morning, a decision that I never regretted. Bob Flockhart worked for Wrights up until he retired. He still enjoys good health and this allows him time to work on and maintain his collection of Austin 7 vintage cars.

The management at Bedford advised Mr Wright that they would like the company to consider manufacturing a luxury coach on a new Bedford coach chassis that would be launched the following year. It was Bedford's intention that this coach would compete with the products of Duple and Plaxton, both of which were well established in the United Kingdom market and also with European imports such as those of Van Hool. Bedford had an opening in the design studies before their next project and they were willing to assist in the design and styling of the Wrights product. Geoff Lawson, who was

1983 and Wrights enter the luxury coach market with the Contour, a coach ahead of its time in styling terms.

later to join Jaguar to develop the then new S series styling, played a key role, assisted by Wrights own Design Engineer, Trevor Erskine, in the development of what became the very stylish Contour coach.

Wrights invested heavily in this project, both in time and money, over a two-year period. The Bedford coach dealers were kept fully informed on the progress of the new coach's development, often visiting the styling studio to view the new product. Bedford had promised a minimum order of 50 coaches, with stock chassis to support the development/sales programme.

The new Contour coach was superb and was extremely well received by both the trade-press and the potential customers. Alas, neither Bedford nor its dealer network honoured their agreement. At the product launch, in the showrooms of SMT, to coincide with the Scottish Commercial Motor show when orders could have been secured, no Bedford chassis were available. The reason given was that the Bedford Dealer Network had failed to order the chassis in time to meet our build programme, and the new Venturer coach chassis had thus been further delayed. Valuable sales opportunities were lost. However, when chassis became available a few months later the order book had firmed up and production commenced.

The Contour coaches built on Bedford chassis featured farings on the wheelarches at rear.

At the same time as Bedford launched the new Wright Contour coach, Leyland launched a new Plaxton Paramount-bodied coach. There were many similarities between the two products and many industry professionals were of the opinion that the Contour coach was the more stylish of the two. All the windows on the Contour top specification models were double-glazed and, for the first time, the windows were bonded, as opposed to gasket glazed. This gave the Contour a very modern, stylish appearance that projected quality. It also provided our competitors with a story that they mischievously used to their advantage when in discussion with customers – that there was a doubt about the long-term structural strength and durability of the bonding adhesive.

Worse was to follow. No sooner had we got production of the Contour up to the agreed targets than volume orders stopped coming from the dealer network. The reason was plain and simple – there had been trouble in Europe, with rioting in major cities and this was threatening to spill over into the United Kingdom. With no visitors from overseas and with fewer from Great Britain going to Europe on holiday, operators were postponing the purchasing of new coaches until their business improved. Coach dealers were sitting with thousands of pounds of new and old stock that was not moving and while that situation remained they would not be ordering any stock vehicles.

The Bedford coach chassis was viewed as a lightweight by the major operators. There was always a question mark on the reliability of the chassis, engine and driveline and the after sales support for Bedford in Europe was far from satisfactory. Wrights, having taken a decision to increase market share, also offered the Contour on the Leyland Tiger chassis. This was developed with the first vehicles, four 57-seaters with gasket-glazed bodies, going into service with Ulsterbus Tours in 1984/5.

Wrights manufactured a total of 36 Contour coaches on Bedford, ACE Ford and Leyland chassis of varying lengths, with the last one being built on a Volvo B10M coach chassis. This vehicle was purchased by Liddell's Coaches at Auchinleck, in Scotland and I understand that, at the time of compiling the information for this book, it was still in use. This particular Contour was built to a high-floor design with increased luggage space. It was destined to remain unique. Due to the lack of sales and the recession in the coach market Duple closed up shop never to open again. Wrights, however, decided to mothball the Contour until trading conditions improved. Shortly afterwards, in 1989, the company had a major fire at the Ballymena plant forcing them to move to a new site, where the company is now located. A considerable number of the moulds, including the main fibreglass moulds perished in the fire. Unfortunately, this forced the company to make the decision that they would not build or develop products for that segment of the market in the foreseeable future.

In 1984/5, Ulsterbus took delivery of four 12m, 57-seat Contours on Leyland Tiger chassis. No 544 is seen here on the pier at Donaghadee, Co Down. *(G Irvine Millar collection)*

The last Contour built was rather a special vehicle being the only high-floor example and the only one built on the Volvo B10M chassis. It was given the suffix *Imperial* to distinguish it from the low height model.

The author and Trevor Erskine with the Contour Imperial.

When compiling this book, I received a call from Edward Doherty, an operator based in Irvine who had purchased a Contour coach. I was pleasantly surprised to hear that the Imperial was still at work with Liddell's Coaches at Auchinleck, who had purchased it new in 1984. *(Liddell's Coaches)*

The company's good relationship and reputation with the senior management of Bedford was a major benefit to both parties down through the years. Wrights sales team worked closely with both the United Kingdom and export sales teams at Bedford who provided Wrights with valuable enquiries, many from overseas.

One such overseas enquiry was from an operator based in Bermuda. A senior manager of the island transport company was visiting the United Kingdom to examine what was on offer from United Kingdom manufacturers and Bedford kindly directed him to call Wrights and make arrangements to visit the company, view the products and discuss his company's requirements. The arrangements were made and, in due course, I met him at Belfast International Airport. On the way from the airport to the factory, the gentleman informed me that he would only be stopping over for the one night, the reason being that there was too much bombing and shooting for him to feel safe. He also had other companies in the United Kingdom that he planned to visit.

We discussed his operational requirements, which were not what we had assumed. The engineers were asked to prepare revised drawings for the following morning. They informed me that they could have these completed, including the costings, for 10.00 am. I then decided, as I did on many occasions, to let the gentleman see a little of Northern Ireland during his visit. It was a beautiful, sunny afternoon and we visited Portstewart, Portrush and then on to Bushmills, on the scenic North Antrim coast. On seeing a road sign as we approached, he advised me that the top whiskey in his country was, surprisingly, called Bushmills. Only as we approached the village did I inform him that the whiskey was distilled here in County Antrim, at the oldest whiskey distillery in the world. As it was the evening

In 1985, Ulsterbus purchased two 11m Contour-bodied Tigers, Nos 537/8, for use on its Irish and Welsh tour programmes. No 538 was later sold to Don Reddin, at Muff, Co Donegal. It must be one of the few Contours left in service anywhere, and probably the only one in Ireland. (Richard Newman)

Ulsterbus also acquired a Contour-bodied Tiger, No 540, from a dealer. This was differed from its own order in that it was a 53-seater and featured bonded glazing. It also had the Hydracyclic gearbox option, which made it non-standard in the Ulsterbus fleet. It later passed to the London Borough of Havering having gone back through Wrights factory to be fitted with an additional door and a wheelchair lift, making it the first accessible coach in the United Kingdom.
(Paul Savage)

and the distillery was closed we travelled on to the world famous Giant's Causeway, a major tourist attraction in Northern Ireland.

The Causeway itself is situated approximately one mile from the visitors centre and, as it was late evening, the tourist bus was not running so we walked down to view the rock formations. As we walked back up to the car park, a cuckoo was calling from the mountainside; it was a beautiful evening, the sun was shining, and the waves were breaking on the shoreline. The gentleman stopped and referred to it being God's Garden so I jokingly asked him had he noticed there had been no gun battles today!

We were to meet at 11.00 am the following morning to view the drawings before his departure for the airport. When we met, he informed me that he had gone into Ballymena town centre and was pleasantly surprised at the friendly welcome he received from a number of people who had stopped with him. This was something entirely new to him as back home everyone went about their business and did not talk or, on reflection, welcome strangers. He then informed me that he had changed his plans as he wanted to see more of 'God's Garden', so could I get a hire car for him. I arranged insurance and provided maps and lots of instructions. He arrived on Monday and left on Saturday to go to London for the weekend before returning home. Two

Around 1984, and with the assistance of Bedford, Wrights supplied 25 TT-bodied buses to a customer, Federated Motor Industries, in Africa. They were all built to a similar specification but on at least two different chassis types.

months later Wrights received an order for four luxury coaches, to be built on Bedford chassis. I have always felt that the welcome this gentleman received from the local people in Ulster during his brief visit, contributed to Wrights' success in winning this order.

A major order worth mentioning was negotiated with the assistance of Bedford, this time to a major customer in Africa – Federated Motors Industries. This order consisted of 25 buses all built to a similar specification, the colour of external livery being the main difference. Before they were all delivered, the political climate changed, structures became unstable and FMI shipped the remainder to another country. My reason for remembering this contract so well has nothing to do with the sales but, rather, the transportation of the product. We were instructed to ship the product through Dublin. We advised the company that all radio equipment should be removed after installation, re-packaged and delivered

separately, as from experience this type of equipment could easily go missing. The answer was, "No, install and commission all equipment prior to gate release." The buses were delivered to what was supposed to be a secure compound in Dublin Port prior to onward shipping and, yes, all the radio equipment did go missing! This happened not once but twice before they listened to Wrights' advice.

When General Motors closed the Bedford commercial operations in the United Kingdom, Wrights lost a valuable ally. Both Bedford and Leyland had developed extensive overseas markets as well as the home market. It is my view that these two should have been combined into one major commercial vehicle manufacturing company and given financial assistance if required, allowing them to compete with the major continental manufacturers.

Vision was lacking and with the demise of these two, plus Ford, the United Kingdom had no longer a bus or coach manufacturing company, other than Dennis, whose main business at that time was the manufacture of fire engines and refuse collection vehicles, although that would later change significantly. In future, the main suppliers of bus and coach chassis would all come from overseas – Volvo, Scania, DAF with a few from Mercedes and MAN.

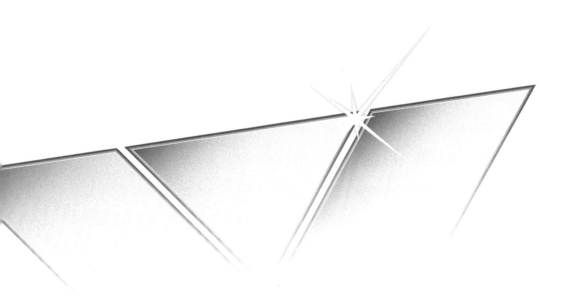

Phil Margrave
Group Engineering Director,
Go-Ahead Group

My earliest memory of Wrights is a visit to Northern Ireland in the late 1980s during those difficult times. Having landed at Belfast International Airport, the taxi followed a milk tanker out of the exit road only to be stopped by soldiers. I was sitting in the back of a car at a security barrier awaiting clearance when a soldier who was on security at the airport, moved to the back of the milk tanker and proceeded to fill a bottle with milk one presumes for his morning coffee. An uneventful trip then on to the factory resulted in my arrival in the car park only to witness members of the product development team hurling bricks at some aluminium framework / panels – you can imagine my nervousness!

My reluctance at this time to purchase any Wrights vehicles was due to their higher cost compared to the competition and despite protestations from a certain larger than life Sales Manager, I still refused to be drawn. One of the conversations with the said Sales Manager was that 'I am not going to retire until I have sold Phil Margrave a bus', but more about this later.

Visits to view production continued, a highlight of which was 'a new bus for London' – deja vu here – where we viewed a Handybus-bodied Dennis Dart, which resembled the front of a tube train, and of which Trevor Erskine was extremely proud; allegedly Peter Hendy liked it as well! A redesign of these vehicles some time later featured the inclusion of a one piece front screen which moved it from looking like a tube train to more of an overground example.

The theme of expensive vehicles continued and I was only ever able to afford, being a poor London bus operator, a number of second-hand variants of these vehicles which, I might add, were very good service vehicles and, unusually, despite the high mileage, had no rattles, something that Wrights can justifiably be proud of.

After pressure and persuasion from chassis manufacturers I bought a single vehicle (well, only leased it). It was a Wright Crusader midi bus on a Volvo B6LE, and I remember Jack being so pleased when he went to his Board Meeting to tell them that at last he had sold Phil Margrave a bus – actually he did not mention the fact that it was only one bus but this came out some time later. (Roger Turner was mortified when he found out about the agreed specification and has been reluctant to allow me to go to body builders on my own ever since!)

A major step forward was when Jack turned up in my office with a proposal to build double-deck buses and, despite the fact they were more expensive than I would have liked, I could not resist and we now have nearly 400 examples in service.

My relationship with Wrights grew and you can say this, it is exactly like dealing with family because that is what Wrights is – one big family that draws you in, convincing you of the 'Wright' way and then introduces you to William who attaches the handcuffs that never come off!

Phil Margrave

Steve Clayton

MEMORIES OF WRIGHTS
some musings by Steve Clayton (ex-Arriva plc)

My first contact with Wrights followed the purchase of a large fleet (over 100) of Wright-bodied minibuses by Peter Hendy when he converted London routes 28 and 31 from crew operation in the late 1980s. The Dart was new on the scene and I found myself in the company of Peter, Geoff Chamberlain and Arthur Burroughs reviewing the design for the Handy (not Hendy!) Bus. Trevor Erskine was the first person I ever met from Wrights, the soft spoken genteel Director of Design whose attention to detail and polite challenging of existing wisdom was, and still is, impressive. Trevor picked us up from Belfast airport on my first visit and treated us to a detailed commentary on the many incidents that had recently occurred on our route back to Ballymena. Despite my initial apprehension his calm manner left me completely at ease.

The factory in the late 1980s, whilst impressive, was nothing to the sophisticated plant that exists today. We discussed the design of the Dart, with its distinctive split windscreen (which was soon superseded by a more conventional one piece arrangement), in great detail over a series of visits. On every occasion Trevor had acted on every comment made at our previous meeting. As London operators we were all keen to see the development of a robust lightweight single-deck vehicle. The Alusuisse construction adopted by Wrights at that time, whilst heavier than conventional construction, had all the attractions of ease of repair, robustness (you could throw a brick at a panel and not even scratch the paint – I know, as along with many others I was invited to try when at the plant), and great strength and rigidity. On one occasion Peter, Geoff and I went to the plant in the evening to road test a prototype at night for windscreen glare. A very patient engineer accompanied us as we drove all around Ballymena and its environs without a care in the world and at risk of getting hopelessly lost – all at a time in Northern Ireland's history when it was not as at peace with itself as it is now.

On one occasion Peter took a ticket machine over and had great fun getting it through security at Heathrow as hand baggage only to be robustly interrogated in Belfast Airport by a policeman who wanted to know what he thought he was doing. Behind the scenes of course was a rather impish Trevor Erskine who had put the officer up to it!

Wrights grew from strength to strength, and deservedly so. Sadly in the early years their 'after care' service lagged behind. I once had a very full and frank discussion with Jack Kernohan over lunch in the White Horse Hotel in Hertingfordbury in Hertfordshire. The conversation was so robust that I seriously began to worry that I had deeply offended Jack (even though I was the customer that had not been my intention) and was fearful of his reaction. He looked me straight in the eye – quite fearsomely – and conceded without offering any excuses that after sales was not up

to scratch and accepted that something needed to be done. Shortly afterwards the company developed Customcare which, combined with their reputation for build quality, helped Wrights to increase the scale of their business.

Jack is wonderful man with a great sense of humour (not always intentional, I think). He is the only man who has invited me out to dinner to a restaurant that was closed for the evening! However, I can assure you that everyone who visited the company never went away hungry, what with dinner in the evening followed by a Ulster Fry the following morning for breakfast. Equally, Jack is an immensely thoughtful man who constantly challenged us. It was Jack who persuaded Mark Bowd and I to abandon bench seating and adopt modern individual seats as standard across all our new vehicle orders. Jack demonstrated that the customer did not always know what was in its best interests – many a deal with Jack was sealed with a shake of the hand. Equally, Jack put the fear of God into me one day when we went Skeet shooting. I had just scored 24 out of 25 when Jack strolled up quite nonchalantly with a loaded shotgun under his arm that was pointing rather too closely in my direction. I scored 12 the next time – but Jack got his order!

When Wrights decided it was time to consider building double-deckers, I was among those consulted. Trevor Erskine, then semi retired (I recall), was part of the team that came and quizzed us about what we wanted. I was not sure that it was the correct thing for Wrights and told them so. I was worried that they might overreach themselves and lose the essential qualities that we all held so dear. It was a tough time in the manufacturing industry and I learned subsequently that Jeff Wright, who was running the business at the time, had serious concerns for its future. I had so much faith in the double-deck design and the ability of the team at Wrights to deliver the quality on time that I and Mark Bowd ordered the very first fifty from the drawing board, on Volvo chassis. The Eclipse Gemini design is much loved by all. I am proud to have played a role being the first to bring it and its earlier low floor competitor the ALX400 to market.

No reminiscence of Wrights would be complete without a mention of William. Justly revered throughout the industry it is, I am sure, William that has been largely responsible for the ethos of engineering excellence in both design and construction at the company. He has a closely enquiring mind that is constantly reviewing the possibilities and technologies of the future, willing to challenge accepted practices from both a constructor's and operator's viewpoint. In my many visits over the years William frequently accompanied us and always knew what was going on. He is a man devoted to what he does and to the people who work for him and the business. Now a new team of managers is carrying on the Wright tradition (ably assisted by an ageless William). Mark Nodder has done a great job in selling that tradition into a wider market place and I am pleased to note that Wrights built almost half of Arriva's 2009 vehicle intake in the UK.

Steve Clayton

FIRE!! – Company Relocates to Galgorm

On the morning of Friday 23 November 1989 I was awakened by a phone call from the local police who advised me that residents adjacent to the Cushendall Road factory had alerted them that there was a major fire at the premises. I was suffering from flu, with a temperature of 103°, but having received this news, and knowing that there was a large number of buses awaiting despatch, hurriedly dressed and went, with my son, to the factory complex to see flames coming through the roof of a section of the main building of the South Factory. This section of the building was the production area where all chassis modifications, including the body sub-frames, were assembled. It was evident that the chassis in the first two development bays could not be saved. However, there was a considerable number of chassis in the other section of the factory. The members of the Royal Ulster Constabulary, being the first at the scene, had evaluated the situation and were in the process of using their cars to pull out chassis from the building. All of the midibus chassis were in the process of being worked on the previous day, and the rear wheels had been removed but this did not prevent their removal!

To the rear of the factory was a new housing development, Shane Court. One resident, Richard McCook, had been awakened by the sound of crackling timbers; he immediately alerted his neighbour, Thomas Smyth and they called the fire service. Together they warned all of their neighbours of the hazard, which loomed just a matter of a few feet away from their houses. As the flames intensified, they used their garden hoses to cool down the timbers of their homes. Within eight minutes of them making the call, two fire engines arrived at the scene. One was directed to the front of the factory and the other into Shane Court to ensure that the private residences

The aftermath of the fire at the Cushendall Road site.

were made safe and then they attacked the blaze within the factory complex from both front and rear.

I might add that with all the excitement in fighting the fire, extracting chassis from the burning workshops etc, I forgot for a period of time that I had flu and it was not until two hours later that I began to feel the effects and went home to recover.

As daylight broke it became clear that half of the South Factory complex was completely gutted and the other half would be out of commission for a considerable time whilst major repairs were carried out. In typical Wright fashion, by 9.00am the same morning full production was being maintained by moving chassis development to another area of the North Factory. The losses of specialist equipment and workers' tools were soon replaced and it was business as usual.

The £3.5 million contract, which had recently been signed, had led to the creation of a further 10 jobs, bringing up the workforce total to 130. Sixteen of these new midibuses had been delivered the previous week and others were awaiting MOT certification and so deliveries to our customers were not affected.

Forensic experts established that the fire had occurred due to a fault in the heat exchanger in a large workshop heater, which ducted hot air to all the work bays. Chassis were purchased to replace those lost in the fire; it was vitally important that these chassis were delivered on time to ensure that the company would meet its delivery commitment to our customer.

The workforce, with the assistance of the production manager, Albert Hanna, rose to the challenge, and all the midibuses were delivered to the agreed schedule and, equally as important, within budget. The Industrial Development Board (IDB), on hearing the news of the fire, which was reported widely both on radio and television, called William Wright offering

The Galgorm site has been expanded on to sites to the left and right of this photo.

whatever assistance was required, to ensure that none of the employees would lose out. It was at one of those meetings that William approached them about a vacant factory, which had been built for the textile industry, at Galgorm Industrial Estate. Due to the demise of the textile business there were few opportunities for this plant to reopen in the near future. The building would require a number of fairly extensive modifications if Wrights was to consider relocation.

The location of the Cushendall Road/Hugomount site, were it to be rebuilt, would limit the company's growth potential. However, to purchase the new factory, carry out the necessary structural modifications and install the entire specialist equipment also had a risk factor. The management, having looked at the cost of rebuilding the South Factory and realising with the new housing developments they would be land locked with no opportunity to expand, took what was then a major decision – to purchase the factory complex at Galgorm. Looking back now, it was one of William Wright's better decisions. I might also add that the valuable assistance offered by the IDB also helped, by promoting jobs and local industry in Ballymena. Up until the recession of 2009, no other local company had, to my knowledge, over the previous fifteen years increased its workforce year on year to compare with Wrightbus.

The ink had not dried on the agreement with the IDB to proceed with the purchase of the factory, before Albert had construction teams carrying out the initial structural changes required to adapt the building and install the specialist equipment to meet his operational requirements. Within a matter of a few weeks, production had commenced at Galgorm and soon we were to see the benefits of having increased space and the total build all completed under one roof. No longer would the company be handicapped by having to work on both sides of a main road! Over a period of time production was completely transferred to Galgorm and the existing factory, including the two sites, was sold off as small commercial units, one of which has fairly recently been re-sold for private housing development.

Wrights targets the GB PSV Market

I n the early 1980s, Wrights had still a substantial order book for traditional coach-built products from school and health care authorities both in Ireland and the United Kingdom.

Market intelligence was indicating to the management that if the company was to expand it must develop a range of products for the PSV market. After deregulation in Great Britain in 1986 and the subsequent 'Ford Transit revolution', there was a growing market for a range of better built midibuses as operators strove to increase market share by increased frequencies. The two chassis favoured by operators were the Mercedes (709D/811D models) and the Renault S75. Having built buses on these chassis for both the school bus and the welfare markets it was relatively easy to develop a product for PSV operation.

I was tasked with developing a totally new sales/customer base, targeting the bus companies operating in all the major cities in the United Kingdom

With the relative success that the company was having in the GB welfare sector, it was decided that the time was right to target the PSV market. This Renault demonstrator was built to PSV specification and shown to operators around GB.

and in Ireland. My sales assistant, Cyril Reid, dedicated his time to servicing all of the company's existing customers in Northern Ireland. At a later date Cyril started up his own company, Drumack Coachworks, in Rasharkin, and continued to provide a quality product and an excellent service to customers. Cyril will freely admit that he benefited a lot from his training on the workshop floor and latterly from his experience in the sales team whilst at Wrights.

I can tell you that it was extremely difficult for me as a representative of a relatively unknown coachbuilder to get an appointment with the key decision makers of major bus companies, and those difficulties did not end there as:

- Prospective customers in the United Kingdom did not know the company name;

- No products available to show customers in Great Britain;

- No buses in the local Ulsterbus fleet for customers to view when they were visiting the factory in Northern Ireland;

- I myself was not known to the management of the companies; and

- Wrights had not built buses for the public service segment of the United Kingdom bus industry.

One other factor, which was a major problem, was the ongoing terrorist activity in the Province. The Troubles had started in 1969 and by the late 1970s/early 1980s they were at their worst. Every day the news reports consisted of street riots, another bombing, fires in major stores and, last but not least, the murder of civilians and members of the police and security forces. However, if and when I was able to persuade the management of bus companies to come to Northern Ireland, see what Wrights could offer and, hopefully, influence their purchasing policy, there were three questions I was often asked:

- What about security of supply?

- With all the riots, bombing, etc, would the factory be there if they were to consider placing an order?

- Why should I risk coming to Northern Ireland, where anything could happen, when I can visit my current supplier, within a few hours by train or bus, with no concerns about my safety?

A journalist once told me that the only good news is bad news so the positive news about Northern Ireland was rarely highlighted on the national news bulletins or in the national newspapers. Obviously there was a reticence among many to visit this part of the United Kingdom. However, those managers from the various bus companies who were persuaded to visit Wrights found an entirely different country to that portrayed on the TV screens or in their newspapers. Wrights has a lot to be thankful for, especially the fact that throughout the Troubles we had few problems in and around Ballymena, which was obviously a major benefit.

If the company was to gain a significant market share the management had to make some major strategic decisions. One way to gain market share is to undercut your competitor's product price but that was never an option for Wrights for a number of reasons:

- The costs of transporting the chassis to the factory and, when completed, back to Great Britain;

- The transport costs of shipping all the raw materials and components;

- Labour costs were similar to Great Britain;

- Engineering and development costs; and

- Product Certification to Great Britain standards. (The local Inspectorate in Northern Ireland operated to different standards so Wrights had to fly someone from Great Britain, at its cost, to inspect each and every bus. I contacted the Minster then responsible for Regional Transport, Rev. Martin Smyth, MP, and, when briefed, he took up the case on behalf of the company. Three years later, after many meetings, Wrights were successful in winning something that we in Northern Ireland should always have had – a local Inspectorate trained to and working to the same standard as the rest of the United Kingdom.)

The one benefit we had at that time was that in Northern Ireland we did not pay the same rates on the factory buildings; this was offset, by the fact that we had much higher energy costs, plus the additional costs of transporting the chassis and materials to and from the mainland.

Based on these facts the company could not reduce its selling price to gain entry into this growing market. The management, having examined the market and listened to the potential customers, took what was then a major decision – to engineer and design a product superior to all our competitors incorporating many innovative ideas offering:

- Greater durability;

- Longer life expectancy;

- Substantially lower life-time costs;

- Reduce accident repair costs with greatly reduced downtime;

- Easier to clean;

- Twelve year structural warranty (subject to the agreed terms); and

- Superb after sales service.

Wrights new products were introduced with:

- All aluminium corrosion resistant construction;

- All bolted construction for ease of repair;

- Quick fit easily replaceable lower panels (time 5 to 10 min);

- Quick Fit rear bottom corner panels (time 5 min);

- Frontal panelling (6 components) (time 10 min);

- Replace a headlight bulb (in chassis compound) (time 3 min); and

- Modern, stylish design, with the interior trim and floor coverings easily cleaned.

They were introduced at a premium price of £2000 on a single-deck and, later, considerably more on a double-deck, with a no quibble warranty and superb after sales service, above that of our competitors.

London has by far the largest number of buses per head of population in the United Kingdom and therefore offered Wrights the greatest opportunity. London Transport specified and purchased all the buses; these were then allocated to the operating districts/companies. As Wrights was not known and had no track record in the PSV market, it was a case of getting on to London Transport's tender list, then proving the company had a product equal or better than our competitors.

Price was important. Equally so was the ability to deliver on time and support the product, especially when you were dealing with the volumes that London Transport was purchasing. We had tendered for a small number of midibuses on Mercedes chassis. During our negotiations, it become apparent that because we were offering three standees less than our competitors, we could not be considered. We then asked to examine the competitor's product with a view to establishing that we were offering like for like and, particularly, why they could offer three additional standees. We also asked the management at London Transport to give us a few days to come up with an answer.

We examined our competitor's product and were not impressed. There were major structural weaknesses in the underframe design which were already beginning to show structural defects in the bodywork. The London Transport engineer, when shown the problem, expressed his concerns and was asked, if given a choice, would he prefer to have a vehicle with three fewer

Unhappy with what it was then purchasing, Centrewest, in London, ordered 90 midibuses on the Renault S75 chassis. The bodies featured a wider entrance to ease passenger flow. RW15 is seen here by the shores of Lough Neagh, at Antrim, in this pre-delivery photograph.

Wrights have been long time supporters of the Irish Transport Trust's annual Bus and Coach Rally. At the 1990 event, the company won the Concours d'Elegance award, sponsored by Walter Alexander and Co; Rodney Mark and Stephen Francey pose with the trophy.

standees or one with long-term structural problems. That meeting and vehicle examination was to have a major impact both on the design of the products and Wrights standing with London Transport.

While we were with the engineer we discovered that accidental damage to lower panelling front, sides and rear was a major problem to the operating companies, resulting in excessive downtime and expensive repairs. It was back to the drawing board again, and here we had the advantage of Alusuisse who had previously designed an easily replaceable panel system. Drawings were prepared and submitted to London Transport, plus a report on our findings. We offered the easily replaceable panel system to them for this contract, at no extra cost, for them to trial. We had won the contract, and having achieved our first order, it was now up to Production Services to deliver the product and the after sales support. This order was the first of many. London Transport was delighted with the product and the after sales service. Orders for both Mercedes and Renaults with a seating capacity of 24/29 were coming from many of the operating companies, all of whom saw the advantage of having a 'Quick Fit' replacement panel system.

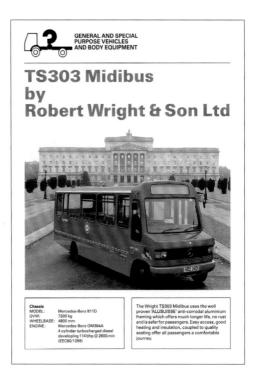

GENERAL AND SPECIAL PURPOSE VEHICLES AND BODY EQUIPMENT

TS303 Midibus by Robert Wright & Son Ltd

Chassis		The Wright TS303 Midibus uses the well
MODEL:	Mercedes-Benz 811D	proven 'ALUSUISSE' anti-corrodal aluminium framing which offers much longer life, no rust and is safer for passengers. Easy access, good heating and insulation, coupled to quality seating offer all passengers a comfortable journey.
GVW:	7200 kg	
WHEELBASE:	4800 mm	
ENGINE:	Mercedes-Benz OM364A	
	4 cylinder turbocharged diesel developing 114 bhp @ 2600 min (EEC80/1269)	

A small number of similarly-bodied Mercedes 811Ds were supplied to London.

Ulsterbus took a small number of 23/25-seat Mercedes 709Ds for use on town services and lightly-loaded rural routes. No 825 was used for publicity photographs and is seen in Ballymena's Wellington Street.

One of London Transport's operating companies, CentreWest, had requested 90 midibuses and we knew we had a fight on our hands if we were to win this business. Price was important, but more important was the delivery schedule. We had to take on the larger well-established companies and prove we could deliver. Based on our tendered price and the agreed delivery schedule we won the order on Renault S75 chassis. The problem now was to deliver, as we had already a substantial order book, but, as usual, Albert Hanna and his team performed a miracle and all the buses were delivered on time and, more importantly, within budget. Many years later John Whitworth (Chief Engineer at CentreWest) advised me that when these buses were being sold on, despite the fact that the Renault chassis was not the most popular with potential buyers, the vehicles sold easily because of the outstanding condition of the bodywork.

The demand for midibuses was growing not only in Great Britain but also closer to home. Ulsterbus saw the many benefits gained by the operators of midibuses and asked Wrights to put forward proposals based on the Mercedes 709D chassis. These were built as 23/25 seaters and were put to use on a mix of town services, rural routes and lightly-used services, a very different approach to that taken by operators in Great Britain. They were given a brighter livery with the branding *Busybus*. The last of these vehicles delivered between 1989 and 1992 was withdrawn in 2006. Several are now in use with operators in County Donegal.

Mr Ken Middleton (Chief Engineer) called me one day to advise me that one of their Mercedes 709D midibuses had been severely damaged in an Army controlled explosion. I asked could I see it and later that week went to view the damage, which was fairly extensive. The bomb had been detonated at floor level and most of the internal and external panelling had either disappeared or ballooned outwards. The side and roof framework was intact, though. However, what did surprise us was the fact that the roof had been raised approximately 50mm by the blast; we established this by the fact that none of the vertical stanchions were in their roof sockets. The engine and driveline were not damaged and, after a period awaiting a decision on its future, the body builders in Ulsterbus' Duncrue Street workshops removed the damaged body and built a replica of a 1930s charabanc on the overhauled chassis.

In August 1992, Ulsterbus No 840, a TS-bodied Mercedes, was hijacked in Londonderry. A suspect package was placed on board and consequently Army Ammunition Technical Officers were called out. This is the result of their 'controlled' explosion. *(Will Hughes)*

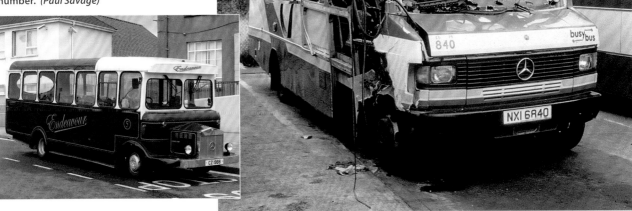

No 840 was rebuilt by Ulsterbus as a replica charabanc, even being re-registered with an appropriate 1930s number. *(Paul Savage)*

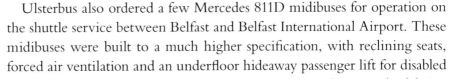

Later deliveries to Ulsterbus featured a revised frontal arrangement, with the windscreen brought forward to the edge of the bonnet. This design was known as 'fast front'.

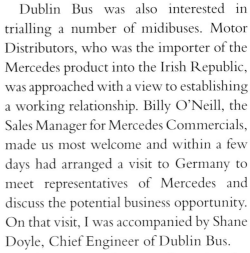

Ulsterbus also ordered a few Mercedes 811D midibuses for operation on the shuttle service between Belfast and Belfast International Airport. These midibuses were built to a much higher specification, with reclining seats, forced air ventilation and an underfloor hideaway passenger lift for disabled passengers, including those in wheelchairs.

Dublin Bus was also interested in trialling a number of midibuses. Motor Distributors, who was the importer of the Mercedes product into the Irish Republic, was approached with a view to establishing a working relationship. Billy O'Neill, the Sales Manager for Mercedes Commercials, made us most welcome and within a few days had arranged a visit to Germany to meet representatives of Mercedes and discuss the potential business opportunity. On that visit, I was accompanied by Shane Doyle, Chief Engineer of Dublin Bus.

When we got down to discussing the

Another customer for the TS/Nimbus body on the Mercedes chassis was British Airways, which specified them with wider entrances and increased luggage space for use on crew transfer duties.

vehicle specification, it was discovered that operators could have a number of different options, which would greatly improve the product that was currently being offered in the United Kingdom. The Mercedes midibus chassis was based around a commercial chassis, basically the same as used on a delivery van. For bus operations, with constant stop/start, operating in arduous conditions, we needed to look at what was available to improve passenger comfort whilst also improving the driver's environment. Twelve options were agreed, which were not offered in the UK.

Two of the most important options selected by Dublin Bus were the comfort suspension and the air over hydraulic braking system and what a difference they made to these buses, especially when compared to what was being offered in the United Kingdom – and they were considerably cheaper!

When the first of the new midibuses for Dublin Bus was completed, we demonstrated the new product to the representatives of London Buses (Arthur Burrows) and Ulsterbus (Ken Middleton). Both later approached

Dublin Bus purchased Wright-bodied Mercedes in 1990. No MW8 is seen at Dublin Airport on route 230 thence to Malahide. *(Paul Savage)*

Mercedes Benz demanding that future products for the United Kingdom be upgraded to include the options available to Dublin Bus. Ken Middleton sent me a copy of the letter he had forwarded to Mercedes Benz United Kingdom stating that if they would not supply chassis to a similar specification then all future Ulsterbus orders would be placed with the Mercedes agents in Dublin.

Mercedes Benz (UK) upgraded the specification, but did nothing about the considerable price differential. Operators were delighted that at last they could now specify a midibus with air operated doors and improved suspension, offering a much more comfortable journey. Wrights continued to build minibuses for operators all over the United Kingdom, but the key customer base for volume orders of these products was with London Buses.

The Dennis Dart Revolution

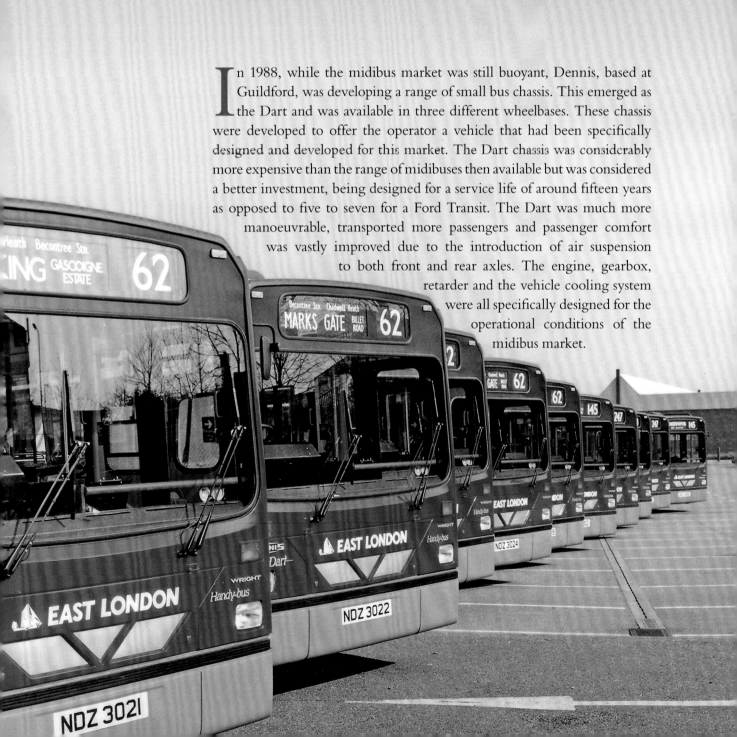

In 1988, while the midibus market was still buoyant, Dennis, based at Guildford, was developing a range of small bus chassis. This emerged as the Dart and was available in three different wheelbases. These chassis were developed to offer the operator a vehicle that had been specifically designed and developed for this market. The Dart chassis was considerably more expensive than the range of midibuses then available but was considered a better investment, being designed for a service life of around fifteen years as opposed to five to seven for a Ford Transit. The Dart was much more manoeuvrable, transported more passengers and passenger comfort was vastly improved due to the introduction of air suspension to both front and rear axles. The engine, gearbox, retarder and the vehicle cooling system were all specifically designed for the operational conditions of the midibus market.

The Dennis Dart was becoming more and more acceptable, with more of Wrights customers asking them to develop a midibus on this chassis. Initially, the Dart was only available from Dennis with the Duple Dartline body. Later, Carlyle acquired the Duple body design and the manufacturing rights. Soon after Carlyle had assembled the jigs to manufacture the body, London Transport tendered for a substantial number of Dart midibuses. Those London bus operators who had purchased the Duple/Carlyle product were finding that the all-bonded panelling on that product was difficult to repair. Downtime was thus a major problem; when damage did occur the bus was in the garage much longer and, whilst there, was not earning any revenue.

Looking back now, London really was an easy target and, in 1990, Wrights offered its new Handybus on all three versions of the chassis. The Handybus was designed and engineered using the well proven Alusuisse M5438 system. All bottom panels were easily detachable and could be removed and replaced in approximately ten minutes. The split windscreen, the driver's side raked back to reduce reflection, could be replaced in minutes and then only cost £50. It actually took longer to remove the broken glass!

One of the early Wright Handybus Darts for CentreWest, DW2, is seen in this pre-delivery photograph at Dunluce Castle, on Northern Ireland's scenic North Antrim coast. Note the split windscreen, which didn't help the look of the vehicle.

Wrights had caught the market with the right product at the right time and soon Handybuses were flowing from the plant to operators all over the UK. Engineering managers liked the simplicity of the product and accountants liked the maintenance figures. The Go-Ahead Group in Newcastle ordered a substantial number of Handybuses but they disliked the appearance of the two piece split windscreen, so the production engineers developed a one-piece windscreen within the same standard front moulding.

These Handy Buses were very well received by both drivers and passengers. We asked companies to send over a number of their maintenance teams consisting of electrical engineers, bodybuilders and stores management to familiarise themselves with the product before the buses were delivered. Peter Lanfrancie (Engineering Manager) reported to me that the bus maintenance team from Go-Ahead were very impressed with the Alusuisse System and they were looking forward to the day when they were asked to carry out a major repair. That opportunity came much sooner than anyone expected.

A few weeks later one of the new midibuses was involved in an accident; if my memory serves me right, a cement mixer collided with the front offside of the bus. It was a major accident that entailed the maintenance team replacing the entire front and offside framework. A representative from Wrights visited Go-Ahead's workshop to view the progress and was surprised to find a group of very happy men who had all but completed the task. They expressed how valuable they had found the training they had received in the repair procedure and how simple the new system was to repair, when compared to traditionally built products.

Go-Ahead ordered a substantial number of Handybus-bodied Darts for its operations in north-east England.

Wrights had learned a valuable lesson, in that, if we were to succeed in the United Kingdom market, we must involve both the management, at all levels, and the service teams. From then on, the garage service teams were expected to come and view the product in build, prior to delivery and to complete a two-day course on the maintenance and repair of the buses for each and every order we received from a new location in the UK and Ireland.

It was at an ALBUM conference in 1991 – always supported by the suppliers to the bus industry – that I met a gentleman who was to play a significant role in the growth of the company in the future. Wrights was showing a Handybus and Plaxton was demonstrating its Pointer, a similar product. Charles Moseby was representing Plaxton. During the interval we got talking. Charles had worked at Reeve Burgess, a small company, not unlike Wrights, manufacturing ambulances, welfare buses and midibuses before it had been taken over by Plaxton.

Charles had reported directly to Harry Reeve, whom he held in high regard, as did most people in the industry. The more I talked to Charles, the more I discovered that he was not happy working for the Plaxton management. I was well aware that if we were to add to our customer base I needed assistance. In Charles I saw a young man with great potential. He was from a similar background within our industry. I asked him to come over and view the range of products and meet with William Wright and myself, with a view to him joining the company. He agreed and came over to view the production facilities at the factory. We discussed his potential role within the company and within a few weeks Charles joined Wrights

Charles Moseby joined Wrights in 1991 as United Kingdom Sales Manager.

The 1000th Dart chassis was delivered to Yorkshire Traction and carried a Handybus body.

A small number of Handybus bodies were built on the Leyland Swift chassis, among them this one for Stevensons of Uttoxeter. *(Will Hughes collection)*

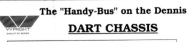

The "Handy-Bus" on the Dennis
DART CHASSIS

Robert Wright & Son
GIVE YOU QUALITY BY DESIGN

INCLUDES

- **The Alusuisse Structal System** - Today Alusuisse have more than 40,000 buses on the road worldwide, of which 6000 have been built using the Structal System.

- **Aluminium Bolted Construction** - Which is 50% stronger than a welded construction.

- **Passenger and Driver Safety** - Due to the immense strength and durability of the Aluminium Alusuisse Body.

- **Ease of Repair** - It takes on average 14 minutes to replace a complete set of near side panels on the 'Handybus'.

- **Low Cost Spares** - Compare our windscreen prices to our competitors!

- **Longer Life Expectancy** - The Alusuisse Body is built for a lifetime minimum of 15 years, without the need for structural renovation.

as United Kingdom Sales Manager. I remember him telling me that one of his biggest problems was the difference in the two dialects; he found the Ballymena Scots dialect was difficult to fully understand, or at least that was his excuse.

Of the many decisions I made, I never regretted asking Charles to join the Wrights sales team. He was a major asset to the company; customers liked him, always having an open door when he called. Equally, the company's office staff, both sales and service, liked him and were very helpful in assisting Charles in his role as United Kingdom Sales Manager to increase the company's customer base. From joining Wrights in 1991 he saw many changes, including the product range the company was offering. He also saw major changes to the customer base as the direct result of company take-overs and buy-outs. Charles also worked very closely with all of the chassis manufacturers sales teams, particularly those at Mercedes, Dennis, Scania, VDL and Volvo.

Wrights local operators Ulsterbus and Citybus took a batch of 40 Darts between them. Ulsterbus No 601, seen here in Lisburn, wears the standard blue and ivory livery applied to these vehicles.

A small number, such as No 612, were given BusyBus logos and an additional yellow stripe. They were used to increase capacity on local routes where passenger numbers had outgrown the size of the Mercedes minibuses.
(Paul Savage)

London Buses subsidiary, Westlink, based around Kingston-upon-Thames, received a batch of intermediate length Darts. DWL1 is seen near Galgorm prior to delivery to London.

The Dennis Dart came in three lengths, those for West Midlands Travel being to the intermediate 9.2m length. WMT also specified the one piece windscreen body style.

Doug Jack

Specialist Consultant
to the bus industry

I first met William Wright in Glasgow in the winter of 1982. At that time, I was Sales and Marketing Director of Duple. SMT Sales and Service were the main Bedford dealers for Scotland and had a showroom in Finnieston Street, right on the banks of the Clyde. They had organised an exhibition of new and used coaches.

William had come across with the first Contour coach body. It looked quite attractive, especially from the front, but was unusual in having an aluminium construction. That gave it advantages in unladen weight and resistance to corrosion.

The Contour had one big disadvantage which, in fairness to William, he had probably not foreseen. At that time, the coach trade for independent operators was controlled by a small group of very powerful dealers. They had enjoyed tremendous success in the 1970s, when most operators bought lightweight Bedford and Ford coaches. Only a comparatively small number of independents bought heavyweight models from AEC and Leyland. DAF and Volvo had come into the market, with the latter starting to make substantial sales. Continental bodywork was also starting to find favour, because coaching is, to some extent, a fashion business.

As the market started to decline, partly because of the switch from lightweight to heavyweight models, larger dealers squeezed the manufacturers for deeper discounts. They also dictated the residual values of vehicles offered in part exchange. They could easily find buyers for used Plaxton and Duple coaches, but could also decide the fate of newcomers to the market. That was probably the main reason why the Contour only sold in small numbers.

Nowadays, the picture is quite different. Most of the manufacturers control their dealer outlets. They are necessary because used vehicles are often traded in part exchange for new ones. Profit is not normally made until the last vehicle in the chain has been sold. It is a very specialised business, which only a few people really understand.

Wrights had diversified into bus bodywork in the 1980's, mainly in the welfare sector and for the education boards in Northern Ireland. The operating industry in the United Kingdom went through a period of great upheaval following the Transport Act 1985. Many public sector bus companies were sold, either to their management teams or to emerging new players like British Bus and Stagecoach. Bus services were deregulated, except in London and Northern Ireland. Minibuses became very popular because of low capital cost and the ability to provide very frequent services. Wrights bodied chassis such as the Iveco Daily, Renault S75 and Mercedes-Benz 709/811D and that gave the company its first contacts with mainstream bus operators.

In 1989, in response to the demand for larger and more durable medium size vehicles, Dennis launched the Dart. Wrights developed the Handybus body and sold quite large numbers into London. While they came out of service in the capital years ago, many are still running with small operators.

On the continent, there was a move towards buses with a large part of the floor only one step above the ground. This not only made buses accessible to people in wheelchairs, but also more useable by parents with baby buggies, people with luggage, the elderly and infirm. Because people could get on and off more easily, buses spent less time at stops. William Wight correctly predicted that low floor buses were the way ahead, although it was a few years before they became mandatory.

I regularly saw William at various exhibitions on the continent. Iveco and Kassbohrer had decided jointly to develop a full low floor city bus. One was on display in an exhibition in Germany in 1994. I was looking around it when I noticed a pair of polished Irish brogues sticking out from just ahead of the rear axle. It had to be somebody with a very lean frame who had gone that far under the vehicle. A few moments later, William pulled himself out onto the stand, remarking that he was very impressed with the design and how it had been put together! (The following year, Kassbohrer was acquired by Mercedes-Benz, forming EvoBus and Iveco took the project forward on its own, as the CityClass.)

About the same time, two Scania engineers told me of a visit that they had made to Ballymena when they were working with Wrights on the first joint low floor vehicles. Chassis manufacturers like to keep production times down by producing standardised products. The two Swedes explained their chassis and told William that his company had to do this, that and the next thing to the chassis in preparation for bodying. They were somewhat chastened to be told by William that it was their chassis, so they could take it away and do all the work, and deliver it ready for Wrights to mount the bodywork!

William Wright also correctly predicted that there would be demand for hybrid buses. He first experimented with a Dennis Dart extensively modified and developed to accept large numbers of lead-acid batteries under the floor. It was extremely quiet, but had relatively limited range on fully charged batteries.

The next stage was to introduce a thermal engine and a generator so that the batteries could be continually charged, thus greatly extending the operating range of the vehicle. In January 2001, Wrights launched the Electrocity in the new ECOS Centre on the outskirts of Ballymena. One of the guests was a lady of Indian origin from Powershift, a Government agency, which William hoped, would pay up to 75 percent of the difference in price of the Electrocity, compared with a standard diesel bus.

When he gets animated and enthusiastic about a project, William talks faster and his Northern Irish accent becomes really broad. The poor lady was struggling to understand what he was saying, especially when he mentioned Powershift, so I found it was the only time that I ever translated from English into English!

When Wrights went into volume production of bodywork, they chose the Alusuisse bolted aluminium structural system. Whenever any customer of Alusuisse wanted to build on a new chassis, Alusuisse had to approve the design and the dimensions of all the structural members. Once the designs were approved, they went into Alusuisse's records. That greatly helped Alusuisse if another customer wanted to build on the same chassis.

William was not happy with this arrangement and was deeply upset when he saw photographs of a body built by Volgren, an Australian licensee of Alusuisse, that even had the stylised Wrights 'W' on the front panel!

Not long after that, Wrights launched their own patented Aluminique structural system. One of the major advantages was the ease of repair of accident damage.

One of the most influential people has been Trevor Erskine. Trevor has had a very distinguished career in the automotive industry and Wrights were fortunate to find him when he wanted to return to Northern Ireland. Trevor is not only a gifted designer, but understands the practicalities of putting vehicles together.

Doug Jack

The Endeavour was built to bus specification on the Scania K93 chassis, for Yorkshire Traction.

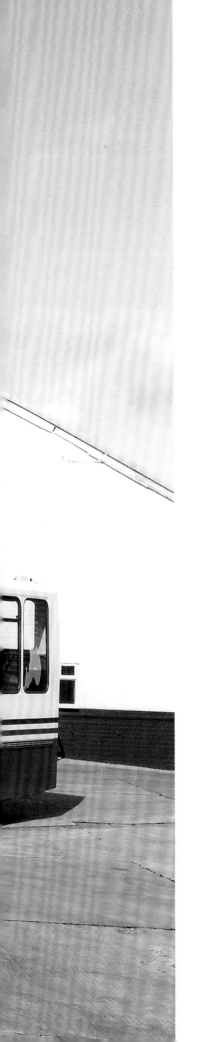

Below: In 1990, Ulsterbus relaunched its express service network as *Goldline*. The enhanced network grew passenger numbers and new vehicles were required. Wrights offered the high-specification Endeavour on the Volvo-engined Leyland Tiger chassis. No 1417 is seen near Ballymena when new on a demonstration run for members of the Irish Transport Trust. *(Paul Savage)*

Big Buses

While the Handybus/Dennis product, like the Nimbus on the Mercedes chassis, fulfilled the needs of a major segment of the PSV market, Wrights was being asked by customers to develop a range of heavy duty, 12m buses, incorporating the many benefits of the all bolted aluminium system, now recognised by many professional engineers for the benefits it offered.

In 1990, Ulsterbus enhanced its express service network, branding it *Goldline* and using new Alexander-bodied Leyland Tigers. Such was the success of this relaunch that a batch of Tigers being built at Alexanders, for service work, was fitted out to *Goldline* standards. As the network continued to grow, additional vehicles were required and Wrights returned to the coach market, although not with a vehicle to the luxury specification of the Contour. Ulsterbus ordered 25 of the Endeavour model, on the Leyland Tiger chassis fitted with a Volvo engine. Volvo, the large Swedish commercial vehicle manufacturer, had taken over the Leyland bus and coach division,

Interior of the Endeavour buses built for Yorkshire Traction.

with Leyland's commercial vehicle side in the United Kingdom being sold to DAF. Volvo immediately replaced all the Leyland engines with their own product. It has been said that the Volvo engine in a Leyland Tiger chassis gave one of the smoothest running coach chassis available at the time, even superior to Volvo's own B10M!

The Chairman/Managing Director of Yorkshire Traction, Frank Carter, asked Charles Moseby to provide him with the costings for a 12m bus on the Scania K93 chassis. Charles met with Frank providing him with a build specification and outline drawings. Frank ordered the bus, the chassis duly arrived and a few weeks later Frank received the new vehicle. I remember Frank visiting the factory to examine the bus in build. On entering the bus,

Frank, in his own flamboyant way, asked one of the apprentices if the vehicle could be completed by the weekend. The apprentice, who shall remain nameless, answered by suggesting that if he gave them all a fiver each they would try. Frank enjoyed the young lad's answer.

Having delivered large orders to London, the Wright name and company logo was now much more familiar to transport people in Great Britain. Dr Robert Dawson, Engineering Director of MTL Trust Holdings Ltd (later MTL Services plc), a major bus company based in Liverpool, contacted Wrights and was invited over to view the production facilities and discuss his company's future operational requirements. I met Robert on his arrival at Belfast International Airport and, having introduced myself, asked if he would like to go to the hotel or for a short run that evening and see a little of Northern Ireland before he returned back to base; he chose the latter.

Our travels that evening took us along the scenic coast road via Carrickfergus, Larne, through Carnlough to Waterfoot, where we turned left towards Ballymena. Having travelled up one of County Antrim's famous glens, we called in at the Manor Lodge where we were welcomed by the manager. Having ordered our meal and advised the manager we would be back in forty-five minutes, we set off up the walkway to the famous waterfall. The walk gave us both a very good appetite to enjoy the sirloin steaks we had ordered earlier! Over dinner Dr Dawson informed me that he had been asked by his Chief Executive, Peter Coombes, to make contact with Wrights and to investigate the products/construction of the buses being built in Ballymena.

This had come about because Mr Coombes who was new to the industry, had been at a dinner and had been seated beside Ted Hesketh (of Translink – Ulsterbus/Citybus/NI Railways). During their conversation, he had advised Ted that MTL would have to reduce the age profile of its fleet if it was to reduce operational costs. Ted, always one to promote Northern Ireland businesses, advised him to have a look at the new products being produced by Wrights in Ballymena when they decided to purchase new buses. I am sure that was not the first or the last time that Ted Hesketh promoted Northern Ireland industry!

Anyway, having enjoyed our walk and our meal, we then travelled on to the hotel where Robert was staying.

You may well wonder why I relate a story like this but, as mentioned earlier, the perceptions of people living in Great Britain about Northern Ireland, were major contributory factors to Wrights gaining orders. If a manager was to consider investing in Northern Ireland he needed to have confidence that the company in which he was investing in, or to which he was considering placing a major order, had a long term future and could fulfil that order, ie that there would be security of supply. Therefore, I took every opportunity to show clients that Northern Ireland was not all that they had been led to believe. Perhaps I should having been working for the Tourist Board on the side!!

The following morning Dr Dawson met with Wrights management, viewed the products then in build and discussed MTL's future operational requirements. Within a very short period of time Charles Moseby was favoured with a substantial order for Endurance city buses on the well-proven Volvo B10B chassis. The following year MTL placed a similar order. The company delivered 13 Endurance city buses in 1993, 62 in 1994, 25 in 1995 with the last three of the Endurance models supplied in 1996. The new Endurance city buses performed well in Liverpool and the Wright logo on the grille area was a familiar sight in the city and surrounding districts. In 1994 MTL also took delivery of 50 Crusader midibuses on the Volvo B6LE chassis.

Grampian Regional Transport forwarded an enquiry asking for product information and pricing for a substantial number of buses on a range of chassis. The detailed specification, which had been prepared by the Chief Engineer, Gordon Mills, was asking for city buses built to a very high specification. A response was duly prepared and submitted for consideration. Interestingly, a number of the buses were to be operated in Falkirk, the home of Walter Alexander, a major competitor. I was not holding my breath waiting for this

MTL placed several orders for the Endurance body on the Volvo B10B chassis, allocating them to various areas in the company's operation and branding them accordingly. Three of the Merseybus-branded examples were posed for official photographs when new. *(Bob Dawson collection)*

No 6507, with Lancashire Travel, branding is seen in service when not long new. *(Will Hughes collection)*

The first vehicle of the order for MTL is handed over by William Wright. In the picture are Steve Dewhurst (Volvo Bus), Dermot Reeve (Warwickshire Cricket Captain), Bob Dawson (MTL) and Thomson Baxter (Volvo Bus).

order, however we did give it our best shot.

I received a call the following Thursday afternoon from the Managing Director of Grampian Regional Transport, Moir Lockhead, inviting me over the following morning to meet with Mercedes at 9.00 am, followed by another meeting, scheduled for 12.30 pm, with Scania. Moir told me to come fully prepared to discuss business. He also told me to call his secretary who would make all the arrangements for travel to and from the airport, hotel accommodation, etc, once I had finalised my travel plans. I had only an hour to put together all the technical information and data, including product pricing, that I would require during our negotiations the following morning. The meeting that morning concentrated on the build specification of the product, to ensure that Wrights' specification complied with all that GRT had asked for, the interface with the Mercedes O405 chassis and lastly with regards product pricing and delivery.

Grampian Regional Transport, being based in Aberdeen on the northeast coast of Scotland, was specifying that a Webasto preheater be fitted in every bus. Moir Lockhead quite rightly questioned the price of this option, stating that Wrights quote was much too expensive. I advised him of the model of the heater we were proposing to fit. I also advised him of the costs we had received from Webasto and the installation costs. Moir asked me to call Webasto, advise them who the heater was for and expect a substantial discount. I was later able to advise Gordon of a satisfactory outcome to my discussions!

The development Cityranger was later sold to Stevensons of Uttoxeter as it wasn't to the specification agreed with Grampian. *(Will Hughes collection)*

One of the Cityrangers, on Mercedes O405, supplied to Grampian Regional Transport.

The second meeting, which was attended by Scania, represented by Jim Newman, was along similar lines. However, because we had already gone through all of the specification it was a much shorter meeting. Moir Lockhead then advised me that he would forward two orders to the company, one for 20 Cityrangers on Mercedes O405 and a further order for 20 Endurance city buses on Scania N113 chassis. I was, of course, to advise Gordon of the outcome of my discussion with Webasto. These orders were the first of many to come from Moir Lockhead, most recently in his position as Chief Executive of FirstGroup, whose subsidiary companies up and down the United Kingdom now operate 3000 plus Wright-bodied vehicles.

Mercedes had a stock O405 chassis which, although not to the Grampian's precise specification, allowed Wrights' engineers to commence building a prototype model. The build programme for the Cityrangers was underway and the delivery schedule was on target. The initial prototype model was examined by GRT management and tested by its engineers. It was later sold to Stevenson's of Uttoxeter.

I must take this opportunity to thank Gordon Mills for his valuable assistance during the initial build programme. Gordon always aimed to have a high quality, durable product which offered the company's customers unrivalled levels of comfort during their journeys.

While the Cityrangers were in build, Wrights engineers were preparing drawings, for approval by Alusuisse, for a body on the Scania N113 chassis. This was to be based on the Endurance model, which was so successful on the Volvo B10B. Alusuisse would not sign off the drawings because of the loads imposed on the framework by the Scania's transverse engine. Numerous drawings were submitted for appraisal and, with no solution in sight, Wrights then had a major problem.

During my negotiations with Moir Lockhead and Scania, I was to meet a man who, unknown to him, was to leave me with a lasting impression. That man was Fergus Leitch, then Managing Director of Reliable Vehicles, the Scania dealer based in Edinburgh. Fergus had delivered about 10 chassis and at that point in time I could not advise him, because of the difficulty we were having getting the framework drawings signed off by Alusuisse, when we would start building, never mind when we could deliver.

Fergus Leitch

Chassis are expensive to stock and to finance yet Fergus simply stated that it was better to ensure that the framework was structurally sound. Obviously it is imperative that you get it right; the structural framework of the bus must be engineered to last the lifetime of the bus. Any other company supplying chassis would have been much more aggressive. Stocking the chassis until we had solved the problem was costing Reliable Vehicles money and yet Fergus never once raised his voice. Both Moir Lockhead and Fergus Leitch were kept fully informed throughout, but this delay was posing major problems, not only to our customer but also to our production management team.

Then we had a breakthrough. The engineers working on the experimental ultra low floor bus were using the same chassis, but were experiencing considerably less lifting loads on the chassis, the reason being that Wrights had designed and constructed the entire lower centre frame of the chassis. The body was also fitted with bonded glazing. Wrights were made aware by Alusuisse that they had experienced similar problems with another company which had used the same Scania chassis. Alusuisse was approached again and asked if the drawings submitted to them for the Grampian contract showed the bodies were to be fitted with bonded glazing, would they be happy to sign off those drawings? The answer was yes and we were back in business – if Moir Lockhead would accept bonded glazing. (Bonded glazing adds considerable additional structural strength to the framework.) The problem and the solution we proposed were fully discussed, the structural integrity of the bus obviously being vital to both operator and manufacturer, and were accepted by Moir Lockhead.

The buses were built and delivered to Grampian Regional Transport but, due to the problems of the structural sign off, our delivery schedule was later

The Endurance body was also built on the Scania N113 chassis for Grampian. No 552 is seen here running with the subsidiary Midland Bluebird company. *(Will Hughes collection)*

Greater Manchester Buses took delivery of 20 Endurance-bodied Volvo B10Bs, painting them in a bright, new, livery, branded Superbus.

than promised. I discovered later that both the management of Scania and Grampian Regional Transport were impressed with Wrights approach to the problem. By keeping them fully informed during the process they were aware of the problem and all the issues arising. More importantly, the buses went into operation and in the test of time have proven to provide excellent service. Moir Lockhead was delighted with the stylish upmarket appearance of the bonded windows and the much better finish of the interior. All buses ordered by Grampian from then onwards had to have flush bonded glazing; later this evolved to double glazing to further increase passenger comfort and security.

Dr Alan Westwell, then Chief Executive of Greater Manchester Buses, expressed an interest in visiting the manufacturing plant to view the products and the build process. During his tour around the factory, it became obvious that he was a man who had immense knowledge of the industry. He advised that he had a requirement for 20 twelve-metre city buses, preferably on Volvo chassis. He was advised there and then that Wrights could offer him 20 build slots, but only if both the order and the specification could be agreed within seven days. A price for the buses, built to the standard specification, was agreed that afternoon, subject to any options specified incurring additional charges. What Wrights were not fully prepared for was the number of changes and the options Alan wanted!

The following week Alan came over in the evening and discussed fully his company's operational requirements. Alan was very impressed with the exterior and interior finish of the bonded, double glazed, tinted windows. Greater Manchester PTE had its own set specification based around step heights, seating spaces, etc, etc which had to be complied with, as well as meeting the requirements of the certification officers. It was agreed that, to be on the safe side, Wrights would prepare drawings and he would have these approved by the PTE. We had achieved specification sign off, now all we needed was the seating plan to be confirmed. I went over the following week and, with the assistance of Charles Moseby, we had the seating plan approved by the management of Greater Manchester Passenger Transport Executive.

The new Endurance city buses, on the well proven Volvo B10B chassis, were delivered on schedule, painted in an entirely new livery. When they appeared on the streets for the first time, they were clearly identified by the large lettering *Superbus*. These buses set new standards for passenger transport in Manchester, with passengers asking themselves why they would travel with 'Joe Bloggs' when they could travel on the new Superbus for the same money. They were an immediate success.

However it was another part of the livery that was to cause the local PTE to approach the London Bus Disability Unit – the use of a Low Floor logo to the rear of the entrance door, similar to that to be used on London buses. The local Passenger Transport Executive was very annoyed about the Greater Manchester buses using this logo on what they deemed was not a low floor bus. However they had under-estimated Alan Westwell's knowledge of the local market place. He informed them that the logo was not the property of London Buses and, much more importantly, he advised them of the floor heights of all the competitors buses operating in Manchester and competing

Although this photograph looks similar to that opposite (it's even the same bus!), we included it to show the change in the branding – from 'low floor' to 'floor line'! *(Will Hughes collection)*

with GMB; the floor height and step heights on GMB's Wright-bodied Volvos were the lowest of all the buses then in operation.

The management of West Midlands Travel, which provides most of the public transport in Birmingham, had intimated to Charles Moseby, who had been working closely with Steve Dewhurst, United Kingdom Sales Manager of Volvo Bus, that they were in the market for a substantial number of 12m city buses. Charles co-ordinated a visit to the factory by a number of WMT's senior management team to view the production assembly line of Volvo buses, particularly the model they were interested in purchasing, the Endurance on the Volvo B10B. Having discussed their operational requirements, a detailed specification was forwarded to Volvo, who put forward a supply offer to the management of West Midlands Travel. In due course, and after a meeting of the management of all three companies, attended by Sandy Glennie, Managing Director of Volvo, Steve Dewhurst, then UK Sales Manager for Volvo Bus GB Ltd, Don Colston, Managing Director of West Midlands Travel and Andy Woolner, his Engineering Director, a substantial order for 250 vehicles was agreed.

Dr Robert Dawson

I first encountered the Wrightbus operation in about 1994. At the time I was Engineering Director for MTL Trust Holdings Limited, the last privatised bus company, unique in being employee owned. MTL had a fleet of approximately 1500 buses across Merseyside, Southport and the Wirral, mainly aging Atlantean double decks. I was determined that, as soon as we could afford new buses, we would invest in the best to bring quality and style to the assets, pride to the people of Merseyside and operational excellence to drivers, passengers and maintenance staff. I carried out an in-depth analysis of products on the market and couldn't settle on anything that met my aspirations. It was then that I came across those lovable leprechauns Jack Kernohan, Wrights Sales Director and Charles Moseby his Sales Manager. At that time Wrights had a very limited pedigree in bus design and manufacture, especially large buses of the type we were looking for. However Jack wove his spell over me and invited me to see what they were up to in Ballymena. I saw a business that was poised to move in a new direction. Its patriarch, William Wright, had decided to employ a professional design engineer, Trevor Erskine, to bring a new concept into the UK market. It would be manufactured using Alusuisse construction and feature aircraft-derived interior styling. Their acknowledged weak spot was in fully understanding those design features that enable driving/fare collecting, passenger ergonomics and operations to be optimized. This is where we came in. And so was born a wonderful collaboration which, though not unique (because similar was happening with Greater Manchester Buses), yielded some fantastic products, The Endurance full size single deck vehicle as a prime example.

MTL invested in several hundred of these buses and was proud to have them on routes throughout Liverpool and surrounding areas. I recall a veritable cavalcade of them rolling out of our Edge Lane Maintenance Depot to attend a photo shoot by the Docks in Liverpool. It was a crisp Spring morning (rush hour!) and the kind hearted motorist who waved out the first bus had no idea that he would spend the next hour watching bus after bus take to the road ahead. The new buses were arriving at the Pier Head as others were still leaving the depot! A sight that many in Liverpool will never forget.

For Robert Wright and Son this will be but a small part of their history but from a personal viewpoint it seemed to be one of those pivotal periods when relationships are stuck, confidence is built and promises are delivered. Through a busy and productive five year period I would meet with my colleagues at Wrights, sharing ideas and seeing their business flourish. Jack, forever modest, plays down his role but don't be fooled, his networking with customers throughout the UK was central to Wrights growth, and a more honorable gentleman will never be found. However, I have already mentioned William Wright and need to say more about this man. As I approach the age of 60, I am minded that men of these years are generally a little slower of late in every department. Not so William. Initially the powerhouse of the business, William delegated the day-to-day running of the business to his able son,

Jeff, and proceeded to spearhead the product strategy in exciting new directions. During my contact and subsequent years Wrights have initiated more novel products into the market than any other UK bus manufacturer. Other chapters in this book will describe what these are but they include forays into turbine, battery, fuel cell and hybrid power. Not all came to full fruition but those that did have taken the market by storm. It is William Wright, in his senior years, who carries the accolade for such achievements as well as for the development of the business into the international arena.

My own small involvement leaves me with a total respect for those at Wrights and a pride in having perhaps played a small part in their business' development. Throughout the period of huge growth Wrights managed to maintain their values and keep the Customer foremost in their thinking. The relationships built during that time are as durable as the buses built by Robert Wright & Son.

Dr Robert Dawson

Dr Alan Westwell,
OBE, PhD, MSc, CEng,
MIMechE, MIEE, FCILT

MY BUSINESS EXPERIENCE WITH WRIGHTS – THE COACHBUILDERS

The Wright coachbuilding business first came to my notice when Jack Kernohan visited me when I was Chief Engineer and Director General at Strathclyde. Jack was demonstrating a typical minibus, which was then essentially the Company's main product. I sampled a road test and inspected the vehicle and was very impressed with the high quality of the product. The focus was not the large Public Transport System in the West of Scotland but the large fleet of minibuses operated by Local Government at that time.

As a result, I always took an interest in the Company's developments and highly rated the Wright Company's high quality products in terms of design, construction and quality of finish. With time I noticed that the Company developed it's product range, moving into single-deck buses. During such years I did not get the opportunity to acquire such products. Then to my delight as a result of new company ownership came the opportunity to purchase the Wright Product. After years of under investment in the company pre and post deregulation and, as MD, I wanted new buses urgently for Greater Manchester. I was making technical enquiries around the Manufacturers when Jack Kernohan responded that they could meet my requirement for swift delivery. I made a visit to the factory to satisfy my self that the quality of product was as good as I had rated it years earlier and was very impressed with what I found. It then emerged that Sandie Glennie and Steve Dewhurst of Volvo Bus had taken a decision to place an order to Wrights to build buses for stock without a customer being involved. I snapped up this opportunity to buy these Volvo B I0B – large 12m single-deck vehicles – and, in a period of days, negotiated with Jack Kernohan a high standard specification, incorporating such quality features as double glazing.

I was pleased that my initial and successive orders led to my Company having placed one of the largest orders for such buses with the Wright Company at that time. Later orders included large orders for the Volvo B6 high capacity midibus product which I had an input to the concept as it was designed. It was a breath of fresh air as the Wright Company was prepared to listen to the customer and endeavour to meet my requirements rather than me being given reasons why things could not be agreed to. Having become a customer of the company I was very impressed with the emphasis which the Wright family put upon customer relationships. Whenever I visited the Company and factory the Chairman, William Wright, would make his business to personally come and have a chat with me and update me on the ongoing developments. He and the family members involved with the business had a genuine down to earth manner. William's son, Jeff, as MD of the production of the business was in the driving seat in the early years and was so pleased to reveal and explain the quality assurance systems he had introduced and continually updated them in order to be at the leading edge of quality production. His team's attention under his leadership achieved the highest quality of product. Mark Nodder followed his example in maintaining the high standards set. The workers were fully in the picture regarding targets and achievements by simple visual means in their workstations and hence the accountability and reason for maintaining the desired quality of product.

Due to the success of the company's product range, William Wright told me that he wanted to respond to the potential increase in customer demand by expanding the factory capacity for which he had produced a Development Plan. I was pleased to provide a reference in support of the proposed development and responded to the various agencies accordingly as they made contact. I was pleased that the project was approved and led to increased production capacity to meet increased customer orders. It was also good to visit the company subsequently to inspect the new premises. This was the workshop area where some years later, when MD in Dublin, I visited the factory to see the vehicles which were part of an order for a quantity of single-deck articulated buses passing along the production lines.

Periodically I would participate in the Company's brain storming sessions, both at the Company and into the late hours, when Jack Kernohan visited me regarding vehicle concepts, design, construction techniques and first hand feed back from the operation of Wrights vehicles in service. I also shared my extensive experience regarding the design, maintenance and repair of double-deck buses when Wrights were assessing whether they should move into the double-deck market and start producing 'deckers as well as single and artic type buses. The Company prided itself being at the leading edge in bus Design and producing futuristic external designs for the company's products which have made a significant impact upon the bus industry,

I am pleased to have been asked to make a contribution towards recording the history of the Wright Group which William developed to what it is today which was started as a small coachbuilding business by his father over sixty years ago.

Alan R Westwell

Dr Alan Westwell, OBE

Pathfinder 320
The low floor revolution begins

Pathfinder brochure

If a company is to be successful, it cannot stand still. What it is producing today will be history tomorrow. William Wright was blessed with an innovative mind and was always looking at what the company should be developing to meet its customers' future operational needs. William had been looking at accessibility issues – for the elderly, mothers with prams and the person in a wheelchair. The idea was discussed with the management of London Buses, who were very interested in developing the project further.

Volvo would have been Wrights first choice as partner. However, on this occasion they declined, the reason being that they thought the UK market was not ready for this product simply because of the additional costs involved in building low floor accessible buses. This, they believed, would make the product uncompetitive in the UK.

Wrights then approached Dennis, whose initial response was cool. However, when London Transport was introduced into the partnership, Dennis then saw a major opportunity to engineer and design a 12m, low floor, accessible chassis and soon bought into the project. Wrights would then develop a low floor, fully accessible, city bus with the support of London Transport.

Dennis prepared drawings of the chassis whilst Wrights engineers worked with Ann Frye from the Mobility and Inclusion Unit at the Department for Transport and Andrew Braddock, Head of Access and Mobility at London

**Artist's impression of the
proposed low floor bus**

Transport (latterly Transport for London). The company's engineers prepared the initial drawings for discussion purposes only. As there would be no chassis available for some time, Wrights development engineers decided to build a full scale mock up of the frontal area of the bus. This included the front entrance and the mid-entrance/exit, as the buses for London were being specified with a mid-exit door which would also be used by wheelchair users to access the vehicle.

Wrights was fortunate that close by the factory there was then a special school where young adults with a range of disabilities received tuition towards helping them live their lives as normally as possible. I asked the principal if she could help us by asking her wheelchair-bound students if they would be prepared to assist in developing the accessible bus concept. They were delighted at being asked and I was informed that they had twelve volunteers who would be prepared to assist our engineering team.

We learned a lot from listening and talking to them, such as the ideal degree of slope on the ramp to be used at the entrance and exit door, the location of the grab handles and bell pushes, etc. We also experimented with full frontal kneel rather than side kneel and the passengers all reported that side kneel was affecting the wheelchair's stability and wheel grip, especially on a wet surface. This information resulted in the buses for London with centre doors being fitted with full kneel facilities on both axles. It is worth pointing out that, at that point in time, there was no legislation available to assist our engineers, so we involved the Department of Transport based in Swansea. We knew mothers with prams and buggies would benefit greatly from the development of accessible buses, so they had to be taken into consideration, too. Having had the feedback from all of the groups, the initial prototype was modified.

A meeting was then called with representatives from London Transport, its Disability Unit, the chassis manufacturers, and the Department of Transport.

I was tasked with preparing an agenda for the meeting so that everyone achieved his or her objectives. Over the years I had prepared many such agendas; however I did find this one a particularly difficult task. Having made a number of attempts, I was far from satisfied and decided to start from a new clean sheet and based my agenda around what I needed to know and do. I went and got a wheelchair, positioned myself in front of the prototype model of the bus and whilst sitting in the chair prepared the agenda for this very important meeting, for example:

- What did the wheelchair passenger, or his/her attendant, need to know?

- What does the driver need to know and do?

- What did the other passengers need to know?

- What did the company operating the buses need to know and do?

- What had the Passenger Transport Executives/city authorities to do to encourage investment in accessible transport?

- On selected routes where speed ramps are in place, these must be to acceptable design standards, so that there will be no long-term damage to the structure of the bus.

- Street furniture repositioned to accommodate accessible buses.

- Access to bus stops to ensure the buses are able to approach the bus stop correctly with the entrance door opposite the wheelchair location at the bus stop.

That time spent sitting in the wheelchair looking at the problems was to benefit all who attended the engineering/development meeting and we were able to agree a common strategy to address all of the points raised.

One of the most important items to Wrights was that local authorities within cities initially provided financial support to all operators who were willing to invest in providing accessible transport. Remember, this was at a time when no operator wanted to invest in buses that would seat fewer passengers, be much more expensive to purchase and, being lower to the ground, were perceived would suffer much more damage.

The prototype chassis arrived and the product development team commenced assembly of the framework; the floor was fitted and bonded to the chassis and the windscreen, window glasses, etc, bonded in situ before dispatching the prototype model to MIRA for a full structural test. This vehicle would be used only as a test bed for the chassis and the driveline components, the body design and construction and would never be completed or be driven on public roads. The prototype model had two large doors placed front and centre providing the weakest structure for the test programme.

Midway through the test the engineers at London Transport decided that they would reduce the front door width, resulting in a much shorter front overhang and extend the wheelbase, providing greater seat spacing on the lower floor. This was ideal for London because they had specified two doors with the wheelchair entering and exiting the centre door whilst all the passengers entered through the front door, exiting through the middle door.

To ensure that the low floor project would be viable in engineering terms, Wrights constructed a 'test bed' body on a Dennis Lance SLF chassis. This vehicle was then put through a series of 'shake down' tests at the Motor Industry Research Association.

These major changes resulted in additional work for both Dennis and Wrights. Both companies had made production drawings and jigs for the assembly of the prototype chassis based on the initial proposals, but the substantial changes resulted in both having to design and manufacture new jigs etc, prior to recommencing production. This resulted in major delays in chassis deliveries just at a time when our production teams were preparing to build. They were now left with a major gap in the build programme so we had to move fast to fill the gap. We were fortunate in that we had received an enquiry but, if low floor production had been on schedule, we couldn't have met that customer's operational delivery programme. So, with the delay in the Dennis chassis deliveries, we were now able to offer a improved delivery schedule. Wrights won that order, filled the gap in its production schedule and had a full production programme until the Dennis chassis become available.

Stephen Hewitt

Proper financial control is very important to the success of any company and for as long as I can remember this Company has been reinvesting its profits back into the business. William Wright, though, always had the necessary controls in place to ensure that when increased expenditure was required, he knew exactly what he could afford.

The Company finances had been looked after by William's sister Muriel but, with a young family to care for, she stepped down and her place was taken by Brian McCaugherty, who became Finance Director at a time when the business was changing dramatically. Brian left the Company to start his own business in 1992.

Charlie Stewart, a non-executive Director, approached Stephen Hewitt, with whom he had previously worked. They knew each other well and respected each other's capabilities. Charlie was a very shrewd man. He made no promises; he just asked Stephen to call William as there might just be an opportunity for an experienced financial accountant.

Stephen did that, had an interview and he took over the accountant's role 1992. Promoted to Finance Director, he retired from the company in May 2002. However, like Albert Hanna, Trevor Erskine and me, William asked Stephen to work part-time in other roles within the company. He finally left in 2008, having worked a total of sixteen years. During that period, when I needed any financial advice, his door was always open.

1993 and Wrights win major orders from London Transport for low floor accessible buses

The Pathfinders for the East London company were on the Scania N113 chassis, which didn't offer such a tidy internal layout. SLW17 was photographed, by the Thames, at the North Woolwich terminus of route 101 from Wanstead Station. *(Paul Savage)*

London Transport decided to split its order for low floor vehicles between Dennis and Scania, and Wrights won the orders for both, with a similar body design on the Scania N113 chassis. Scania refused to modify the chassis to accommodate a shorter front overhang, given the number of chassis ordered. This resulted in the Scania buses having a slightly different entrance layout, with seat spacing in the main saloon not being as generous as the Dennis product. With the engine driveline across the rear of the Scania, the rear seating was not as customer

The first Pathfinders to take up service in London did so with London United. LLW9, a Dennis Lance SLF, is seen leaving the bus station at Hounslow en route to Northolt Station. *(Paul Savage)*

friendly. Although the Dennis product was much more customer friendly, there was no comparison when it came to reliability. The Scania being a well-proven and tested product was superior. As a manufacturer one may comment on the comfort of the rear seating, but one should ask, "Who sits on the rear seat of buses and do they really care?" Indeed, many of those sitting on the rear seats would not mind the higher seat positions or the additional step.

The Scania driveline was much easier to service being across the rear of the chassis and with all the componentry facing the engineer as soon as the rear access door is opened.

During the negotiations with London Transport, Nick Leach, who was then working very hard developing Scania sales in Great Britain, had built up a special relationship with William Wright, a relationship built on trust and one that was to benefit both companies sooner than expected.

The Go-Ahead Group, based in Newcastle, was the first company outside London to show an interest in having a number of low floor accessible buses. I had kept my good friend Peter Lanfrancie informed of the developments, consulting with him on both the chassis and body design. Peter was looking for the earliest possible delivery. The company was contracted to deliver all of the London order before we could consider building for any other company and that included the order we had received from London Transport for accessible buses on Scania N113 chassis.

Deliveries of the new low floor accessible buses to London began in 1993 and the vehicles were well received by both operators and passengers especially those with mobility problems. Very few wheelchair-bound passengers use the buses daily after they have had an initial journey to evaluate the transport system, so the elderly who had difficulty with steps, and mothers with baby buggies and shopping were the main beneficiaries.

Wrights trained operators' engineers in the factory to provide a local support service. Parts manuals and supply lines were agreed to ensure that downtime in the event of a breakdown or an accident would be reduced and kept to a minimum.

Having delivered the first consignment of accessible buses to London, Wrights then developed a similar product for the Go-Ahead Group, but on this occasion they wanted a low floor accessible bus with the passengers all entering and exiting through the front door with no mid door (unlike London). This required a number of major changes to the chassis and the body. With the wheelchair passenger entering and exiting the bus through the front door the bus kneels on the front suspension only. With a mid door, to achieve the desired step height the bus has to kneel on both axles. This involves additional compressors and additional air reservoir capacity etc.

Thus, the seating arrangement on the Go-Ahead vehicles was totally different. Wrights had by this time consulted with a number of key customers; all wanted to maximise the seating capacity whilst ensuring that they could assist the lady with the baby buggy, but few really wanted to carry wheelchair passengers. The Go-Ahead Group would have liked to develop a bus that could carry two wheelchairs, the reason being that on the proposed route there was a major hospital. They did not want the drivers to be in the position of having to refuse a wheelchair passenger should there be two at the stop. It expressed the opinion that if a driver was confronted with this, he would allow the other wheelchair passenger to enter and take up the space reserved for mothers with prams. Interestingly, there was no legislation for low floor buses in the UK preventing the driver carrying two wheelchair passengers. I doubt if a driver was often confronted with the problem, though!

Like London, the new Pathfinder 320 accessible buses were delivered to Newcastle and were well received by both management and passengers. One of the major problems encountered by drivers was the numbers of cars being parked on the approach to bus stops. This prevented the bus aligning properly with the footpath to allow the powered ramp to be deployed at the bus stop. When we delivered the buses I travelled around the route on a Pathfinder accompanied by Peter Lanfrancie and a traffic warden, to look at the problem.

On the route there were no less than seven bus stops where the approach was blocked due to cars being parked illegally and, believe it or not, two of the cars were displaying Disabled Parking Badges! The management of the Go-Ahead Group agreed a plan with the local parking attendants that in return for their assistance in stopping indiscriminate parking they could travel free throughout the city while on duty. This was to prove a major success, ensuring that bus stops on the route were kept relatively clear, thus making the job of the drivers much easier and helping to reduce journey times.

A Go-Ahead Coastline Dennis Lance SLF/Pathfinder is seen on route 326, the one that was plagued by parked cars during the proving run.

While Dennis was engineering and developing the chassis, I had a call from Andrew Roberts, the City Engineer of Canterbury City Council. The initial call was asking for information regarding products we built using Alusuisse construction. During the call I informed him what we were developing and how it would improve the service he could offer the general public. This was a major opportunity, as I believed that the accessible bus was ideal for park and ride operations. Families did not want the hassle of trying to find a parking space. They simply lifted the child from the seat in the car, strapped the child in the buggy and wheeled it onto the bus. Every one benefited – fewer cars parked in the streets, traffic flow in city centres speeded up, less congestion resulting in a healthier environment and the child travelled in greater safety by not having to leave the pram.

Having expressed an interest in the company's new product, Andrew visited Ballymena within two weeks. As we had at that point in time not received a chassis, the project was still in the development stage. We discussed the project, examined both the drawings of the chassis and the body design but especially potential seating layouts, as he was of the opinion that they may require more space for mums with prams. We then examined the development mock-up, which we had used for market research. This was to give him a feel for the project and to demonstrate the many advantages to be gained by providing low-floor, easy-access buses.

However, his was a future need for this product (they hoped to introduce a new Park and Ride route into the city), but if they got planning permission they would certainly be looking at offering accessible buses. He asked to be kept fully informed on the progress and expressed an interest in having an operational bus as soon as possible to demonstrate to the local authorities. I wrote to Dennis asking them to invite our potential customer to their factory as soon as they had the chassis engineered and assembled. I kept in regular contact with my customer to determine what progress he was having in getting planning approval and to keep him advised on the chassis developments.

One problem, though, was that with the orders from both London Buses and the Go-Ahead Group, we were not in a position to promise an early delivery schedule. As Canterbury had not received planning permission, they were not at that moment in time able to ask companies for quotations to operate this route.

When the second prototype model of the Pathfinder 320, as it had now been officially named and which was to be the company demonstrator, was completed, tilt tested and certified, we demonstrated the product to the full council at Canterbury. They were very impressed with the versatility of this new development in passenger transport, which offered many passenger improvements over the existing bus. They asked if they could use one of the Pathfinder photographs they had taken, when they were placing a advertisement for a bus company to operate the route, although they as yet had not received planning approval. Tenders were received and, after due diligence, East Kent was selected as the operator.

After discussion with Roger Heard (Dennis Sales Director) we agreed that Dennis would act as prime contractor. Prices were submitted and they were awarded the business. Delivery of the new Pathfinder 320 in October 1993 was accepted as ideal in that the operating company could use traditional buses if they got the operation up and running before then. With the Christmas rush this would be an ideal time to introduce the new

Pathfinder 320 accessible buses, as they would make a major impact and (hopefully) result in everyone leaving their cars out of the city as it was usually grid-locked at that time of year.

A few weeks later, I had been over in Great Britain on business and on returning was advised by Mr Wright that he had been informed by Dennis that we had lost the contract in Canterbury, due to fact that the delivery date of the new buses was not acceptable. This I knew to be incorrect and, on reflection, I suspected it to be a move to enable Dennis to move the business to a European manufacturer. To say that I was annoyed would be a understatement; this was an order that we had developed from an enquiry about the type of construction we used, to supplying potentially the first operator in the UK to provide an accessible Park and Ride transport system.

I now accept some blame in that I should have known better from past experiences. I had put my trust in the Dennis management and, by allowing them to be prime contractor, we lost control of the business. Wrights had spent thousands of pounds working with Dennis developing the low floor bus and now, when both companies should have been working as a team, they moved the order to a mainland European coachbuilder (Berkhof) in the belief that they would assist them to sell the new Dennis Lance SLF chassis in mainland Europe. Incidentally, the buses for the new park and ride were not delivered to the customer on time.

The sales of the Dennis Lance SLF chassis, which should have been a major success for Great Britain evaporated overnight. The only orders that I am aware of for that body/chassis combination were those sold to East Kent in Canterbury, Ribble in Preston and from Speedlink Airport Services for British Airports Authority ground operations at Heathrow.

Having decided that Dennis was more interested in developing the European market and certainly not interested in being a partner with Wrights, we had to look for a new partner. I would have no hesitation in stating that this one act by Dennis, after the work the company put into developing the first accessible bus with them, was the biggest disappointment of my career in the bus industry. On mature reflection they were the losers.

At the risk of being accused of repeating myself, I have already stated that William Wright had developed a close working relationship with Nick Leach at Scania, which was finding the going tough in getting established in the UK. The Scania N113CRL chassis, although not the most passenger friendly, was considered to be reliable and parts supply was good, but deemed expensive. If they were reliable then they would require fewer replacement parts anyway and downtime would be greatly reduced.

A meeting with Nick was arranged and within a few days an agreement was drafted and signed. With the initial order secured from London Buses we were now back in business. So started a new era for the company and soon orders were flowing in for the new Scania product.

To compete with the Dennis chassis, we looked at the range of Scania chassis available to the company that could be developed. Whilst the N113 was ideal for those wanting a body with mid doors, the L94 model was much more cost effective and an ideal product for most operators. With a direct drive from an inclined engine driveline module, customers could be offered a proven driveline, which, when packaged into the bus body, offered a much-improved customer friendly, seating permutation. With the Scania L94, we had now a reliable product, providing excellent accessibility, excellent seating arrangements and with service support covering all of the UK.

The major bus companies operating outside London, at that time, really wanted nothing to do with the transportation of passengers in wheelchairs. In my initial sales approach with the key customers, I was showing them drawings with 37 seats (subject to chassis) when they were currently operating buses with upwards of 49 seats. Most of our customers were not interested in a bus that cost more yet carried 20% fewer seated passengers. And when you mentioned the wheelchair passenger you were virtually shown the door; they were simply not interested.

One must give credit to the determination of Ann Frye, Andrew Braddock and latterly Donald McDonald for their leadership and determination in pushing the boundaries of accessible public transport in the United Kingdom. While it is right to recognise them for their leadership and for providing financial support from London Transport and the various Government Departments to assist operators to provide and develop the customers awareness of the benefits, one must not forget the man with the vision, who saw an opportunity and, against the odds, pioneered accessible transport in the United Kingdom – William Wright.

At that time, William did not receive the credit he should have had from the passenger transport industry in the United Kingdom, for having the vision and determination to develop the transport system and for pioneering accessible transport for all, nor would he have wanted it. Now his reward comes from seeing all the Wright buses (so easily recognised by the company logo incorporated into the front panel design) travelling around London and all the major cities in the UK. He derives great satisfaction from local people coming up to him and saying that they had been on holiday somewhere in the UK and all the buses operated there were from Ballymena!

If one had been carrying out market research with our potential customers, asking them in simple terms:

- Was there a need for Accessible Transport? The answer would have been "No".

- Was there a need to provide Public Transport wheelchair accessibility? "No". There were other support groups who could and were willing to provide that service, for example Dial-A-Ride.

- Was there a need for easy access, with an allocated space for mums with baby buggies in buses of the future? I suspect that if the truth was told the answer would have been "Yes", but not if it meant losing seat spaces or increasing the cost of the buses.

- Would you purchase buses, which, although offering additional features to enhance the journey for all those travelling by bus, would cost 10% more? The answer would have been "No".

- Would you pay extra for a bus with these additional features? The answer would have been probably "No" from 90% of operators.

Considering all of the evidence from virtually all of our customers, which I suspect would have clearly illustrated that they would not have been in favour of developing this concept of public transport, one must commend William Wright for having the tenacity and grit to proceed with the project – and backing it with substantial sums of his own money.

All of the major chassis manufacturers initially declined when consulted about developing the product for the UK market. Dennis only came aboard when William, supported by John Craven Griffiths of London Transport, called a meeting at Wrightbus and advised them that London Transport wanted to provide accessible transport for all and hoped that the supplier would be a British partnership of chassis and coachbuilder. Scania had not been initially been consulted, but Nick Leach was hungry for business and was keen to proceed if the initial order was of sufficient size to justify the development expenditure on the project.

Volvo was consulted and their answer was similar to what most operators would have given if they had been consulted – the UK market is not ready for this type of bus, it would be much too expensive for the UK market and the UK operators were not getting financial support from the local authority's like they do in mainland Europe. To develop a low floor city bus for London only could not at that moment in time be justified.

As interest increased and more and more Transport Authorities/Passengers Transport Executives and others supported initially with a few pounds from the Government purse, the scene was set for growth in this sector of the market and once again Wrights had set the standards. Our UK competitors had nothing to offer, and I believe they initially thought that this was one of these ideas that would not gain customer approval. How wrong they were!

More and more of Wrights customers were seeing the benefits to be gained by operating passenger friendly buses. Passenger Transport Executives were now specifying low floor city buses in all of the major UK cities and legislation was the final hurdle.

With legislation setting out the time scales for the introduction of accessible transport, anyone who had doubted the future impact of accessible transport, be they operator, chassis manufacturer or coachbuilder, was now left in no doubt it was the future.

Famed for its fleet of ancient, heavy rebuilt buses, the Mediterranean island of Malta is now home to one of the first low floor buses to come out of Ballymena, a Pathfinder 320-bodied Dennis Lance new to London in 1993/4. *(John Durey)*

There was still a strong demand for the Endurance city bus on the Volvo B10B chassis, it being by far the customers' preferred model. Operators in most of the UK major cities were then still ordering tested and well–proven products. With the business relationship with Dennis no longer operational, it was imperative that Wrights filled the gap in its product range. So, an agreement with Scania was finalised and an initial project chassis was programmed for delivery.

The new Scania L94 chassis was delivered in 1994 and the project team, under the very capable leadership of Production Director, Albert Hanna, assisted by Damian McGarry who had prepared the assembly drawings and the bill of materials, got stuck right in to the job. No product, before or since, has been developed faster. William Wright played a major role in the development of this bus, as it was vital to the company's future. From receipt of the chassis to completion of build took only seven weeks! The product was then thoroughly tested at MIRA.

Wrights now had an alternative 12m, low floor, accessible city bus

Jeff Wright with the first Scania
L94/Axcess Ultra Low.

product, one that was reliable, used well proven driveline components and, probably more important, one that was perceived by operators as a heavy duty chassis that would give years of service, with minimum downtime. Osrders for the new Axcess Ultra Low on the Scania chassis were slow to start, not because of the product, but because the operators had still not accepted that accessible transport was here to stay.

Volvo had, in the meantime, licensed Alexander's at their Mallusk Plant in Northern Ireland to assemble the Saffle all aluminium bus body, using an assembly system not unlike the Alusuisse system used by Wrights on the Volvo B10L chassis. Orders didn't flood in. Northampton Transport and West Midlands Travel purchased a relatively small number of these chassis, some powered with engines using LPG. These buses were not the success hoped for and only one other order was placed with Alexander's; that was by Translink (Citybus/Ulsterbus) based in Belfast. Wrights were asked to quote for the initial small trial batch but due to the company's delivery commitments at that time, could not meet the Citybus/Ulsterbus delivery schedule, much as we would have liked.

The company's relationship with the management of Volvo Bus in the UK had proven to be very successful to both companies at all levels. We could meet with the engineers and discuss any problems we encountered. The Sales Teams met regularly to discuss any problems they were having and also examined potential business opportunities to ensure that all Volvo customers were supplied.

Sandy Glennie was then a major player in the UK bus market. I will freely admit that I learned a lot from listening to him; he was one of the most persuasive salesmen and the best negotiator that I met during my career in the bus industry. But more important to me in all my negotiations with him was the fact that I could trust his word; not once in all my negotiations with him was I deceived. On the one occasion when he had to amend an agreement, he called William Wright and requested a meeting that evening at Belfast International Airport. He came over, met with William, advised him of his problem, negotiated a new agreement and flew back on a later flight that same evening. He easily could have lifted the phone and made the call, but that was not Sandy's way of doing business.

On the subject of trust, it was vital to the success of both the companies and the customers. Our customers had to have trust in Wrights, that we would support the product. Wrights Development Engineers, whilst discussing each of the projects with the different chassis manufacturers, ensured that these were not revealed to the other parties. Everyone involved in a project had to sign confidentiality agreements.

On one occasion, Steve Dewhurst (Volvo Bus), having lost a very valuable order to the new Scania low floor accessible bus, and being quite annoyed, asked me what Wrights were playing at. Why we had not advised him that the company was developing a new product on the Scania chassis? I fully understood Steve's concerns. However, I replied to his question, by simply asking him, "Would you have ever trusted me, the engineering staff, the sales team or the management of the company if any of us had revealed what we were developing for our other partners?" I confirmed the company's commitment/confidentiality to Steve and to Volvo, both in new product developments, and equally as important, the allocation of build slots. I reminded Steve of the confidential agreements that we all sign up to and hoped next time that Volvo would be the winner. Now looking back at the many products we developed with Volvo, they were often the winners!

Before the adoption of First corporate livery, Scania L94/Axcess Ultra Low SS9 is seen in service on Glasgow's Overground network. *(Will Hughes collection)*

Alan Millar
Editor, Buses

As a journalist, I first became aware of Wrights in the early 1980s. I was news editor of the weekly *Commercial Motor*, and William Wright – ever the ambassador for his ambitious company – had made contact with Noel Millier, our passenger transport editor, to make the UK mainland aware of its innovative approach to bus bodybuilding.

Although the bus operating industry was still regulated and largely in public ownership, new players – large and small, most of them based in continental Europe – were pushing at a potentially wide open door to break practices and secure a slice of the market for the industry's buses and coaches. Several displayed more ambition than ability to deliver, and I guess we were not very sure about Wrights, either. Could a small family business in rural Northern Ireland building small numbers of vehicles really make its presence felt?

Our perception changed when it won an order from Maidstone Borough to body some Bedford YMTs. This was a breakthrough, for although Maidstone took a much less traditional approach than many operators; until then it had bought most of its bodies from Duple and Wadham Stringer, long established English bodybuilders. As a council undertaking, its order gave Wrights a foothold in what counted then as the establishment.

The Contour coach proved that its ambitions were undimmed and while the bigger volume manufacturers experienced some very difficult years as the operating industry was deregulated and privatised, Wrights plugged away and began to be taken a lot more seriously when it secured a succession of ever larger orders for minibuses and midibuses from London Buses. This was business at the heart of the establishment.

Around 1992, by which time I was a freelance journalist with several different strings to my professional bow, Wrights approached me to ask for a quote to provide it with a press relations service. The words that impressed me most then came from Jeff Wright, who spoke of the company aiming to be as big as Plaxton, which then dominated the coach and small bus market. It was an ambitious aim, and to be honest I'm not sure that I was yet convinced it could get there, but it left no doubt in my mind that this was a company that intended to make its mark – and that its mark would be a memorable one.

A couple of years later, when it came back and signed up my services, it had just kicked off the accessible low-floor bus revolution with the first Pathfinders for London and was on a twin-pronged crusade to convert the UK bus industry. One prong was to convert operators to the Wright product range; the other to sell the virtues of low-floor to a still sceptical audience. The social argument in favour of a bus that could accommodate wheelchair users was the easy part; the one that might turn an expensive obligation into an attractive commercial opportunity was to talk up the possibility of accommodating fare-paying shoppers with baby buggies, and the ambulant disabled, and of enlarging the overall market for bus travel.

Some of the most cheering things to see were how Wrights sales team steadily won new customers for its products, how the proportion of low-floor products increased rapidly and how its innovation led often larger competitors to follow in its wake. The commercial argument proved to be no empty PR claim. It was true. These buses were helping attract passengers.

Over the seven years I was most closely involved with Wrights, I was constantly aware that this was a business different from most of its competitors. It was innovative and confident enough in its strengths not to secure a sale at any price. It sold not just its products but a love-you-to-death approach to its customers that delivered a standard of aftersales support few could genuinely rival. But above all, when someone bought a Wrights bus – or hundreds of them, it mattered not whether the customer was small or large – that someone bought into a family business with incorruptible ethics and a genuinely human approach to all its dealings.

Now that I view it again from the outside, editing a magazine that follows the myriad movements of the bus operating and manufacturing industry, it is impressive to see how that multi-faceted approach has propelled the company farther forward – developing double-deckers, StreetCars and into the leading edge of the hybrid revolution. It was never afraid to go beyond the family circle to provide itself with the people to drive it forward, and has attracted world class professionals to its team. Yet it remains a family-own, family-run company with rock solid family values.

Alan Millar

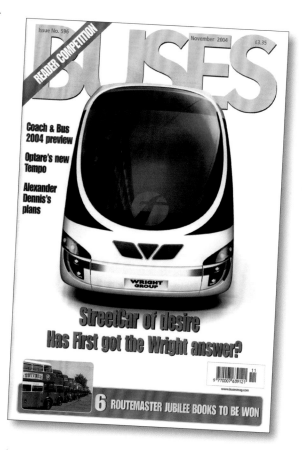

Volvo 12m Accessible City Buses

Our Endurance 12m city bus, on the Volvo B10B chassis, had by far the largest share of the bus market, both in the UK and in Ireland. Wrights was aware that Volvo was going to lose a significant share of that market if it did not develop a 12m accessible single-deck city bus. Volvo customers preferred the Volvo B10B chassis to the B10L and Scania, with its simpler L94 chassis, was gaining an increasing market share. We had earlier carried out a feasibility study of how best we could develop a low entry accessible bus using a modified Volvo B10B.

Volvo were late in deciding to enter what was then a small, but highly significant, segment of the market. They developed three B10BLE chassis and sent one to Plaxton, one to Walter Alexander (Falkirk) and one to Wrights. Volvo products were being supplied by all three companies and, as the major supplier of buses on the then current B10B, we were disappointed that in the allocation of chassis we were the last to receive a prototype. However, when I made that point to a member of the Volvo management team, he laughed, commenting, "Wrights will have the bus built while the others are studying the drawings." That was not to be the case on this particular project, for a very good reason!

The Volvo B10B chassis, like the Dennis, had a conventional driveline and if we were to have

A naked Volvo B10BLE chassis showing the galvanised Floline centre section inserted by Wrights.

The ease of access to the Renown is clearly demonstrated here. The vehicle was destined for service in Manchester.

a low entry step at 320mm high and an entirely flat floor, the design would have two steps over the rear axle. This was acceptable. However, Jeff Wright came to me with a suggestion of a very simple improvement that was to have a significant impact on the sales of this product.

Under the regulations being enforced at that time, the floor should be entirely flat. However, with a bus kneeling approximately 70mm to provide easier access, one has to ask, "What is a flat floor?" Jeff Wright suggested having a very gentle slope in the floor, running from the entrance step to the first step over the rear axle, thus eliminating one of the two steps. This would require the approval of the Disabled Persons Transport Advisory Committee (DiPTAC) if we were to market the product in the UK.

Having erected a subframe on the chassis, and tested the walkway, it was decided to build the bus incorporating Jeff's idea of eliminating one step. The bus was built and completed well ahead of schedule. However

Members of the Wright family could always be relied upon when necessary to demonstrate the company's products. Here Bob Wright's daughter, Muriel (Finlay) pushes her grandchild's buggy off the bus without difficulty.

we also knew that our two competitors were in the process of building their prototype models. If we were to reveal the design improvements to Volvo, or DiPTAC, there was every chance that they could accidentally, or otherwise, advise our competitors. Plaxton were the first to launch its new product to the industry with the conventional two steps.

Sandy Glennie was then invited over to the factory to view the progress of the new Wright Renown city bus. As we walked down through the buses on the production line, Sandy was of the opinion that the bus would be in the finishing shop. I asked Sandy to come with me to look at this new product, not knowing that it was the new Volvo. He took one look at the floor line and the seating layout and asked me whose chassis this was. When told that it was the new Volvo, he walked down the aisle to look at the instrumentation, this being the only way he could identify the chassis from inside the bus. He then turned to me with a smile and asked how did we design this bus with only one step, having not realised that there was a slight slope in the floor. When we advised him how we had achieved the 'Floline' floor, he expressed his delight that this innovation was to be introduced on the new Volvo chassis, commenting that we had a winner.

Arrangements were made to launch the product at Volvo's headquarters at Warwick, but first we had to have the new Floline floor concept approved by DiPTAC. This was not to prove an easy task.

The senior management of DiPTAC were invited over to view the new city bus and they were pleasantly surprised with the new product. They accepted that the Floline floor and seating proposals were ideal for the UK market place, where the vast majority of operators use buses with the entrance/exit door forward of the front axle. It was a cost-effective chassis and, being a derivative of the current B10B, would be very acceptable to all of Volvo customers currently operating the Endurance/Volvo product.

DiPTAC realised that one of its key objectives was to sell the benefits of operating accessible buses to operators. Product pricing and customer acceptance was vitally important if operators were to accept and develop an accessible transport system in the cities. Legislation was forcing both operators and transport authorities to ensure that a fully accessible system would be adopted as the standard for future passenger transport requirements.

DiPTAC saw the benefits and realised the new Renown city bus offered many advantages and with that in mind they asked to have the bus demonstrated to the full committee in London. We agreed, but asked Ann Frye to ensure that David Quainton, who was Chairman of DiPTAC, was not at the presentation, as we felt this

We just thought this a nice picture of the demonstration Renown so we included it. And it gets Robin Barr's picture onto these pages – more of him later!

would be totally unfair as he (working for a competitor) could have influenced the other representatives of the Committee. The presentation went ahead and the Renown was approved by DiPTAC, setting new standards for the United Kingdom market on a chassis that virtually all the operators accepted as being their preferred chassis.

Operators, realising that the market was moving away from the traditional bus to the new accessible transport system, were very interested in the new Renown on the Volvo B10BLE chassis, especially as all of their service personnel were very familiar with this chassis. Now that Wrights had a competitively priced product, orders started to flow from all over the UK and Ireland.

Jeff Wright's idea of a Floline floor was to prove a real winner both for Volvo Bus and Wrightbus. With only one step in the gangway, the engineering/operational managers approved of it. The company accountants liked the product's overall costs, including daily running costs, and passengers gave the thumbs up to the bus that was to set the standard for easy access.

West Midlands Travel (WMT) had been operating the Endurance city bus and was reluctant to move to any other chassis. During the 1995 Bus and Coach Show, at the National Exhibition Centre, a local wheelchair lobby group had secured themselves, by chains and padlocks, to the railings outside the entrance as a show of solidarity against WMT management and the local Passenger Transport Executive, in that neither specified accessible buses. WMT management hurriedly called a meeting with William Wright and told him they were issuing a press release that evening and appearing on local TV to state that all future bus purchases would be more customer friendly and be easily accessible to all.

This was great news, but for the fact that they also wanted the change to take effect immediately, including the current order, stating that all buses going into build would be low floor. This was not possible for a number of reasons:

- The chassis build programme / model change
- materials wouldn't be in stock or readily available from suppliers; and
- production services needed time to co-ordinate the new bill of materials to allow production of the low floor accessible Renown to commence.

WMT was fairly adamant that the product change be implemented as soon as possible. They also wanted the buses built using gasket glazing, not bonded, simply because of the additional time spent replacing a broken pane, but this demand was impossible to meet. We advised them that we were aware that UK operator's preference would be for gasket glazing, but until we had engineered, developed and fully tested the modification, this option was at least two years away from production. Knowing that gasket glazing was important to WMT, Wrights developed and tested a bus structure on a 12m Renown city bus to accept this style of glazing. And this was completed within one year, rather than the anticipated two!

Volvo made the necessary changes to the chassis build programme and West Midlands Travel took delivery of 67 Endurance City Buses in 1995. Having changed the order to low floor, accessible buses, WMT chose the Volvo B10L, as the B10BLE was not then available. They received 110 Liberators on Volvo B10L chassis during September/October 1997. When

Travel West Midlands was the biggest customer for the Liberator, which was built on the Volvo B10L. Outwardly similar to the B10BLE the Volvo B10L provided a greater length of step free floor in the saloon. *(Will Hughes collection)*

the new Renown with the Floline floor had completed the structural tests and been signed off for production, West Midlands Travel ordered this new product taking delivery of 10 in January 1998 with a further 15 for their operations in Dundee.

Initially, customers were reluctant to accept bonded glazing. However, as time went by the Customcare Team developed a fast, efficient service, including operator training on the replacement of window glass. By the time we had engineered and developed the bus framework structure to take gasket glazing the management of most companies had by then accepted and preferred bonded!

The new Renown city bus was the operators' preferred product. When customers specified buses with a mid exit door, they were now offered the Volvo B10L; this chassis, with the engine fitted off centre to the nearside rear of the bus, was the ideal chassis if this option was required. Sales of the new Renown continued to grow.

I remember the Managing Director of one of the major bus companies in London telling me quite forcibly that he would never purchase a low floor, accessible bus simply because of the additional costs, stressing London Transport's fixed rates would not cover those costs. A small wager was placed, that he would order low floor accessible buses within twelve months. Six weeks later I had a call from him stating that London Transport were providing financial assistance and asking when could we deliver. I might add that when we delivered the bus the wager was overlooked!

Ulsterbus operate buses throughout Northern Ireland. It was a very profitable company and had accumulated considerable funds but the Government confiscated these profits to finance non bus-related activities. So, for a number of years, there was little expenditure supporting public transport, either into the railways or into buses. Ulsterbus management was left trying to provide a public transport system with a fleet of buses that were well past their sell by date.

Under direct rule, ministers were not in the least interested in how the general public travelled to and from their work; they were not dependent on the votes of the people in Northern Ireland to return them to office. That all changed when Northern Ireland got its own elected assembly Those elected were well aware of the problem and took up the challenge, and today we have new trains and a considerable number of new accessible buses and coaches now in daily use.

In 1999, Ulsterbus had not purchased any new service buses for approximately three years and when it went out to tender it was for a fairly large volume. After examining the offers from various suppliers Wrights were awarded a significant order for new buses on Volvo B10BLE chassis. Ted Hesketh (Managing Director) of Translink wanted to ensure that the general public recognised the new image of both Ulsterbus and Citybus and instructed

Ulsterbus No 2850, a Volvo B10BLE/Renown, which wears the latest Ocean Blue, grey and white, was photographed in Portrush en route to Coleraine. *(Paul Savage)*

Adorned in First's corporate colours, Badgerline Volvo B10BLE/Renown R902 BOU looks good as it's parked up for its official photograph.

his marketing department to employ a professional company to prepare a number of proposals for consideration. After due process they presented us with a striking new image of both the exterior livery and an equally modern interior.

Ulsterbus and Citybus operated different types of bus and another of Ted Hesketh's key objectives was to develop a bus that would meet the aspirations of both companies. Wrights, with the assistance of the management of Ulsterbus and Citybus, achieved that objective, with the only difference being one single colour on the exterior to distinguish the operating company; all the other components were now to the one standard. This was much more difficult to achieve than one would have expected simply because we were working with two different management teams and two different drivers' trades unions. One must pay tribute to both James Erwin (Engineering Department) of Ulsterbus and to David McCaughey (Contracts Manager) of Wrights and to the management of

Ninety Renowns on the Volvo B10BLE were delivered to Citybus and Ulsterbus. Citybus No 2798, in Metro magenta, grey and white, is seen in Belfast's Royal Avenue. *(Paul Savage)*

both companies for achieving this objective. William Moore, Translink's Procurement Manager, had stipulated a firm delivery date and he reminded me on a number of occasions that the management might have wanted a totally new image etc but he wanted the buses delivered to the agreed schedule. The company's objectives were achieved and were the first of many new buses supplied to Translink. Ninety Renown City Buses on Volvo B10BLE chassis were delivered between September 1999 and May 2000

Thomson Baxter

Thomson Baxter

Whilst looking at the many photographs and recalling the negotiations we had with our many (potential) customers, there is one name that keeps forcing its way into my thought; I refer to my good friend, Thomson Baxter.

I first got to know Thomson when he was working with David Bryant at Renault, developing that company's bus sales. On many occasions, I asked Thomson to come over to Ballymena but he always refused, saying that there was no way he was coming over in one of those petrol-engined budgies; he was referring to the Shorts SD360, a small plane that was used in those days by several airlines on their flights between the regional airports in Great Britain and Belfast (and another successful product developed and built in Northern Ireland!).

Thomson then joined Volvo Bus and since then he has been over on many occasions with customers; the planes got bigger! Everyone in the bus industry knows Thomson for the character he is; there is never a dull moment when he's around. A natural born salesman, he has brought a large amount of business to Volvo Bus, and to Wrightbus, and I must put on record my appreciation to him, and his colleagues, who assisted both Charles Moseby and I get Wrightbus established in Great Britain. Long may Thomson Baxter continue in his current role within Volvo Bus. This world would be a much duller place without him. And many of his customers would agree!

Before I finish, I must relate two tales to illustrate a couple of the points I've made about Thomson:

On one visit to Northern Ireland, Thomson had bother getting into a well-known pub in Bushmills, as it was a few minutes before opening time. However, Thomson's ability at opening doors soon had us at the bar and two hours later he was in full song, thoroughly enjoying himself. Later that evening, when we were leaving, one of the locals followed us from the bar and advised that should Thomson ever be in Bushmills again he would be made very welcome. Since that evening Thomson is now a firm believer in the benefits of Black Bush whisky, which is distilled in the village; he tells me it improves your vocal chords!

On a business note, I was approached by John Halpenny, of Blackrock, near Dundalk in the Republic of Ireland, who had decided that he wanted to purchase a new single-deck bus, the first the family had ever purchased having in the past only bought second-hand buses for its service between Blackrock and Dundalk. The only day he could visit the factory was Saturday and when I called Thomson, gave him the facts, he agreed, after his usual banter, to come over and meet the customer and return back later that evening. We met at the factory the following Saturday morning and within an hour a deal had been done. And more importantly, that customer has since purchased several more new buses and coaches from Thomson. This is just typical of the man we all hold in such high regard.

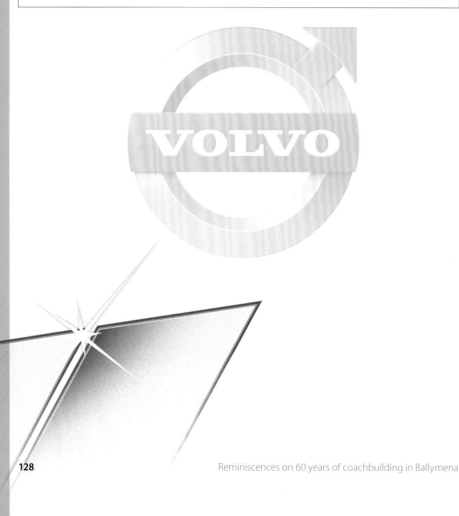

WRIGHTS PARTNERSHIP WITH VOLVO

AJM (Sandy) Glennie

Wrights quarter century relationship with Volvo started in Irvine in 1980 when three enthusiastic gentlemen from Ballymena called in to introduce their quality aluminium body system based on the Swiss Alusuisse design. It was not so much the clever system that impressed me but the sheer, open enthusiasm for the industry and products that the visitors projected. They were William Wright, Managing Director Trevor Eskine, Technical Director, and Jack Kernohan, Sales Director. The team was refreshing as my usual contacts were rather dull finance and mechanical people who did not see further than the factory gates. By contrast the conversations were about the customer – what did the passenger/customer need and how could they help the operator, especially in service and maintenance, a topic near to my heart.

The first product agreed was the Contour coach on the Coach Show exhibit B10M.

Wrights, however, realised the complexities of the coach industry very quickly and put their formidable efforts into the bus business where marketing was direct.

Jack Kernohan travelled the length and breadth of UK asking customers, "What do you really want from a bus?" and reporting diligently back to William and Trevor so a wanted list could be addressed and designed.

Volvo had nothing significant to offer Wrights until the B6R was launched in 1991 and Wrights launched the Crusader having already met good bus operator reaction with the Handybus. Immediately the innovative product developers, led unceasingly by William, proposed the B6RLE, a one step entry midi which was being requested by the various passenger lobbies and so arguably UK's first low entry bus. The relationship was spurred on by the opening of the Irvine bus plant for Olympian, B10M and B6RLE.

Always pushing the envelope, William Wright was visiting as many international bus shows as he could manage, engaging himself with the de-regulated bus companies and fostering ideas for the future. As early as 1993 he approached me on the Olympian but, advising that the double-deck body industry was over-supplied, I indicated that there was no UK articulated bus manufacturer and that there would be a specialist market in that product once privatisation had settled down. No doubt behind the scenes work on artics was commenced.

William's team were great respecters of the competition and he was not shy in introducing himself to all managing directors and asking direct questions like, "How do you do that?" and "How do the customers find it?" On some exhibition stands he was often seen lying under exhibits, shoes only visible, to see how they were constructed. His motive was to make them better.

The big partnership success came in the search for a UK definitive heavy duty, single-deck bus, with high reliability. This was the Volvo B10B and was a success

story for both companies, being bought in large numbers for service in Manchester, Birmingham, Liverpool and Glasgow. It would be fair to say it became the mainstay of the operating industry. The B10B was followed in 1997 by the B10BLE, a one step low entry city bus. Wrights developed the Floline floor concept, which provided a totally low floor, with only one step over the rear axle. This provided the maximum seating capacity whilst offering the best space for the passenger, a vehicle again designed for comfort, safety and operator economy – the hallmarks of Wrights.

The close relationship continued with artics for FirstGroup, the Eclipse Gemini in 2002 becoming market leader, and the double-deckers for Hong Kong.

The most ground breaking programme with Volvo was the Streetcar which encapsulated all of Wrights product development expertise and which has now led them into complete bus manufacture for the first time in a highly demanding US market.

A further measure of Wrights quality focus was the development of modern supply chain and the bringing in-house of consistent quality fibreglass manufacture in 2006 to maximise quality and minimise delivery delays.

William Wright understood in the 1990s the need to develop fuel/carbon saving bus products, an understanding nurtured by his visits and discussions with operators, legislators and governments. The result is that two significant products, Electrocity and Streetcar hybrid, have been delivered and are in the vanguard of public transport developments.

Wrights today is Volvo's biggest independent European bodybuilder partner and with 1000 units produced in 2007 are amongst the top five in Europe.

A company focused on product excellence, customer service and ceaseless product development, privately owned and managed with a mission, that's Wrights!

AJM (Sandy) Glennie

A Volvo B7RLE/Eclipse Urban on demonstration with Ulsterbus. Obviously the destination Bournemouth is from a period on loan elsewhere! (Paul Savage)

Introducing The Crusader

By 1989, London Buses was demanding a low floor, accessible midibus. Dennis was engineering and developing a range of midibuses (the Dart) of 8.5m, 9.0m, 10.2m and 10.6m length, offering a range of seat permutations. These chassis were all fitted with the same axles, suspensions, automatic gearboxes and engines. This resulted in little difference in the cost of producing each of the chassis, but the bodies did cost more due to the length/seating capacities and so had a greater effect on the overall price. The key to product pricing was based on volume production.

The first Volvo B6LE/ Wright Crusader on display at a public event. *(Will Hughes collection)*

A number of Wrights key customers had experience with its range of minibuses on both Mercedes and Renault chassis and wanted the company to develop an accessible midibus on the Dennis Dart chassis. There being no alternative, if we wanted to supply our customers we had to develop a product on the Dennis Dart chassis. Dennis was now supplying this chassis to a number of UK coachbuilders.

This segment of the market was very competitive and over the time we supplied it, the company found it difficult to make a profit on this product. Our customers wanted Wrights buses, but many were unwilling to pay more than our competitors' prices. From information received from market research we believed that we were being charged several thousand pounds more per chassis than our main competitor. Many of our customers, knowing the quality of the product and the after sales service, purchased from us anyway, being prepared to pay a premium just to have a Wrights body!

When our customers wanted to purchase accessible midibuses we were not competitively priced in the UK market yet those customers wanted an alternative to the Dart.

We looked at a traditional Volvo B6 chassis when Wrights was on the Volvo stand at the Kortrijk Bus and Coach show; Volvo was exhibiting a midicoach on the B6 chassis. The coachbuilder, with the approval of Volvo, had removed the centre frame of the chassis and dropped it much lower to provide a large luggage compartment. On closer examination of the chassis we established that if we were to drop the centre frame of the chassis we could offer a low entry chassis. The chassis having been fitted with independent front/rear air suspension could be easily adapted to provide an excellent low floor, fully accessible midibus. This chassis, when adapted, would comply with the legislation current at that time.

The larger 10.4 m Dart chassis was viewed by a good number of engineers as being a lightweight product, having a four-cylinder engine and Allison automatic gearbox. The Telma retarder was not fitted on the initial chassis and the braking system without the Telma was considered by many to be very costly to maintain, as the brake shoes had to be replaced regularly. However, the Dennis Dart chassis was built to a price and performed well in a very tough market place, especially London.

On our return from the show, drawings were prepared of the Volvo B6LE chassis and the new accessible midibus body, named Crusader, all in all a real heavy-duty package compared to the Dennis Dart. The one failing the product had was that the same chassis had been introduced by other coachbuilders in a conventional bus format and had a number of problems. Sales were limited, as this chassis was only available in one wheelbase giving a maximum overall length of 10.6m.

However, with London Transport asking for 10.2m models, the Volvo midibus did not meet London specification. When the presentation package was prepared, we arranged a meeting with Sandy Glennie and Steve Dewhurst. Having examined the drawings and knowing that they had no product for this segment of the market, Volvo was very keen to bring it to the market as soon as possible. The Volvo B6LE chassis, incorporating a number of improvements, would be designed, engineered and built at the Volvo assembly plant at Irvine, in Scotland.

Both companies working together, along with the chassis design engineer Hammy Watson from Irvine, agreed the chassis design modifications required. These were then signed off by Volvo management in Sweden. While they were producing the prototype chassis, our product development engineers were preparing product drawings and bills of materials for the Product Development Team. The frameworks, sides, roofs etc were all assembled prior to the chassis being delivered.

In due course, the initial chassis was delivered, production commenced and a few weeks later the first Crusader midibus rolled off the assembly line. After structural road tests were completed, the new Wright Crusader accessible midibus was displayed at Volvo headquarters in Warwickshire to all of the UK Trade Press and to the management of a large number of Volvo key account customers. The new Crusader midibus was well received by both operators and the press, so it was now up to both companies' sales teams to progress orders.

Volvo had programmed chassis deliveries and Wrights management had agreed build slots to ensure that product deliveries of the new Crusader would meet both companies' and customers' expectations. The Volvo B6LE chassis was much more expensive. However, when engineers compared the driveline and braking specification of the Volvo with the Dennis Dart there was no comparison. With the introduction of the new Volvo midibus, Wrights customers were now being offered an alternative low floor, accessible, midibus product.

Sales of the Crusader midibus were above our expectations. We had expected the cost

Mike Ball, Gary Raven, Jan Engstrom and Lars Blorn with a B6BLE destined for First.

difference to be a bigger problem, but with the strength of Volvo marketing, combined with the Volvo support package, customers were supporting the Volvo/Wright product.

Crusader midibus sales continued to expand with a number of the buses going into London where they performed very well. Steve Dewhurst advised me that Volvo was finding that some of the problems experienced on the chassis with other bus body manufacturers were not apparent on the Crusader product. The structural strength of the body could affected the life expectancy of the chassis componentry (such as steering, suspension and anti roll bar bushes), but these items were performing much better on the Wright product.

With future legislation forcing engine manufactures to engineer and develop all future engines to comply with Euro 4 legislation, it was Volvo's intention to fit a new Euro 4 engine to the prototype model. Bus chassis are a very small segment of the total Volvo product range and virtually the only product engineered, developed and built in-house is the engine. We now know that was about to change. Volvo was developing a totally new range of engines in conjunction with companies in which it had a major share, or owned outright. These engines would have a major effect on the design of all future bus products. The then current range of Volvo bus engines was not being developed to comply with future environmental legislation and therefore the Volvo B6LE chassis would cease production on the introduction of Euro 4 legislation. Volvo at that point in time had no plans to replace it.

Wrights had pioneered low floor accessible buses and had built up a significant number of customers who purchased its earlier products and wanted to purchase their midibuses from the company. Therefore it was vitally important that the company find another partner who had or could build a similar chassis.

Top: Mike Ball (Volvo Bus) hands over a Crusader-bodied Volvo B6 destined for service in Cork to Bus Eireann's MD, Bill Lilley.

Bottom: Dublin Bus chose the Crusader to enhance capacity on its Imp network. This one was photographed in Dubin's O'Connell Street en route to Marino. *(Paul Savage)*

Above: The Crusader was also built on a relatively small number of Dennis Darts. Delivered new to London United, VDZ 8004 had migrated to sister Transdev company, Yellow Buses, in Bournemouth when caught by the photographer. *(Paul Savage)*

Below: A number of Darts was also delivered to Ulsterbus for use on the Airbus service between Belfast and its International Airport and also on a network of accessible services in towns across the Province. No 651 had been transferred across to Citybus for use on Park & Ride services but here had been pressed into use on normal service.
(Paul Savage)

Right: A similarly-styled body was also built on the Mercedes OH1416 chassis and named Urbanranger. Only a small number of these stepped-entrance models were built, including this example delivered to Universitybus at Hatfield.

Below: An Urbanranger in school service with the Western Education and Library Board, Northern Ireland. *(Will Hughes)*

New Cadet midibus on DAF SB120

Knowing that DAF had been involved in the development and build of the Metro Rider chassis, Wrights knew they had the technical expertise and the ability to build a quality product. Through their UK distributor (Arriva Bus and Coach) contact was made and, in 1997, a meeting was arranged to discuss developing a product.

Bob McLeod, the Managing Director of Arriva Bus and Coach, accompanied the senior management team from Wrights to a meeting with DAF to discuss the business potential. Bob was very interested, knowing that Arriva purchased a good number of Dennis Darts every year. DAF was very interested too. It had the capacity and all the technical engineering management expertise in house. And so, within a matter of a few weeks, an agreement was signed to design, engineer and develop a new accessible midibus for the UK market.

A project team from both companies met and agreed a product development strategy. It was agreed that Bob McLeod would brief a number of Arriva's Operational Engineers from different companies within the group, including those operating within London, who would have experienced different problems. They were to come to the meeting having each prepared a list of the problems they were encountering operating the Dennis Dart chassis, and to advise us of any product improvements to both chassis and bus body that they would like to have incorporated in future products for Arriva.

The meeting was well attended and very educational. Yes, they were having problems. Yes, they were fairly simple, but all would add additional costs to the chassis. However, all agreed that the small increase in the cost of the chassis would be insignificant if, as they believed, it would eliminate many of the problems that operators were frequently encountering.

For example DAF would install larger capacity alternators combined with greater battery capacity; this would ensure that in winter, with all the lights, heaters, wipers, etc working at full capacity, there would always be adequate power. They also enhanced the braking system to a modern disc system which would provide a greater life expectancy and require less downtime in the garage. These modifications, if incorporated, would address most of the complaints from the engineers from London, who because of their operational problems due to traffic conditions, were suffering greater brake wear. These additional costs combined with the reduced downtime to supply and fit replacements justified the extra initial costs.

The chassis build specification for the new midi-bus was agreed and signed off to allow the chassis to be designed, engineered and developed for the UK market. It was decided that an 8.5m model was not a profitable product, after comparing the market price for 8.5m Dart and a similar product seating a similar number of passengers from the Optare product range. It was agreed that we jointly develop and market a range of midibus products starting with a model of 10.2m overall length (this still being

A DAF SB chassis

This SB120/Cadet was delivered to Arriva in 2002 for service in northeast London.

the preferred length for London), followed by a 10.6m model, all with four cylinder engines, and should we find that there was sufficient demand, we would also develop the 8.5m/9.2m models. A number of customers asked if we could offer the larger model with a six cylinder engine. Having examined the driveline proposals, it was decided to develop an 11.3m model with the more powerful six-cylinder engine. This chassis was to be designated the SB200, with the new bus body being referred to as the Commander, the other, smaller chassis being referred to as the SB120 model, with the bus body design named Cadet. DAF engineers had a very professional approach to new product development; each and every component used in the product was evaluated and checked to ensure that the problems identified on the Dennis products were eliminated.

Progress on the concept design drawing went very smoothly. One of the many changes to the chassis that Wrights requested, was for DAF to construct the chassis using the Floline concept that Wrights had developed in the larger buses. The Floline chassis/floor resulted in the bus having one less step, up to the rear saloon seating. This was much safer, more passenger friendly, and as all our competitors had two steps to rear of the saloon, was viewed as a major benefit by operational engineers when purchasing vehicles. I might add that other suppliers soon adopted a similar concept with only one step in the rear saloon.

The DAF midibus chassis is an excellent product; sadly to date it has not achieved the sales success that it should have. I put this down to two reasons – firstly the market demand for midibuses has peaked for the present and, secondly, DAF (Eindhoven) should have marketed the product in the UK and Ireland. A number of the large bus companies refused to purchase chassis from Arriva Bus and Coach, a subsidiary company of a major competitor. The sales and marketing of the DAF bus products, including the UK after sales service, did not compare with the other established companies with whom it was trying to compete. However Arriva operating companies, especially in London, purchased considerable numbers of the new Cadet on the DAF SB120 chassis. They have performed well and all of the operational engineers were well pleased with the reliability of the new product.

The fact that each chassis, when manufactured, was produced to a specified length, was to prove to be very costly to transport and to provide adequate stock levels. It was decided that because the front and rear modules were

Arriva's London companies took the Cadet in several lengths, including the shortest (version as illustrated by DWS6. *(Paul Savage)*

The SB120 was also taken by several Arriva companies outside London.

identical, DAF would supply these, eliminating the mid centre section. This allowed Wrights to reduce chassis stock levels. With front and rear modules in stock, and our engineers producing and fitting the centre section, we could supply any of the three models off the shelf! This resulted in chassis stock levels being reduced by over 30%. The other major benefit was that the carrier transporting the chassis was now able to transport three chassis at a time, when previously it could only transport two. With the additional costs involved in providing and installing the centre chassis frame, plus the savings on transport costs, one would have expected considerable savings to be reflected in the chassis pricing; these savings never materialised.

The DAF SB120/Cadet was launched in the United Kingdom in 2000.

Bus Éireann, Ireland's national bus company, having looked at all the midibus chassis available, placed a substantial order with the local DAF dealer in Dublin. When these were completed they were allocated to different centres in the Republic of Ireland, Letterkenny, Dundalk, Limerick and Galway being four major areas where they operate daily.

The Cadet midibus has opened new doors to mothers with baby buggies, elderly people and the disabled, who would have had difficulty getting up into older buses with two or three steps. The Cadet offers one other major benefit, it only being 2450mm wide. This allows it to operate much more easily in congested inner city traffic, through large housing complexes or on narrow streets/roads.

Minor accident damage, such as replacing broken glasses and lower side,

DAF was eventually convinced to supply chassis without the mid section. This allowed us to reduce stock levels and the carrier to transport three chassis at a time, instead of two.

Bus Eireann was a major customer for the SB120/Cadet. This example is on a local service at Sligo. *(Paul Rafferty)*

front and rear panels are two of the major problems that all operators have to budget for. The Cadet was designed to reduce these costs by keeping the downtime to a minimum. Replacing one of the lower skirt panels should take no more than ten minutes. All windows glasses can be gasket glazed, again reducing downtime while fitting replacement glasses. Bus engineers were delighted with the Cadet. Wrights continued to listen, to resolve problems and develop cost savings. While the Cadet might cost more initially, its lower lifetime cost would be a major benefit to its customers. That's a fine strategy if you're always selling to engineers; however it doesn't have the same appeal to company accountants who are often only concerned with the initial outlay!

The body fitted to the longer, more powerful version of the SB120 – the SB200 – was known as Commander and has proved a popular choice with operators in the independent sector, as with Kimes of Folkingham and Claribels in the West Midlands.

Mike Morgan
Editor, routeONE

MEET THE INNOVATORS

Wright's of Ballymena may have a history going back sixty years, but I've always felt that there's more to Wrights than meets the eye. To my mind it is more than just another bus builder, it is a true innovator.

Throughout the past six decades the company's remarkable growth is punctuated by decisive moments as the business introduced innovation after innovation as part of an instinctive desire to keep ahead of the market.

Despite being a relative newcomer to the business of bus building, its list of market leading initiatives is remarkable. And they all flow from that instinct for what the market needs next.

It was not by accident that it led the way in 1994 with the aptly-named Pathfinder low-floor body on Dennis Lance SLF and Scania N113 underframes.

Who else would have had the vision (and the courage) to develop the futuristic StreetCar, leading to the diesel/electric parallel hybrid version for Las Vegas.

Meanwhile, some would say that it continues to punch above its weight by conducting development work on hybrids as the next generation of drivelines for UK buses.

It's a steep learning curve and a brave path to take for a company that specialises in bus bodies rather than complete vehicles but, as William Wright has been heard to remark, "Wrights didn't get where it is today without taking risks."

Mike Morgan

routeone
SERVING THE NEEDS OF THE COACH AND BUS OPERATOR

ISSUE 317   21 JANUARY 2010

A Wright good performer

The Wrightbus Gemini 2 DL is winning the respect of lead customer Arriva. It's a significant new double-deck design that is also available in low-height configuration and the first examples with 4.23m-high bodies are running for Arriva Yorkshire at Selby. Pages 32-34

TOP STORIES IN THIS ISSUE

POLITICS IN THE MARKET	COACHMARQUE CLOSE TO 50	PREPARED TO TAKE A STAND	SAFE, FUEL EFFICIENT DRIVING
Manufacturers suffer fallout. Pages 4-7	Accreditation that counts. Pages 12-13	Steve Whiteway is CPT President. Pages 25-26	Taking the SAFED solution. Pages 29-30

Sandra Whitelaw
Managing Director

WHITELAWS
COACHES

WHITELAW'S COACHES LTD OF STONEHOUSE SCOTLAND

The question I asked myself was, "How would we, Whitelaw's Coaches, be viewed at Wrightbus?" I needn't have worried. As my brothers and I arrived to look at the products being built at Ballymena, the sign in the reception foyer wishing us a very warm welcome to Wrightbus said it all. We were welcome and valued visitors.

We were then greeted by the ever energetic and enthusiastic Jack Kernohan, who told us more about the products available and demonstrated the quality and innovative products that the company had to offer.

Whilst we were being given the factory visit, Mr William Wright could be seen in the distance overseeing some activity, a sight that became common place on a visit to Ballymena and it wasn't long until he paced across the factory floor to welcome us.

There was no doubt that these well built, quality, innovative vehicles were exactly what we wanted to buy to fit with our business needs and desires. The family passion showed in the product, which was something we could clearly relate to in our own business.

It was very evident from those early days, back in 1998, that we, a small operator, were very important customers and offered valued business to the company – Small, family business = Valued customer.

It was also recognised that our needs and operational requirements may be different and these were always explored and incorporated into vehicles being built for our business.

This was the start of a strong business relationship between Whitelaw's and Wrightbus that still holds true to this very day. Wrights have become the preferred bodybuilder for our vehicles.

The team at Wrightbus have always worked very hard to retain our business, deliver products on time and provide us with the aftersales support that we need to keep our vehicles operational.

Every order has just been as valuable as the next, regardless of the order size. They didn't only want to win the business, they want to keep the business.

As an operator, it is important that we are listened to and that our comments and requirements are reflected in the end product that will be used to deliver the services we provide to our customers. Often these comments have resulted in product changes or improvements, which has shown that it is not just selling you the vehicle that counts, your opinion on the product is equally important, and where improvements can be made, they will.

We are proud to be associated with Wrightbus, and we hope that Whitelaw's will see many more Wright products introduced into the fleet for many years to come.

A forward thinking, professional, successful, family business that embraces their customers – that is Wrights. We wish the family and everyone at Wrights every success for the future.

Sandra Whitelaw

Supplying the smaller operators

On my recommendation, Wrights management decided that the company would make every effort to supply the small operator as well as the larger ones. The man wanting one bus received the same treatment as the operator requesting bigger numbers. The price was based on volume and therefore it was important that the small customer purchased a product with as few variations as possible from the standard. Items such as internal trim colours were easy to vary.

Some of our competitors were not interested in one-off orders and neglected the smaller operators. Not Wrights! We remembered the days not so long ago when we, like them, were much smaller and were delighted to receive one-off orders. I can think of a number of customers who fell into this category – John White, an operator based on the Shetland Islands, Edward Doherty, based in Irvine, Ayrshire,

Whitelaw's of Stonehouse have been loyal customers for some years now. This Volvo B7L/Eclipse Metro was acquired in 2002.

Above: This TT-bodied Bedford was supplied to Mackie's of Alloa in September 1986. Although intended for bus operation, it was fitted out to a semi-coach specification.

Below: In 1996, John Halpenny of Blackrock, Co Louth, purchased two Endurance-bodied Volvo B10Bs for use on his services in the Dundalk area. This one is seen in 2006 on the stand at Dundalk having just arrived from Newry. *(Paul Savage)*

John Halpenny, at Blackrock in the Republic of Ireland and more recently Lenox Mackie of Alloa in Scotland, whose father had purchased buses from the company.

Whitelaw's of Stonehouse in Scotland is another good example of the smaller operator who provides an excellent local bus service. Sandra Whitelaw operates both luxury touring coaches and service buses and when she needed new accessible buses, Wrights readily provided a product that fully met her expectations.

Many operators, including the management from the larger companies, who I considered to be among my friends, would have called either my colleague, Charles Moseby or myself. My Ulster Scots accent did cause a problem for some of my customers. On one occasion a customer called Charles and asked if he could finalise the deal with him. Charles advised me what he had been asked to do, having informed the customer that he would meet him and finalise the build specification and the overall deal. The reason – that customer couldn't understand my accent and felt much happier with Charles. At least with Charles he knew what he had purchased! More importantly though, together we had secured the business.

Articulated Buses

Wrights build the first articulated city bus
engineered in the United Kingdom.

Artist's impression of the
articulated bus.

During one of our brain storming sessions with Moir Lockhead at First Bus/ Group, looking at the future needs of the UK bus industry, Moir raised the subject of articulated buses, so we looked at the many advantages and disadvantages of this product to the operator. He asked for outline drawings and budget prices to be forwarded to him, for discussion with his senior management. Before we could prepare any drawings we had first to agree the chassis, so Scania and Volvo were contacted and asked to forward chassis drawings.

Scania offered the L94UB, which although an excellent chassis had a number of negative points. The front axle was a drop beam; this resulted in a higher floor level up and over the front axle that was far from acceptable to our product development engineers. With a rear exit door just ahead of the rear axle, again this resulted in an undulating floor dropping from the turntable to the exit door and with three steps up to the rear seats, this chassis was not ideal. Scania would not supply the newer N94 chassis, which would have been acceptable, with the driveline across the rear, stating that this chassis would be much too expensive for the UK market. However, we believed that the real reason was that they had long terms plans to market this product directly into the UK themselves.

Volvo was developing the new B7LA articulated chassis, with independent front suspension, very low turntable and with the engine offset to the nearside rear corner, providing a totally flat floor. On paper this chassis looked ideal.

The customer could have up to three doors on the nearside, but at that moment in time we couldn't see a need for that option in the UK.

Having agreed on a Volvo chassis, I had a brief meeting with Moir in Glasgow to give him an update. Moir was making a keynote speech to the bus industry and I had about twenty minutes after his press meeting to update him on the project. He looked at the drawings, the projected costings and, having examined both, turned to me and stated that he wanted the first of the new articulated buses delivered to London for presentation to the media and the Government transport advisors on 5 October 1999. Having dropped the bombshell that he now wanted the bus so soon, he got up from his seat to go to the airport and as he walked away, he turned and with a smile said, "Don't ring me with any excuses, Jack. Remember the 5th October is your deadline. Sort it out with Volvo."

I knew that Volvo could not deliver the new B7LA chassis in time so we hastily arranged a meeting with Mike Ball and Steve Dewhurst of Volvo to discuss what options were available to us. As I thought, the new Volvo B7LA Chassis Development and Delivery Programme could not meet our production requirements, if we were to deliver on time – and that we had to do. They offered the B10LA, the articulated version of the Volvo B10L chassis (which we already had bodied, but only as a 12m rigid). This chassis had the standard Volvo engine and driveline with which engineers were familiar, and everyone was more than happy with the selection.

The first articulated buses were built on the Volvo B10LA chassis. This is First Glasgow's AV1. *(Will Hughes)*

First also trialled the B10LA at the other end of the country, in Southampton where No 129 is seen working to Glen Eyre.
(Paul Savage)

The first Volvo B10LA chassis could not be delivered until the last week in July 1999, leaving our production teams only six weeks to build, paint and deliver the bus to London.

Earlier in this book I referred to Albert Hanna's ability to motivate men and meet virtually impossible delivery dates. This was one of those occasions. With only six weeks from the delivery of the chassis to having the bus in London was virtually impossible. To anyone else it would have been, but not Albert. He knew that he had to use the weeks leading up to the delivery of the chassis to design and pre-assemble most of the componentry, so that when the chassis arrived it was then an assembly operation only.

The chassis arrived and, within a few days, the chassis modifications were carried out, and the framework assembled on it. When completed the bus was given a check over by the local Volvo dealer, prior to being shipped to London. The new Fusion articulated bus on the Volvo B10LA was shipped on 1 October, arriving in London two days in advance of the deadline given to me a few weeks earlier by Moir Lockhead.

Albert and his production teams had achieved what was considered impossible. Volvo's management team was amazed that Wrights had engineered, developed and delivered the new articulated bus to the agreed schedule. One observation that I might comment on is the fact that when the workforce is given a task such as this, they seem to enjoy the challenge and work to ensure that they deliver. FirstGroup launched the new Fusion articulated bus in London to wide acclaim from the trade press and the management of London Transport, especially Peter Hendy (now Commissioner of Transport for London), who was very enthusiastic about the product.

After the London event, the vehicle, which was in effect a prototype, was taken to MIRA for completion of the structural test programme, prior to the model going into full-scale production.

Stuart Jones

VISION AND INDEPENDENCE

The first Wright bus body I remember seeing was a demonstrator on a Bedford chassis that subsequently went to Maidstone Borough. It had a fresh, clean, purposeful look, but I don't remember getting the impression that this was a bodybuilder that was really going places. What I didn't know then that was 25 years later, all of the established UK manufacturers would either have closed down or be in the hands of new owners.

I was far more impressed when, late in 1982, Houston Ramm, then editor of Coachmart magazine, returned from Northern Ireland with a picture of a new coach design that was being developed. When the Contour itself appeared, the reality looked every bit as eye-catching, though I wondered whether it wasn't a bit too good for a Bedford chassis.

It was 1987 before I first visited Ballymena, despite my mother's attempt at dissuasion, because the 'Troubles' were the only thing most people in England associated with Northern Ireland. The company was still based in its old factory with a work force busily engaged in all manner of diverse projects, some of which I was told (in no uncertain terms) that I was not to write about. There were minibus conversions, fire engines and buses, as well as the purpose of the trip, the Contour Imperial on a Volvo B10M chassis.

On that occasion we didn't go to the Bushmills Distillery, though subsequent invitations, accepted without hesitation, have usually incorporated an opportunity to take in some of Northern Ireland's beautiful scenery. The Wright family were always keen that visitors should gain an appreciation of the country's positive points, and their own activities have also looked beyond the factory gates to a wider role in the community.

Many subsequent visits have been made to the 'new' site on the Galgorm Industrial Estate, and every time the plant has been bigger, there has been more investment, more people have been employed and production figures have risen. A highpoint of visits has been the opportunity to talk with William Wright and Trevor Erskine, the man who designed my first company car, the Ford Fiesta, earlier in his career, and hear their fascinating insights into bus design and how to meet passenger needs. William's interests were always as much taken up with alternative drive systems as they were with bodywork developments.

Consistently punching above its weight, the company, more than any other, fired the demand for low floor technology, supplying the Pathfinder 320 body to London on both Dennis Lance SLF and Scania chassis, with small numbers going elsewhere. Before they were delivered I remember Jack Kernohan and Trevor Erskine taking me out on the prototype, unpainted in bare aluminium panels

with an incomplete interior, and the sense we all had that this was the leading edge of bus technology worldwide.

I wasn't convinced about low floor early on, largely on cost grounds, but William had the vision and could see further ahead, and he was right.

There have been a few products launched that have not entirely convinced the market, such as the Mercedes-Benz based Urbanrider and the previously mentioned Contour, but failures have been rare. Others, particularly in the minibus market where the low floor Vario and the Irisbus Daily LoGo spring to mind, looked like a good idea but were thought better of before the expensive commitment to productionising was undertaken. These aside, there have been very few developments that have not been snapped up in large numbers by operators. Buses like the Eclipse, built using the Aluminique bolted aluminium construction method developed by the company, have melded passenger aspirations with the demand for practicality and durability demanded by engineering departments.

For years William told me that there would be no double-decker and all of a sudden, there it was, the Eclipse Gemini, raising the bar again with its distinctive 'Nokia' look.

Now we are in the early stages of two of the company's most ambitious projects yet, not that William hasn't been steering the company towards them for years. Firstly, the move into offering complete vehicle solutions with both diesel and hybrid drivelines, and secondly, delivering the Streetcar RTV BRT system in the USA; globally one of the most difficult markets to succeed in.

It's an exciting new era and one that will need all the innovative drive, attention to detail, and commitment to customer satisfaction that has earned this once small company the widespread respect it has today.

Stuart Jones

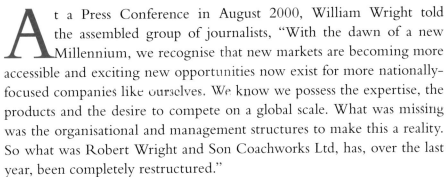

Wrights re-groups for Growth

At a Press Conference in August 2000, William Wright told the assembled group of journalists, "With the dawn of a new Millennium, we recognise that new markets are becoming more accessible and exciting new opportunities now exist for more nationally-focused companies like ourselves. We know we possess the expertise, the products and the desire to compete on a global scale. What was missing was the organisational and management structures to make this a reality. So what was Robert Wright and Son Coachworks Ltd, has, over the last year, been completely restructured."

So what is now The Wright Group comprises four separate entities each with its own management teams, all reporting to the Group Board. These are:

Wrightbus – responsible for the design, engineering, development, the manufacture and sales of all bus bodywork within the United Kingdom and Republic of Ireland;

Customcare – dedicated to providing the after market support for all of Wrightbus range of products, including supply of replacement components, technical support, product training courses etc. Customcare has developed 11 support centres with a further 12 satellite centres. The staff in all of these support centres have been to the factory and been fully trained in the products so as to provide excellent after sales support;

Expotech – a new company originally conceived as a launch platform to show that we were serious about developing new business opportunities for the Wright Group worldwide, from the supply of complete buses, to design and technology transfer and component sales, through to licensing agreements for the Aluminique construction system – ideal for territories which, for economic reasons, demand products be supplied in kits for local assembly. (The initial contract was with Chance, which is now part of North American Bus Industries (NABI). Although Expotech continues to service this original relationship, the wider international opportunities have all been taken directly by Wrightbus.)

Announcing the changes, Mr Wright went on to explain why the management had taken the decisions, "Wrightbus has experienced dramatic growth in the nineties. Output has trebled and there are now nearly 4000 Wrights buses in operation the United Kingdom." (That was in 2000. Now, in 2009, there are approximately 8000 Wright buses operating on the roads and cities of the United Kingdom.) "In managing this growth, we have maintained the quality of our products, increased and broadened our product range, won many new customers and, equally as important, retained most of our existing customers. To strengthen our position at home and to develop new opportunities, it now makes sense to review how we manage the business. This new management structure provides the base for continuing expansion, and gives each departmental manager the autonomy to react quickly to market opportunities as they arise."

Wright Composites - This additional company was formed in 2006 to develop a range of glass-reinforced plastic bespoke solutions. The company had previously sourced these components from local suppliers. The management, in the interest of supplying a quality product at a competitive price, delivered on time to meet Production's operational requirements, set up a new company in a factory adjacent to Wrightbus. Today Wright Composites, which has had phenomenal growth in a short period of time, now employs a total of 133 fully trained, skilled operators.

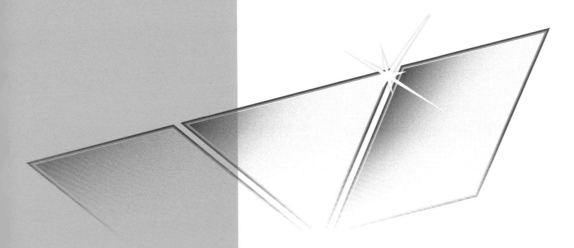

Millennium City Bus sets World Class Standards

Artist's impression of the new Millennium bus

Nothing in this world stands still. That certainly is the case in the bus industry and environmental legislation from the EC led the UK government to impose tighter emission controls. Volvo decided, like a number of manufacturers, to adapt engines from its current truck range but, looking back, that was a disastrous decision from the bus builders' point of view. Gone was an excellent engine (DH10) which was not only reliable, but due to its horizontal layout, was easily packaged into both coaches and buses alike. This was especially useful in the design of a low floor city bus.

Having been advised by Volvo well in advance Wrights decided that now was the time to introduce the totally new bus body that Paul Blair, the company Design Engineer, had been developing along with the engineers. The new Millennium design incorporated many improvements, some of which were not visible to the passenger. However, the totally new styling of both the exterior and interior was to set new standards for the bus industry in the United Kingdom.

Wrights had undertaken a great deal of market research with the management of key customers during their visits to the factory and while visiting with them to find out what improvements they would like incorporated into future bus designs. Experience has been that you will get many constructive suggestions from engineers. They are always very keen to have these incorporated into any new design, that is until you ask them how much extra money they are willing to pay. Then you find out who are the real decision makers in their company!

In my opinion, one man stands head and shoulders above every one else in the UK bus industry. When you sit down with Moir Lockhead, Chief Executive of FirstGroup, and ask him what improvements he would like incorporated into future products, he readily gives his vision of what he wants to provide in the way of Quality Passenger Transport Systems for his customers. That's a challenge to everyone – the chassis manufacturers, the bus manufacturer and, without a doubt, his own senior management, but he doesn't want to pay for the added features unless they benefit his passengers! However, Moir recognises the fact that if you are to improve quality there will be added costs. One example very high on Moir's priority list is extended warranties with the manufacturer accepting liability for its products for upwards of five years. This is not impossible, but policing the extended warranty is another matter.

I met with Moir regularly, consulting with him on Wrights performance, future improvements to enhance that performance (whilst reducing costs) and, very importantly, reducing fleet downtime, for example in bus cleaning, servicing and reducing the costs of repairing accident damage. The one question that is vitally important to Moir in his vision of providing a quality, competitive, cost effective service to all FirstGroup passengers is, "What can be done to improve the public image of buses as a modern, innovative, public transport system?"

Moir Lockhead set the standards in the United Kingdom, even going back to my first visit to Grampian Regional Transport where I saw his input into the buses in Aberdeen. The one major problem he and every other operator has, and I might add this prevents many from achieving their ultimate goal of operating fleets of high quality buses, is vandalism and the attitude of the general public to their own environment, particularly in terms of cleanliness. Both of these have a serious effect on the attitude of staff and all those tasked with ensuring that the fleet is properly cleaned and maintained on a daily basis.

One has to be thankful that the vast majority of bus engineers are professionals trying to do the job to a high standard in a very tough environment. It is getting more difficult to recruit properly trained engineering and operational staff and equally as difficult to get qualified drivers, all of which makes the task much more difficult for the operator who wants to provide modern, clean buses that will attract the general public to leave the car and travel by bus.

Listed below are a few of the improvements that were requested. Most went into production; however a few were ultimately dropped due to lack of demand. Although they would have improved the bus, and in the lifetime of the bus would have been a good investment, they were viewed to be too expensive. I was asked by one purchaser, "Why should I spend extra money which may show savings in the lifetime of the bus, when I may not be with the company this time next year?"

- Design a bus with a greater WOW! factor, to attract more passengers from cars onto more exciting buses, thereby assisting in reducing traffic congestion in inner cities.

- Eliminate interior corners that cannot be easily cleaned.

- Investigate new materials for the internal panelling, seating, floor coverings, etc that can be cleaned more easily and are much more resistant to vandalism.

- Develop and engineer a windscreen wiper system that is less prone to damage in the bus wash and is more robust.

- Engineer and develop a quick fit "Protech Panel System" for all the lower panelling including front and rear corners.

- Design, engineer and develop an easily repair/replacement all bolted framework, to reduce repair costs by up to 75%.

- Replacement of headlamp bulbs etc to take a maximum time of three minutes in garage forecourt (not needing to be over a garage pit).

- Introduce a thermostatically controlled forced air ventilation system, warm in winter and cool in summer preferably with an option of driver's air conditioning to ensure that he is comfortable in all weather conditions and has good vision at all times.

- All electrical motors to be of brushless design to extend the motor's life expectancy.

- Engineer and develop a mid section underframe, fully galvanised eliminating the yearly anti rust treatments to ensure the structural integrity of the bus during its lifetime. Wax treatment would only be required every five years.

- Design and engineer a framework structure, including the underframe, to take the much greater loadings generated by having cantilevered passenger seating. Having cantilevered seating would reduce the cleaning times for a bus by up to 20%.

With the introduction of low floor buses, all the chassis componentry was installed much lower on the chassis underframe. This was to result in having the coolant radiator fitted low, behind the rear wheels and resulted in the radiator core being difficult to keep clean. Engineers complained bitterly about this at every service meeting, but when asked for suggestions few were forthcoming!

In 2000, Volvo Bus introduced the new B7L, a totally low floor bus. The design allowed two full width doors, one fitted at the front and the other just behind the front axle, when offered in the UK market. For the rest of Europe and all left hand drive countries, bodybuilders were able to offer three doors, with the third to the extreme rear, as the engine was fitted off-centre, to the (UK) nearside of the bus. The radiator was now fitted above the engine, and came totally enclosed with its own soundproofing package. This driveline layout resulted in the operator having similar seating capacity to competitor's products, but the total rear enclosure of the radiator, with a box structure, was not acceptable to many Volvo customers. The rear seating was difficult to access and this area of the bus was noisy. In summer, with some of the engine and driveline above floor level, the area was also warm and difficult to ventilate.

Although company engineers now had a chassis offering a totally flat floor, good seating layout (as far as Wrights were concerned), with a radiator away above floor level (which would seldom require cleaning), they weren't

Ulsterbus was supplied with a Volvo B7L on demonstration. Given fleet number 2023, it was allocated to Larne depot. The radiator is behind the rearmost panel in the window line.
(Paul Savage)

In 2002, Arriva unveiled its Bus of The Future – a Wright Eclipse-bodied Volvo B7L. This bus was built to test customer reaction. It featured an enhanced interior with 2+1 seating in the low floor area, better legroom and air conditioning, but would that be enough to woo car drivers onto public transport?

Ulsterbus went with the Scania L94/Solar. Belfast-based No 704 is seen here arriving at the Co. Down village of Killyleagh. *(Paul Savage)*

happy, mostly for the reasons stated above. However, those companies that purchased the new Eclipse Citybus were delighted with the new features and most were happy with the performance of the chassis, but few were pleased with the rear seating arrangements.

When Wrights introduced the new Millennium product on the Scania L94 chassis, it was named Solar. Like the Eclipse, the new Solar city bus was very well received by its customers. They were delighted with all the innovative, cost saving ideas that had been incorporated into the design. Scania's sales team was well aware of customers reaction to the Volvo product and when discussing it they referred to the "rear toilet" which, too often for Volvo's liking, was costing them sales. This was not good for Volvo, or Wrightbus for that matter, as Volvo had by far the largest share of the 12m City Bus market in the UK.

Volvo (Sweden) was not listening to Volvo GB and probably could not understand why the B7L sold in other markets, but was not selling in the UK. The reason was simple really – it was designed for the left hand drive market, where three doors are commonplace and standee buses are more common.

On a visit to Volvo GB, I was discussing the problem with Norman Thomas (Volvo Engineering Manager) and I asked if Volvo had an alternative chassis drive line in their model line up, sold in other world markets, so we could develop an alternative to the B7L. Norman, who I always found to be very helpful, went to his computer and having looked at a number of chassis, printed me off a copy of a Volvo chassis that was later to become the B7RLE. This chassis had a conventional driveline and my first impression was that if we could supply and fit the Floline floor and meet the current legislation, it was ideally suited to the UK market.

Top left: Customers didn't like the interior layout offered by the Volvo B7L chassis so it was decided to offer the B7RLE, in the UK market. This photo shows the framework for the Floline floor fitted on a B7RLE.

This Volvo B7RLE/Eclipse Urban was demonstrated to Ulsterbus in January/February 2007 but this didn't result in any orders. *(Raymond Bell)*

Below: Peter Shipp of East Yorkshire Motor Services takes delivery of five Volvo B7RLEs from Charles Moseby.

Drawings were prepared, seating plans examined and a meeting was arranged with both Steve Dewhurst (Volvo UK Sales Manager) and Norman Thomas to discuss the proposal to develop the Eclipse Urban (twin door, front entrance), whilst retaining the Eclipse Metro on the Volvo B7L for customers specifying a centre exit door. Later we went to Volvo Bus (Sweden) to meet the engineering team, to finalise and discuss the new product, the development programme, including the development timescales. Our engineers always paid a lot of attention to the structural framework of the chassis supporting the rear engine and driveline. This is vitally important to the structural integrity of the bus bodywork. We agreed the development programme, delivery of the prototype chassis and, to speed up the project, Volvo agreed to send their structural engineer over to meet with Adrian Robinson, Wrights' structural stress engineer.

A few weeks later the chassis arrived, closely followed by the structural and chassis engineers from Sweden. The engineering drawings were approved and signed off and, within a few weeks, Volvo had a competitor for the Scania L94/Solar.

The Eclipse Urban was an immediate success for Volvo GB and was soon the market leader in the 12m bus market, which was once again dominated by Volvo, with the B7RLE. Both the Eclipse and the Solar products incorporated the Floline floor plan that had been developed for the Renown.

I briefly mentioned Adrian Robinson the company's structural stress engineer. Adrian is a quiet man who has never received the recognition from Volvo or Scania for the excellence he has achieved, especially when one considers the range of bodies, on

Reading Transport's Scania L94/Solar No 1018 is pictured in the town centre when on its way from Shinfield Park to Caversham Heights.

Trent Barton takes pride in what it does, regarding itself as a retailer and its buses as mobile shops. Its frontline fleet totals 280 vehicles, and more than half are Wright products – 92 Scania L94/Solar (like this one) and 51 Volvo B7/Eclipse! *(Trent Barton)*

For the launch of its More branded services between Poole and Christchurch, Go-Ahead Wilts and Dorset purchased a batch of Eclipse Urban-bodied Volvo B7RLEs, which featured 2+1 seating in the low floor part of the saloon. No 110 is seen loading at Bournemouth's Gervis Place on an eastbound journey. *(Paul Savage)*

For the high profile *fastrack* service linking Dartford with Bluewater/ Gravesend (via Ebbsfleet International station), routes with substantial investment in infrastructure and bus priority, Arriva chose the Volvo B7RLE/ Eclipse Urban.

When it introduced a new link between Glasgow city centre and Glasgow Airport, Arriva Scotland West acquired a batch of Volvo B7RLE/Eclipse Urban in this highly visible colour scheme.

KMP of Llanberis operated several B7RLEs on their route between Bangor and Llandudno, in North Wales. *(Paul Savage)*

different chassis, Wrights has developed – from low floor 12m City Buses to, articulated City Buses and double-deck, all low floor, fully accessible. Adrian had also to take into consideration all the derivatives – such as twin doors, centre doors on both sides for operation at airports, cantilevered seating – whilst assisting the chassis manufacturers to design/develop new chassis and, by doing so, make them much easier for the bodybuilder to construct the bus body on and, at the same time, reducing the overall costs of the new products. The company has not had any structural problems with its products and as anyone in sales will appreciate, this is a major benefit when negotiating contracts.

I would like to personally acknowledge the valuable assistance provided by Adrian Robinson to everyone in the product development and sales teams.

Up in Glasgow, McGill's used the Volvo B7RLE/Eclipse combination on its service thence to Gourock. *(Will Hughes)*

Stagecoach operates many Volvo buses throughout the Group but most of those with Wright bodies have been acquired through take-overs. In June 2009, Stagecoach Cambridge took delivery of ten Volvo B7RLEs with Wrightbus Eclipse 2 bodywork. These vehicles, which feature leather seats, wi-fi, full air conditioning, cctv and real time passenger information are destined for use on the new Cambridge Guided Busway. Andy Campbell, Managing Director of Stagecoach Cambridge (centre) commented, " . . . we felt that the B7RLE with Wrightbus bodywork was the best single-deck vehicle on the market". Also in the photograph are Arthur Argyle, Volvo Bus Regional Commercial Manager (left) and Robert Mason, National Account Manager, Wrightbus. *(Volvo Bus)*

In 2008, the Millennium range was facelifted, one of the first examples being this Volvo B7RLE for loyal customer, Lothian Buses.

Above: Cadet/Commander on the VDL also received a new body as part of the Millennium range. This was the Pulsar. Kimes of Folkingham, who had previously purchased the Commander, took this example for the Peterborough to Oakham route. *(Andy Izatt)*

Left: In 2009 Arriva Scotland West received a batch of Pulsar 2-bodied VDL SB200s, which feature the revised frontal arrangement. *(John Deegan)*

Below: The first VDL SB200/Pulsar was delivered to Arriva.

One product which deserved more success than it actually achieved was the Commuter wheelchair accessible interurban coach. Based on the successful Volvo B7RLE chassis, the Commuter was designed to carry up to 51 seated passengers and one wheelchair user, with ample luggage space provided in side lockers. The industry didn't take to the concept and just four vehicles were built, all of which now operate in Scotland.

Ulsterbus had initially shown an interest in taking ten of the Commuter model, though in the end only one was acquired. It was allocated fleet number 2201 and saw service at Ballymena, Newtownards, Newry and, finally, Londonderry where it was painted in the latest version of fleet livery. (John Durey)

Two vehicles were delivered to Stagecoach Western for the Dumfries and Galloway Council-sponsored upgrade of service 500 between Dumfries and the port town of Stranraer.

Eclipse Fusion

With the introduction of the new Eclipse 12m City Bus, the company decided to expand and develop this new up market design over its entire product range. The first product was the development of the Eclipse Fusion articulated bus on the new Volvo B7LA chassis which had been introduced in 2000.

This chassis was developed for the European market offering up to four doors on the continental nearside of the vehicle. In the UK, we could have offered up to three doors, but most UK operators like to maximise seating capacity, so we offered one door at the front, with an exit door in the rear saloon. The engine size was reduced to 7.5 litres.

All the advantages already detailed in the development of the Eclipse bus were incorporated into the new Eclipse Fusion. FirstGroup placed orders for the new Eclipse Fusion on the Volvo B7LA chassis, with many of these being allocated for operation in Southampton, Manchester and Leeds.

In 2000, Dublin Bus ordered 20 Volvo B7LA/Eclipse Fusion to enhance the transport operation in the city. This was a very important order for Wrights as it was relatively local and therefore the company could easily monitor the product. As this was one of the first orders received for the Eclipse Fusion, we benefited from the valuable assistance of Shane Doyle (Chief Engineer) and his engineering staff, who visited regularly to examine progress and to ensure that all the special requirements of Dublin Bus drivers were incorporated into the design development.

We had demonstrated the Eclipse Fusion in Dublin prior to receiving the order and, on that occasion, the driver was Robin Barr, who over the years has shown the company's products all over the UK. The first demo journey was between Heuston Station and Connolly Station. On that journey we started with 153 passengers, dropping some and collecting others at the various bus stops en route. The following morning we went to one of the large housing complexes on the outskirts of Dublin. We followed that, in the afternoon, with an operational route from one of the larger educational colleges. It was on this journey that the Dublin Bus manager was called on his mobile phone to be told that one of their double-deckers had broken down on that particular route. He advised that help was close at hand – US! When we came to the vehicle that had broken down, the surprised passengers were taken onboard and we made our way back through Dublin, dropping off and picking up passengers at the bus stops, and not having to leave anyone behind.

On a lighter note, on leaving Dublin we were heading for Cork and Robin mistakenly turned left, one street too soon and we finished up at the rear of the Guinness Brewery. Now that would not have been a problem if we had been in a car, but in an 18m articulated bus it was a very big problem. With two-way traffic, cars parked on both sides of the road and a fairly tight bend in the street, I thought, like everyone around us, that we would be there for some time. But I must give credit to the great driving skills of Robin as we finally got around the corner with literally millimetres to spare, without touching any of the parked cars, and headed on our way to Cork.

The demonstration of the manoeuvrability of the Eclipse Fusion over the bridges on the canals, without any inconvenience to other drivers and the

The articulated Volvo B7LAs for Dublin Bus are lined up at Broadstone Garage prior to entering service.

ability of the bus to operate in dense traffic conditions, whilst maximising passenger capacity during peak journeys times, was enough to convince Dublin Bus and the Government transport officials that this was an ideal vehicle for the future.

Wrightbus is the only company to have designed, engineered and manufactured articulated city buses in the United Kingdom.

Scania wanted a competitor to the Eclipse Fusion so it was agreed to build a similar product for them, the Solar Fusion using the Scania L94UA chassis for those customers who wanted Scania products. Whilst the Volvo has sold in reasonable numbers, the Scania has not delivered the sales that were expected, mainly due the fact that this chassis is not an ideal design for articulated buses.

While we developed the market for articulated buses in London by demonstrating the advantages of that product to many of the bus companies and the transport authorities, we lost the business for a number of reasons. Having spent over a year considering the product, London Transport went out to tender asking for delivery to a time scale that we could not achieve, as we already had a large order book, that we were fully committed to delivering. On the other hand, Mercedes was suffering. In its home market in Europe, sales were dramatically down and they was working to reduced capacity. They could deliver and offered an additional discount plus extended warranties to ensure they got the order. Much as Wrights and Volvo would have liked the London order, there was no possibility of either company, either reducing the price and by doing so losing money, when there was other profitable business around, or providing extended warranty in London which we knew from experience, is the toughest operational environment in Europe.

Mercedes needed the business at that point in time, and without doubt bought the business. If they had known that Volvo and Wrights were not in a position to deliver the product on time, I am sure that the deal would have been entirely different!

The Dublin artics later received the blue and yellow livery. *(Paul Savage)*

The Volvo B10LA/Fusions at Southampton were later replaced with B7LA/Eclipse Fusions, although these too, were moved on due to grounding problems with speed bumps. *(Paul Savage)*

Another customer for the Scania Solar Fusion was Nottingham.

The first Fusion on the Scania chassis was delivered to First Manchester for service at Bury. *(Will Hughes)*

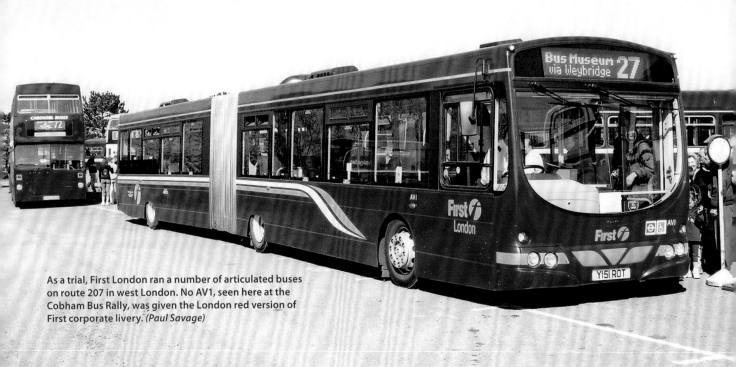

As a trial, First London ran a number of articulated buses on route 207 in west London. No AV1, seen here at the Cobham Bus Rally, was given the London red version of First corporate livery. *(Paul Savage)*

Cyril McIntyre
Editor, *The Omnibus Magazine*

THE OMNIBUS SOCIETY
www.omnibussoc.org

WILLIAM WRIGHT – TRANSPORT INNOVATOR

The re-organisation of CIÉ in 1987 and the resulting establishment of Bus Éireann and Dublin Bus as separate companies within the CIÉ Group ushered in a new era of development of bus services within the Irish Republic. The previous policy of treating bus operations as a subordinate part of a railway network had artificially constrained the growth of intercity bus routes outside Dublin, but now Bus Éireann would be free to develop express coach services on all major interurban corridors.

Growing the market for interurban bus travel was Bus Éireann's main priority in those early years and it was not until the mid-nineties that attention was turned to the Company's city services in Cork, Galway, Limerick and Waterford. Cork was, and still is, Bus Éireann's largest city bus operation with a fleet greater than that of the other three cities combined.

As Media & Public Relations Manager of Bus Éireann at the time, I was already familiar with the innovative designs emanating from Wrights of Ballymena and in particular with the pioneering work of William Wright in developing lowfloor buses fully accessible to wheelchair users. So I was particularly pleased when in 1997 Bus Éireann selected the Volvo/Wright combination for ten new single-deckers for my native city, one of which was of the new fully accessible design with a wheelchair entry ramp. It was a pleasure to work with the Wrightbus team at the official launch of the new buses.

This first fully accessible vehicle in the Bus Éireann fleet underwent intensive trial operation in Cork, where hilly routes, narrow streets and traffic congestion pose their own challenges to bus operation. The enthusiastic commitment of Joe Fitzgerald and his staff together with the active co-operation and input of local groups representing wheelchair users were complemented by outstanding aftersales service and technical support from Wrights. The success of these trials led to a policy decision by Bus Éireann that all future purchases of large capacity city buses would be of fully accessible design, anticipating public demand and legislative requirements by several years.

Today the entire Bus Éireann city bus fleet of 189 vehicles is fully accessible; almost 70% of these are Wright-bodied, thanks to competitive pricing and a high quality of service and support from the team at Ballymena. This is a tribute to the continuing reliability of Wright products. The new Volvo Wright double-deckers going into service this year with both Bus Éireann and Dublin Bus are setting new standards of passenger comfort and enhancing the image of public transport in the 21st century.

I have also enjoyed travelling on Wright buses of other operators; the coach seated double-deckers of Route 36 and The Witch Way in Yorkshire are a particular example of how Wrights tailor designs to suit the needs of individual operators while always raising standards to entice people out of their cars. I have also

travelled on the FTR in Leeds, another example of William Wright's philosophy of innovation in the field of bus rapid transit; where he has led others are now following. The new hybrid powered double-decker now in service with Dublin Bus highlights his pioneering work in developing alternative driveline systems to meet the challenges of environmental change.

My several visits to the Wright factory at Ballymena have always been both enjoyable and inspiring. The warm welcome, the desire to satisfy customer needs and the commitment to quality and innovation are attributes which will sustain the Wright Group through difficult times ahead.

Over 50 years ago, while still at school, I subscribed to *Buses Illustrated* (precursor of today's *Buses* magazine) and read about the innovative pioneers of the bus industry – Henry Spurrier of Leyland Motors, George Rackham of Leyland and later AEC, Colin Curtis of the Routemaster team, to name but a few. Today, William Wright of Ballymena has already earned his place alongside those pioneers of yesteryear.

Cyril McIntyre

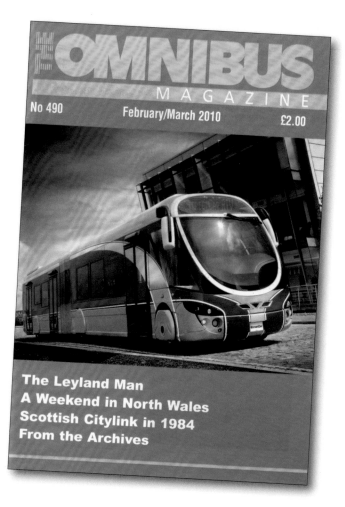

Double-deck developments

Artist's impression of the
Wright double-decker

The Sales Team was always being asked, "When are Wrightbus going to develop a double-deck? We want a company that can supply and support all of our fleet of buses." So there was pressure on the management to engineer, design and develop a double-deck product, incorporating many of the improvements from the new Millennium city bus that were now accepted by engineers as having cost benefits.

By 2000, having spent three years evaluating this market, the products and the competition, Wrights was aware that already the major manufacturers had sufficient capacity to supply the double-deck market. Wrights also were aware that the current products on offer from our competitors were badly in need of a facelift and, moreover, many of our potential customers expressed a desire for a better-engineered product. When asked would they pay more for a totally new product, incorporating many of the improvements already now supplied as standard in our single-deck product range, the answer, as expected, was "No" for a number of reasons. However, when presented with the company's proposals, outline drawings and details of the many improvements, potential customers expressed a desire for the new double-deck product – that was until we mentioned price!

Much of this reluctance came from companies operating in London, where competition for business was tough. To put it bluntly, the reason that our competitors products were perceived to be poor, was down to the fact that operators were unwilling to pay more for a higher quality product. Not only would Wrights have the usual development costs associated with a new a range of buses, but it was going to have to make major structural changes to the factory complex to allow double-deckers to be built. New jigs and fixtures, new preparation and paint shops would also be required. So the total costs before developing any product would be £1.6m. Now you know why the company hesitated before deciding to develop the double-deck range! Eventually we bowed to pressure from our customers and the project got the green light from the Board of Directors.

Surprisingly, Volvo Bus advised against developing the product, based purely on the profit margins in that segment of the market at that time. But the Board had decided that we would build double-deck city buses and, to paraphrase Margaret Thatcher, we were not for turning back now. The management went ahead and, after carefully looking at all the chassis, chose the Volvo B7TL. Volvo has by far the major share of this segment of the market and it has the product support that today's customers demand in this very tough market place. Equally as important, Volvo, having had experience with Wrights other products, knew that the new double-decker would set world class standards and were keen to develop and support the company in the development and sales strategy for this new exciting product.

The company wanted a world leading product engineered and developed at the cutting edge of design. With that in mind, I approached Martin Fisher, an engineer with Travel West Midlands, to assist our engineers in the design, engineering and development of the new product. The company's product development engineers had, up to then, little or no experience of double-deck design. It was vital that we had someone with considerable product knowledge on the team, advising the engineers. Martin Fisher had vast experience of not only operating double-decks, but also repairing and maintaining them. He knew where, over the years, they had encountered structural problems and where greater access was required to service chassis componentry, on different models from different manufacturers. Market research was undertaken to determine what operators ideally wanted to include as standard or as options. The company design engineers, with Martin's assistance, incorporated many of the customers' requested options into the Eclipse Gemini concept. Paul Blair prepared high quality concept drawings of the exterior and interior design of the new Eclipse Gemini; these were well received by Volvo and some of the key decision makers in the industry who were consulted for advice.

The market research had identified many of the problem areas. However, that was no alternative to having hands on experience. Martin Fisher played a significant role in the success of this product. Packaging the seating plan to meet current legislation, including meeting DDA requirements and London Transport operational requirements was a challenge to even the most experienced engineer!

The exterior frontal design was based around the Millennium (Eclipse) single-decker with the stylist/design engineer Paul Blair working with the development engineers to develop a design that would be easily recognised as another Wrightbus product. A key objective was to use as many of the standard components from the single deck in the frontal design and elsewhere to ensure that the company's Customcare Centres had sufficient replacements in stock, ie windscreens. There were a number of constraints, though, on what could be achieved, for example overall height; we ideally wanted a minimum of six feet headroom on the top deck.

Martin Fisher advised Wrights engineers that double-deck buses occasionally suffered severe damage to the side frames/roof and cantrail at the nearside corner by having to pull in very tight to the left hand side of the road, particularly in the leafy suburbs of cities. This resulted in the top deck framework being designed with more of a 'throw in' to the framework, starting at the bottom of the windows on the top deck. The roof had a greater curvature, whilst still providing the desired headroom. These two minor changes resulted in the lowering of the cantrail by approx 100mm, which will reduce damage. The three Rs - Rapid to Repair or Replace - framework system was now fitted as standard. 'Protech' Panels were fitted to front and rear of bus to reduce accident damage costs, including downtime.

As most double-deck buses operate in inner cities, the operational conditions are tough and the environment dirty. To ensure that the bus could be easily cleaned externally and internally, one of the engineering design briefs was to ensure that all corners would have a curvature and all components and materials used in the interior would be dust-resistant.

The first vehicle to be completed was the 10.6m model, which was to be demonstrated by Charles Moseby to major customers all over the UK, but first shown on the Wrightbus stand at the 2001 Bus and Coach Show.

Having been tasked to supply Production Services with the build specification for the Eclipse Gemini demonstrator, including the internal trim colour scheme and the external livery, I found this to be more difficult than anticipated. We wanted the Eclipse Gemini demonstrator to have the WOW! Factor, both externally and internally, and not to be in the fleet livery of any of our customers, so it could, ideally, be sold on directly to a customer with little or no refurbishment. I spent considerable time selecting the specification, the options and the colour schemes, finally selecting metallic silver as the main external colour, with two additional bands, one yellow and the other black. The interior materials and finish were designed to be easily cleaned, easily refurbished and colour co-ordinated.

When completed, the vehicle looked like no other double-deck and when launched at the Bus and Coach Show, at the National Exhibition Centre in Birmingham, it was the star attraction. Wrightbus had never

The demonstration Eclipse Gemini, in its special silver livery, is seen here in Edinburgh. Lothian later became a valued customer purchasing numerous Geminis.

before built a double-deck city bus, and now had a far superior product to any of its competitors. The exhibition was a major success with everyone from managing directors, engineering, operational managers and drivers all wanting in to view the new Eclipse Gemini.

The following morning, the sales team, knowing that the show did not open to the general public until 9.00am, knew that there was every chance our competitors, who like ourselves could gain entrance earlier, would take the opportunity to examine and evaluate the Eclipse Gemini. We went into the exhibition half an hour before the exhibition opened to find the senior management team of one our major competitors all seated on the top deck! I have no doubt they were impressed. However, at that moment they were more embarrassed, but to give them credit, they did comment that the company had built a very impressive bus.

The management of Wrightbus made the strategic decision that, having never before built a double-deck bus, we did not want volume orders, until we had at least one year's experience building the new product. We also wanted sufficient feedback from operators as to how the bus was performing.

The Eclipse Gemini was introduced into the UK market in 2002 at a premium of £6000 above our competitors' prices. After all the hype at the exhibition, this was a major disappointment to Volvo GB. They knew that the product would not be cheap, but were not expecting a differential of this size. Wrights market research had shown that operators were not happy with the products they were then receiving, but we also knew that these companies controlled the product price. If we were going to offer a product incorporating many of the improvements they had asked for and we had designed and engineered into our product range, we had to increase the price. The sales and marketing strategy on product pricing worked; it limited the supply of product to UK operators until we had engineered it for production, trained the production teams personel and, more importantly, we had feedback on the structural tests on completion of the test programme taking place at MIRA initially, and then from those customers operating the buses.

Might I add that when our competition examined the Gemini it was not long until they were back at the drawing board. The Gemini had set the standards, the customers were no longer willing to accept what they had been receiving and were willing to pay more for a better engineered product. Today, all of our competitors are offering a much improved, higher quality product and have had to increase the price of their products. The Gemini still offers many advantages to the operator that our competitors have not included in their standard product build specification.

London Transport was delighted when we informed them that all of the new Eclipse Gemini product would initially be sold to London operators. The reason for this decision was that we required volume orders, to a standard design specification. Having invested so heavily in the factory infrastructure, the product development and the Gemini test programme at MIRA, it was now time to benefit from these investments. Posters all over London featured the new Eclipse Gemini and it soon became a familiar sight with increased output from the factory. They soon became known as the Nokia Buses, simply because the design of the frontal screens was very much like the front display panel of a Nokia mobile phone.

London is a very tough operating environment and we knew from past experience that if the buses performed well in London then we would have no problems in any of the other major cities. Market research highlighted two major complaints from all operators, drivers and customers. Buses operating in inner London travel very slowly, so the interior saloons became

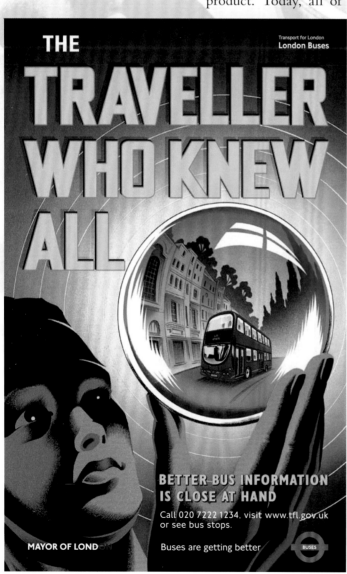

THE TRAVELLER WHO KNEW ALL

Transport for London
London Buses

BETTER BUS INFORMATION IS CLOSE AT HAND

Call 020 7222 1234, visit www.tfl.gov.uk or see bus stops.

MAYOR OF LONDON

Buses are getting better

BUSES

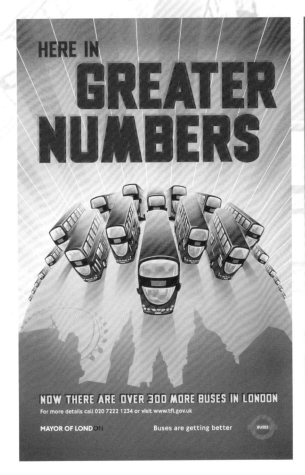

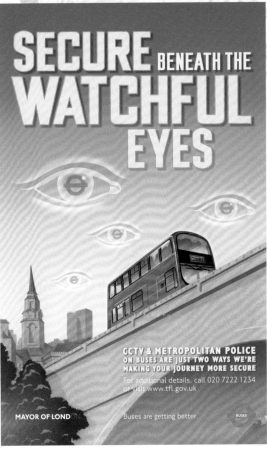

extremely hot and humid in summer and were also cold in the winter. Now, if this was bad for the passengers, who would probably only be on the bus for twenty minutes at the most, just think what it was like for the drivers who were there for the day. With the assistance of our supplier network chain, we highlighted the problem and asked them to bring forward solutions. This resulted in the Gemini gaining a thermostatically controlled, forced air heating and ventilation system fitted as standard on both decks with the option of:

- the driver's cab supplied with full air conditioning;
- the passenger saloon on both decks being fitted with thermostatically controlled air conditioning.

This added considerably to overall price of the Eclipse Gemini, but both operators and the management of London Transport were quick to see the advantages and adopted it into the standard build specification. The driver is ultimately responsible for the safety of the passengers and if he is operating in an environment such as that described earlier, he is not going to be as alert and as attentive as someone who is driving in a fully air conditioned, comfortable environment. Safety all round improves and if you as a driver had a choice, which would you choose? Operators had then, and still have, major problems getting drivers, and having trained them they do not want to lose them. An attractive bus, with an air conditioned saloon and driver's air-conditioning, is a small price to pay to ensure they retain the services of an experienced driver.

When the operator had an accessible, low floor, double-deck bus involved in a side impact accident, unlike the older traditional bus, the framework, including the bonded windows, are very important to the structural integrity of the bus. The Eclipse Gemini incorporated the R3 framework – Rapid to Repair or Replace. This offered the customers major savings. Subject to the severity of the damage, it was estimated to save the customer over 90% of the labour costs and 75% of the materials costs and ensured the structural integrity for the life time of the vehicle. The one other major benefit that should be taken into consideration is the fact that instead of the vehicle being off the road for a considerable amount of time, it could be back in service within a few days with assistance now available from one of the many local Customcare Service Centres.

On a much lighter note, to assist in marketing the R3 framework repair system, I had decided, with the help of Ivan Stewart, to design a tie for gentlemen and a headscarf for ladies, incorporating a design based around the R3 bracketry; these would be given to key customers when they visited the factory. Having had a presentation on the benefits and the cost savings, we would then present each and every one of the visitors with the tie as a reminder of the product. I discussed my requirements with Ivan who, as previously mentioned, is one of the Product Development Engineers. Ivan has a natural ability to "think outside the box" and within a few days he presented me with a number of designs based on the R3 bracketry, illustrated on different colours of background. After some discussions, and slight modifications, we selected the design on two different backgrounds, red and blue, and forwarded these illustrations to a local manufacturer renowned for manufacturing a high quality product. Samples and illustrations were returned within a few days and, having selected the design, the colours and the material, a substantial order was placed.

Over the years I have been presented with many ties that have the company name or logo clearly defined on the tie. I consider this to be a totally useless exercise, as all too often it is never used unless one is visiting that factory/ company. I had asked both Ivan and the manufacturers to design the tie so that it could be worn on all occasions. A few weeks after presenting a tie to a senior member of Bus Éireann, I received a call from him on a Monday morning. He informed me that on the previous Saturday morning, whilst accompanying his wife on a shopping trip, he had been approached by a lady, a complete stranger, who asked him where he had purchased his tie. The lady explained that they had a wedding to attend in the near future and she thought the tie would be very smart with her husband's new suit. As he had been approached unexpectedly and taken unawares, he did not want to say that he had received the tie from Wrightbus, but did inform the lady that he had received it as a gift. We laughed and he advised me that Ivan could always take up artistic design in the clothing manufacturing industry. What it did prove, though, was that we had accomplished what we had set out to do – design a stylish tie that would be noticeable, could be worn on all occasions, would wear well and the wearer would hopefully would always remember the R3 when putting on the tie each morning

Bus Éireann must have liked all of the many benefits. They have continued to place significant orders, for the Eclipse Urban; all include the R3 framework repair system.

Incidentally, none of our competitors can offer a similar repair system and as anyone operating buses in inner cities can tell you, it is not whether a bus will be involved in an accident, but when?

Full-scale production commenced in 2001 and already Wrightbus has over 2000 double-deck buses operating in UK cities and Hong Kong, with a large proportion in London.

Arriva is one of the largest bus companies, operating approximately 7000 buses in the UK with many other of their operating companies based overseas, including the Netherlands. Arriva operates approximately 1000 double-decks in London, of which 325 have been supplied on both Volvo and VDL chassis. Its subsidiary company – Arriva Coach and Bus – is also the importer and distributor for what was originally DAF bus and coach chassis, now known as VDL (named after its owner Mr Van der Leegte).

Many Arriva companies are customers of Wrightbus and wanted the company to build the new Gemini double-deck on a VDL chassis, the well established DB250LF model. Like the Volvo, this was a low floor chassis

A VDL DB250LF chassis for Arriva London.

The 1000th Gemini was built on a VDL DB250LF chassis for Arriva London.

A Gemini in the nude! The substantial Aluminique framing of an Eclipse Gemini under construction at Galgorm is clearly visible in this picture.

engineered and developed for the UK market. The engine and driveline were well packaged, but the chassis configuration did not allow our engineers to package the seating on the lower deck quite as well as on the Volvo. Operators of the VDL DB250 agreed that the chassis was good, reliable and fuel efficient. Wrightbus management, having met with Arriva management, agreed to engineer and develop the Pulsar Gemini on this chassis, subject to being given sufficient orders to justify the development costs.

Bob McLeod (Managing Director) of Arriva Bus and Coach was very keen to have the product on the VDL chassis, to market to both the Arriva operating companies and other bus companies, but it was just a little more difficult to extract an order. However, in the end we did receive a commitment and Arriva received the product. The Pulsar Gemini was well received by the Arriva operating companies, especially those in London and within a short time was to prove a success with passengers.

Production of the Gemini product range on Volvo and VDL chassis was running at approx twelve buses per week.

I personally believe that the VDL product range would sell in greater numbers if it were an entirely independent company and had a service support network similar to that offered by Volvo and Scania. When Volvo purchased the Leyland Bus Division it also inherited the associated dealer support network and Leyland had dominated the volume business, in both trucks and buses in the UK. Since the takeover, Volvo has closed all its manufacturing facilities in the UK and now imports its products from Sweden and more recently from Poland, where most of the bus chassis are

Lothian Buses, in Edinburgh, has specified the Gemini for its recent double-deck deliveries (and the Eclipse for its single-deck orders).

now assembled. Volvo has increased its sales of truck, coach and bus chassis in the UK and, over the intervening years, has totally reorganised the service support for its products. Ideally, customer support is best located close to and easily accessible by the operator, and having this facility has been to Volvo's advantage. Likewise, Scania got round this problem by training the service staff of its local truck distributor to deal with buses.

By 2009, Wrightbus had the capacity to manufacture 16 double-deck buses per week. I am glad that I did not take Steve Dewhurst's advice not to introduce a double-decker into the company's product range and I might add, so is Steve! Volvo has another quality product to offer its customers, both here in the UK and overseas.

Recently Wrightbus' local operator, Translink ordered 125 Eclipse Gemini on the Volvo B9TL, to Euro 4 specification. Having reintroduced the double-decker first in Belfast with Citybus, it has more recently expanded double-deck operation to cope with changes in school transport regulations. Most of these Geminis are fully compliant for school bus operation, having seatbelts fitted.

The first Eclipse Gemini double-deck was delivered in 2001 and with the growth of accessible double-deckers all over the UK today, Wrightbus has captured 43% of the double-deck market and has already almost 2900 operating on the roads of the United Kingdom, on the well proven Volvo B7TL, Volvo BT9TL and DAF DB250LF chassis.

One hundred of the Translink order for 125 vehicles are fitted with three-point seatbelts for use on schools duties. Eighty Geminis, such as No 2249 seen here on The Mall in Armagh, were allocated to Ulsterbus depots where they have proved both useful and popular. *(Paul Savage)*

Dublin Bus VG36 awaits its customers outside Dublin's central bus station, Busaras. This vehicle is dedicated to the Airlink service and wears a special livery. *(John Durey)*

London United, which had run some of the first Pathfinder 320 low floor single-deckers, took a batch of Geminis on the Volvo B7TL. This was among the smartest London liveries.

Citybus, in Belfast, placed its first Eclipse Geminis in service in May 2008. Photographed within hours of taking up its duties, No 2202 is seen in Royal Avenue heading for the shopping centre at Forestside. (Paul Savage)

The Blazefield Group has set new standards for passenger comfort with leather trimmed interiors, murals and stunning liveries on its buses on *Route 36* between Harrogate and Leeds and *The Witch Way* between Burnley and Manchester.

Having already used the Volvo/Eclipse Gemini combination for its route 36 between Harrogate and Leeds, Blazefield Group also took the same combination for its *Yorkshire Coastliner* operations between York and the coastal towns.

Travel West Midlands' Martin Fisher was involved in the development of the Eclipse Gemini. One of that concern's deliveries is seen in central Birmingham. Note the motorist ignoring the bus lane!

East Yorkshire chose the Gemini, on Volvo, for its 2005 deliveries

Above: London is a tough environment for any bus and sometimes it's not too pleasant for the driver and his passengers either. FirstGroup has improved standards with cab air conditioning and thermostically controlled heating and ventilation on both decks, as on First London VNW32666.

Right: Having enhanced its express services fleet, over recent years Bus Eireann has being doing similar with the city and commuter fleets, an example being the purchase of ten Geminis for commuter services in Dublin and Cork. *(John Durey)*

Below: In 2008, to increase capacity on the service between Windsor and central London, First Berkshire placed in service three Volvo B9TLs, finished to a high specification with leather seats, tables and Wi-Fi. *(John Durey)*

With its stunning looks, the Eclipse Gemini has been chosen for operation on several high-profile routes. And a well-designed livery, such as that on this Go-Ahead North East Volvo, makes the Gemini stand out from the crowd.

Having taken an East Yorkshire Gemini on demonstration, Isle of Man Transport purchased eleven, which were delivered in early 2009. Fleet number 65 is seen being passed by one of the Island's historic steam locomotives, No 13 *Kissack*. *(Mark O'Neill)*

Metroline placed its first Wright-bodied double-deckers in service on 27 March 2010 when the first of an order for 22 Eclipse Gemini 2 bodied Volvo B9TLs took up duty on route 237 between Hounslow Heath and White City.

On 28 March 2010, Lothian Buses relaunched its service between central Edinburgh and the airport using 14 Eclipse Gemini 2-bodied Volvo B9TLs, which feature a new livery, high-backed, leather-trimmed seats, tables, wood-effect flooring and luggage racks. *(Lothian Buses)*

The Wrightbus Eclipse Gemini 2, on the Volvo B9TL, is the result of a project between the two companies to deliver an optimised double-decker which meets Transport for London's stringent noise and emission tests. The vehicle makes extensive use of composite material developed by The Wright Group to reduce weight and increase fuel efficiency. The first of 76 for Go-Ahead London was destined to be the 1000th Wrightbus vehicle operating in London. Pictured opposite, left to right, are Richard Harrington, Chief Engineer and Phil Margrave, Group Engineering Director of Go-Ahead Group; Jonathan Poynton, Business Development Director and Mark Nodder, Managing Director of the Wright Group; Phil Owen, Volvo Bus Sales Director.

First London (below) is also receiving Eclipse Gemini 2-bodied Volvo B9TLs.

Going Global

Wrightbus has been to the fore amongst British bus body manufacturers when it comes to achieving export sales.

Various lorries and truck-derived buses were exported to Africa and Saudi Arabia during the 1980s, but the first export sale of modern buses was of 25 Crusader-bodied Dennis Dart SLFs to Canberra, the Australian capital in 1996, an accidental order if the truth be told.

David McCaughey (left) and the author outside the factory with the first Dart SLF about to leave for Canberra, Australia.

In early 1998, Wrights looked at the Hong Kong market to see what was available, but didn't progress the research. However, Mark Nodder believed there was an opportunity and revived the project again in 1999. In an interesting co-incidence, during 2000/1 both Stagecoach and First expanded their overseas portfolios, buying into Hong Kong. The choice of vehicles and bodybuilders for Hong Kong customers was reducing and they were looking for new suppliers.

Action Canberra Dennis Dart No 135 basks in the sun of the Australian capital. *(Paul McNamara)*

Wrights decided to build a double-decker for the Hong Kong market on the Leyland Super Olympian tri-axle chassis. This was planned to be completed before the Gemini for the United Kingdom market, but this decision was reversed to give the company the opportunity to claw back some of the development costs from the bigger London market.

Mark Nodder had invited the companies to visit the Wrightbus stand, and was keen to explore potential business opportunities in Hong Kong, and the Far East in general.

Representatives from several Hong Kong companies, accompanied by the Volvo export sales manager for the area, Mr Don Goodier, spent a considerable time examining the Eclipse Gemini double-deck and discussing the build of the product with Wrights' David Johnson. Over the period of the show, they also visited other suppliers of double-deck vehicles, but they returned to Wrightbus on a number of occasions to look at the Gemini and follow up on this new interesting concept. The new design, the quality of finish, the benefits of an all alloy, all bolted, easy to repair, lightweight framework was of immense interest to them. The Engineering Team from Kowloon Motor Bus (KMB) was very impressed with the new Eclipse Gemini, and before leaving they arranged to come to the factory to view the production facilities and discuss future business opportunities.

The main operators in Hong Kong – Kowloon Motor Bus, Citybus and New World – were all receptive to the new idea. While a chassis had not been chosen for the new design, KMB recommended Volvo, and Volvo needed a new body partner. A prototype was built on the Super Olympian for evaluation, as a forerunner to a potential 200+ bus deal.

The first batch of 40 (of 101 Olympians) was in the course of delivery when Hong Kong got caught up in the Severe Acute Respiratory Syndrome (SARS) epidemic, resulting in a slowdown in the region's economy. The order was then spilt into two batches, with 180 vehicles now delivered. As it happens, only the first 50 were built on the Super Olympian, the chassis being changed to the Volvo B9, which resulted in major changes to the body.

KMB must be the world's most demanding customer and each batch has had specification changes to the bodywork. Hong Kong is a very tough

William and Mrs Ruby Wright, with representatives from Kowloon Motor Bus and Volvo, at the handover of the first *Wright Bus* in 2003. *(Kowloon Motor Bus)*

The first deliveries to Hong Kong were on the Leyland Super Olympian chassis. *(Denis Strange)*

environment and KMB regularly request improvements of both chassis manufacturer and bodybuilder. Operators look closely at design and like to have an input at all levels of engineering so if you can succeed in Hong Kong, you can succeed anywhere!

Unusually, the KMB vehicle doesn't have a name; it's simply known as *The Wright Bus* and is used on high profile routes. KMB loves the style and involved Feng Shui in the design. The smiling face of the front is particularly appreciated.

Wrightbus is now a well established player in Hong Kong and is looking at supplying a completely knocked down (CKD) bus to KMB for assembly in China. This would be based on the Euro 5 Volvo, also in kit form although in 2009, another order was placed for 175 more *Wright Buses* on Volvo B9 chassis. These vehicles are to be delivered during 2009/10.

The success of this challenge to export buses to Hong Kong was a great encouragement to the Sales and Marketing Team. A key objective of the management is to examine world passenger transportation systems and seek niche markets with a view to supplying companies with a superior range of quality products.

The Volvo B9 in tri-axle form as used on the KMB deliveries.

Where it is not possible to supply fully assembled buses due to political pressures, Wrightbus, having established a working relationship with the company and subject to sales potential, will offer a Licence Agreement where Wrightbus will assist them to engineer, design and develop new products for the local market, using the proven Aluminique framework, all bolted technology. Wrightbus will ship all the components as a kit, complete with

Although looking very similar to the body on the Leyland Super Olympian chassis (the casual observer would be hard pressed to tell the difference), major changes had to be engineered into the design when production was shifted to the Volvo B9TL chassis. *(Denis Strange)*

drawings for the local builder to assemble the product, using relatively unskilled labour. Part of that licence agreement will be that Wrightbus will train and increase the skills of the local labour in that company. Subject to the volumes, etc, this package will greatly increase the sales potential for both companies.

KMB's Managing Director, Mr Edmond Ho Tat Man, receives a presentation bowl from Wrightbus' Jonathan Poynton to mark the delivery of the first *Wright Bus* of the 2010 order. *(Kowloon Motor Bus)*

Wrightbus Product Manager David McCaughey and David Johnson (right) with the first of the 2010 delivery of Volvo B9s for Kowloon Motor Bus. The plaque was presented to David Johnson by Volvo Bus in appreciation of his work in Asian markets.

Scott Harvey

Scott Harvey is our man in Hong Kong, where he is responsible for Customcare aftersales and technical support to Kowloon Motor Bus (1933) Ltd and its fleet of Wrightbus tri-axle double-deckers.

Scott began his career with the Company in 1992, when he joined as an apprentice. Guided by Robert Alexander, he was introduced to the Wrightbus family and learned his trade – everything from the importance of simple tasks, such as good housekeeping, through to a command of the Wright refined manufacturing processes. By the time he finished his apprenticeship he understood the end product was not only built on 'Quality by Design' but quality through people skill and attentiveness.

In 1998, Scott joined Darren McCormick and David Johnson on the Opus project then being developed in conjunction with a Wichita, Kansas company then called Chance Coach Incorporated (later Optima Bus Corporation and now part of North American Bus Industries, Incorporated). As part of the total support package for the new Opus vehicles, over a period of two and a half years, Wichita became Scott's 'home from home'.

Returning from the USA in late 2001, and after further personal development through other projects, Scott was offered an opportunity to work in Customcare, providing dedicated aftersales support for the vehicles being developed for Kowloon Motor Bus (1933) Ltd, in Hong Kong. The

Pictured on page 189, before departing on its long journey to the other side of the world, the first of the 2010 delivery of Volvo B9s for Kowloon Motor Bus was then photographed in Hong Kong prior to entering service. This batch of vehicles will feature the re-styled front fitted to the Eclipse Gemini 2.

prototype vehicle for KMB, a Volvo B10TL, was commissioned in March 2003; this was followed by a further 99 similar vehicles. A further order for the Wrightbus product (64 Volvo B9TLs) was delivered in 2005/6.

Customcare support is a wide and varied role. Each day is a learning experience. It is vital to not only work with the customer's various departmental staff but also its shopfloor operatives, as this gives Scott a good insight to operational issues that the end user experiences with its vehicles. In translating this information, the Wrightbus product can be further developed to exceed the customer's expectations.

Scott enjoys many sports, hiking being his favourite activity each weekend. Although many visitors to Hong Kong relate to the big city, it is actually full of many beautiful country parks and mountains. Obviously, language is very important in his life and although still learning, he has developed a good understanding of Cantonese. He notes that Chinese culture is engrained with respect for others – also a Wrightbus ethos! He has made many close friends and colleagues throughout his career and is thankful for being part of the family and their influence on his journey in life.

Now a part of the Wrightbus network for eighteen years, he has his own young and delightful family. He married Tsz in Hong Kong in 2005 and they now have two daughters, Aaliyah Louise (4) and Rihanna Ruth (2).

Chance Coach

Wrights desire to create an export business led to a meeting with Chance Coach, an American concern which had come about through a management buyout by Chance Industries, an amusement ride manufacturer.

From 1998, US companies were looking to Europe for business partners. Bus design in America hadn't changed much in thirty years and low floor would soon be needed due to disability legislation. Smaller companies were trying to drive this change, and that led to the Wichita-based Chance Coach visit to Ballymena.

The Opus was a small, low floor, US compliant, heavy duty bus. The prototype vehicle was launched in 2000 and was well received. The first production vehicles were delivered to Long Beach Transit in 2001. This one was for Sierra Spirit in Nevada.

A project was agreed to design a small, low floor, US compliant, heavy duty bus with a 12-15 year life. As this was a new venture for both parties there was an exchange of technologies, but the prototype vehicle was built in Ballymena. Production was then transferred to Wichita where the staff were trained by Wrights. The components were supplied from Ballymena, completely knocked down (CKD) like a flat pack. The prototype vehicle, named Opus, was launched in 2000 and was well received. It might seem hard to believe, but US transit bosses had never seen coloured hand poles on a bus before! The first production vehicles were delivered to Long Beach Transit in 2001. As an aside, every US transit manager who visited Ballymena to see production fell in love with Northern Ireland and, more importantly, bought buses. At its peak, Wrights were supplying 100-120 kits per year.

Chance Coach was renamed Optima in 2004 and sold to NABI in 2006. The Wichita plant was closed and the Opus production line was moved to Alabama.

An Opus bus in service at Salt Lake City.

The Opus buses delivered to Long Beach work a route serving the liner Queen Mary, now a floating hotel. Other Opus vehicles can be found in Chicago, Miami, Salt Lake City, Austin, Hawaii, Waco and Greenville. Two hybrid versions are now undergoing trials.

Deliveries to Arriva Netherlands included the DAF SB120-based Cadet and the larger SB200-based Commander, one of which is seen here near Rotterdam.
(Paul McNamara)

Netherlands

In 2000, Arriva took over approx a third of the Dutch nationalised fleet. After problems with some Alexander-bodied Dennis Darts, which didn't meet the low noise requirements specified in Holland, Arriva ordered a batch of 20 DAFs – eight SB120s and 12 SB200s – from Wrights which were put them into service at Leeuwarden. The chassis were imported from the Netherlands, bodied in Ballymena, driven back to the Netherlands and placed in service in the hometown of major Dutch coachbuilder, Berkhof. Needless to say, this didn't go down well, but Arriva bought almost 200 before Berkhof came up with a suitable design.

Dubai

Until the global recession of 2009, the Gulf state of Dubai had been planning a massive enhancement of public transport in the country. Wrightbus staff had worked hard to ensure that the company won a substantial share of the 1616 vehicle order from the Dubai Roads and Transport Authority. However, with the collapse of property prices in the state, plans for bus investment were shelved and the contract with Wrightbus and all the other successful bidders were cancelled.

Singapore

August 2009 saw a change for the better with the winning, together with Volvo Bus, of a significant order from SBS Transit of the Island City State of Singapore. The order is for 150 tri-axle, air-conditioned buses on the Volvo B9TL chassis but, after the building in Ballymena of the prototype, the rest of the order will be supplied as completely knocked down (ckd) kits for construction locally. Wright Group engineers on site in Singapore will ensure that the Company's high quality standards will be maintained during the build process, which is scheduled to start in early 2010 and be complete by the end of the year. Supplying buses as ckd kits is, of course, nothing new to the Company as over 500 were supplied to the United States between 2001 and 2006.

Artist's impression of the Volvo B9TL double-deckers for SBS Transit.

Customcare

Demand for Wrightbus products was increasing with buses now based in all the major cities in the UK and Ireland. Wrightbus was aware that operators were not receiving the support they needed, so Charles Moseby (UK Sales Manager) and I were asked to come up with proposals on how best we could best serve our customers' needs.

Historically, the company's manufacturing team had provided after-¬market support and, although the service had been acceptable, increasing demands from customers were suggesting that an entirely new approach was required if, as a company, we were to provide a top quality after-sales service. Most of the company's products were being sold on Volvo chassis and the Volvo Service Centres, both in the UK and Ireland, were providing what was deemed to be, by far, the best service available to operators. Charles produced an outline map of the British Isles, showing the Volvo Service Centres, which also highlighted the customers who operated buses in that area and the number of buses in daily operation.

But there were a number of customers who operated Scania buses and we needed to provide them with support, too. There was no way that a customer operating Scanias would want to take the vehicle (in the event of major structural damage) to a Volvo Service Centre, so first we had to determine what level of support would meet our customer's expectations. We believed that the support we offered to our customers was good. We now needed to know how our customers at both Management and Operational levels viewed the company's after-sales service support and what they really wanted.

Wrightbus commissioned an independent market survey, covering the company's key customers at both levels and after extensive research, the consultant published his report. The in-depth report made very interesting

The Customcare team. Director, Geoff Potter, is front row centre.

reading. (The company names, or who had been interviewed, were not published.) To summarise the results, the service we, as a company, provided was better than most but still left a lot to be desired, simply because the level of support from the industry, in general, was poor. As a company known for the quality of its products, it was vital that Wrightbus' after-market support was vastly improved so that our customers knew, and recognised, the company as a manufacturer of quality buses that offered our customer after-sales service similar to that of the luxury car manufacturers.

Customers wanted a local service that could provide them with excellent parts availability, strong warranty support, parts manuals, both in book form and on CD, to allow them to process orders efficiently. They also wanted operator training in the proper procedures to repair a Wright bus when it was involved in an accident. Also very high in the wish list was operator training in replacing bonded windows, adjustments to the controls operating entrance and exit doors, etc. With the extensive use of multiplex electronics, the operating company's electrical engineers required to be trained in the use of this new technology and how it could benefit them by reducing their labour costs.

It became clear that Wrightbus needed to create an organisation focused purely on the after-market, an organisation which would not be diverted by other priorities. The result was that Wright Customcare was launched in 1997.

In those early days, Customcare consisted of two service personnel on the UK mainland with two dedicated stores personnel both based in the

Galgorm manufacturing plant in Northern Ireland. Rodney Mark, based in the Customcare Centre, had the added responsibility of meeting with the engineers from the various companies and providing hands-on training, with the help of Production Line Managers, to ensure that the technicians were given proper instruction to allow them to carry out in house servicing of the components of the products.

Sam McLaren had joined the company in December 1996 and was tasked with taking overall control of the Customcare after-market field sales support. Sam had many years experience in the bus industry dealing with customer's complaints, whilst ensuring that remedial work was carried out when reported. Service Centres were appointed along the lines that Charles Moseby had suggested, the Volvo Service Centres being keen to develop a closer working relationship with their customers. Customcare Supplier Partnership Agreements were signed, replacement components parts stock levels agreed and operator training, at all levels, including stores personnel, was arranged and action taken to ensure that all those requiring hands-on training received maximum attention. Customcare management had listened to its customers. With Sam McLaren's in-depth knowledge of the bus operator's service requirements, the company's aim was to keep operators' buses on the move and in top condition, whilst minimising cost of ownership and maximising operating profits.

An important aspect of Wrights hands-on training is that it allows the development of strong business relationships. These relationships encourage trainees to comment on technical issues they have had in their day to day work. This continuous customer feedback is a vital element to both production engineering and engineers developing new products. To achieve our ultimate goal, this needs a three-way partnership between the chassis supplier, Customcare and last, but by no means least, the operator.

Customcare expands to meet the challenges ahead

Having recognised that after-sales support is a crucial part of its whole life commitment to the customers, The Wright Group is continuing to expand its industry-leading Customcare network.

Geoff Potter, having been with the company six years, and with immense knowledge in providing after sales service, was appointed a director of Wrightbus. Under Geoff's leadership, Customcare has expanded dramatically and currently has over 40 direct employees and a network of 20 franchised Customcare Service Centres. Gordon Aylmore, Director of Customer Services, Wright Customcare (based in GB), has played a significant role in developing Customcare in the United Kingdom. Gordon

Interior of a Customcare centre

had much experience in dealing with the chassis manufacturers before joining Customcare, having worked with Volvo. His role in developing Customcare Centres, as well as supporting the technical support engineers on the ground, is recognised by all those involved, including the chassis manufacturers.

Tthe latest evolution of the organisation has been designed to keep vehicles on the road, by minimising unplanned downtime. Twenty Mobile Service Engineers, supplemented by the Customcare Centres, are coordinated by four Regional Service Engineers. Our customers can call one number and a Customcare Service Engineer will be in contact within one hour to resolve any issue. A guaranteed next day parts delivery service from a new state of the art distribution facility and a new on-line parts ordering system have also been introduced. An agreement recently signed with DHL specialist automotive team, sees the immediate transfer of existing parts storage and distribution from an ultra Modern 75,000 sq. ft. Logistic Centre at Halewood, Merseyside

Having demonstrated the service commitment to diesel/electric hybrid citybuses in London, the team is now planning the next major step in its development based on providing the total service support package for the new range of Wright Midibuses products which will be introduced in 2010, with production commencing in 2011.

The growth of the Customcare network mirrors the growth in the Wrightbus share of the UK market. Gordon Aylmore explains, "There are now over 9000 Wright buses in service in the UK and Northern Ireland and that number continues to grow weekly. The expansion of our Customcare network recognises the importance of ensuring that all new and existing customers have ready access to a quality after-sales service and support wherever they are. Customcare support is not just limited to the United Kingdom, as Wrightbus products (both CBU and CKD) have been exported to the Netherlands, Hong Kong and to the USA."

Customcare is expanding its range of support contract packages to its customers. The Parts Assurance Package typically provides a five year contract to cover normal `wear and tear items' with Repair and Maintenance Packages, with and without labour, increasing in demand from operators looking to reduce costs and also looking to fix significant elements of their vehicles' operating costs.

The latest investments in training facilities and other initiatives are part of a long term commitment to operator support, providing the best whole life cost proposals. According to Gordon Aylmore, "Whilst we are currently in a market leading position, we can never be complacent and only by being innovative and proactive can we continue to be the market leader in this segment of the market. Customcare, like the parent company has expanded to meet demand and today is the market leader in providing after-sales service to the company's valued customers."

Customcare opens a new Training Centre

Rodney Mark leads a training session for a customer's engineering team.

To keep pace with a growing demand from customers who now clearly see the many benefits to be gained by having their workforce fully trained in the maintenance of their fleet of Wrightbus products, a new training centre was opened at Ballymena in 2008. Located in the new Customcare Centre at the Galgorm factory, the training suite, which was completed at a cost of £500,000, provides classroom and workshop-based environments for dealer staff and engineering technicians from bus operating companies. With the introduction of hybrid powered vehicles there is a greater need for in-house training of engineers, for both the company and for the operator's engineers. With the new training centre, Customcare has now the capacity to provide training for up to 350 technicians per year.

Wrightbus Structural Engineering Expertise

From 1986 to 1996, Wrightbus used Alusuisse aluminium extrusions and castings for the construction of its body designs. This system was supplied under licence and every Wrightbus design proposal was approved by Alusuisse as being structurally adequate.

Of course this meant that Alusuisse expertise ensured the aluminium body and steel chassis combination was fit for purpose in terms of longevity. This proof is imperative as the low floor chassis had dictated the need to package the engine and gearbox at the very rear of the vehicle and the chassis members became slender. The chassis cannot solely support its own componentry; the body is expected to make up the deficit strength and stiffness required to carry the componentry and passenger masses.

By 1996, the Alusuisse patent had expired and the Wrightbus Board made the strategic decision to independently design, source and structurally approve its own body system. This would be similar to the Alusuisse system but with further improvements to enhance the build process, ensuring that both build times and accident repair labour costs are reduced, whilst at the same time minimising weight.

Rather than rely on subcontracted engineering advice, it was decided to expand the company's own in-house core engineering design capabilities and and employ a professional structural engineer.

In September of 1996, Adrian Robinson was recruited. A graduate of Queens University's Aeronautical Engineering Department, Adrian had worked as a Stress Engineer with Shorts Bombardier for ten years.

Structural analysis techniques used in the aircraft industry were then deployed at Wrightbus, the primary

Adrian Robinson (seated) and Sam McCartney

aim being to ensure the chassis and body combination for every new product developed, provides adequate strength for a durable trouble free life of fifteen years.

The main tool used for this analysis work is a mathematical model constructed and processed on computer. Known as Finite Element Modelling, this enables Adrian to literally see predicted stresses and displacements within the bus body and chassis. These are then closely inspected to ensure the stress levels do not exceed known fatigue values and the displacements do not exceed acceptable levels which would interfere with the buses functionality. Too much stress on a body or chassis component would give premature structural failures and too much displacement would lead to breaking glass (bonded in), creaking and breaking internal trimmings and poorly fitting doors. Also, visually, the bus may have unacceptable curvature along the bus length.

This structural analysis has enabled Wrightbus to be competitive in weight and cost through structural material optimisation. The areas that require more strength than others are identified early in the development cycle and the necessary amount of material and components included.

After the design is deemed to be structurally satisfactory, the first vehicle is built. This first vehicle of every new product/design is then taken to Millbrook Proving Ground at Bedford. Here the same technique to that used in aircraft airframe stress measurements is used. Stress gauges are fitted to the areas which have been found to give the higher stresses in the computer simulations. Once these are installed, the vehicle is driven around the test track features and the actual stresses and loads in the vehicle are measured. Particular attention is paid to the stresses incurred as the vehicle goes over speedbumps and around the Ride and Handling Circuit at various speeds. Millbrook return the data to Wrightbus, where it is processed to give the actual life of the structure. Once these final results are derived and deemed to be satisfactory, the design is signed off and full series production of these vehicle types is started.

The evolution of various low floor single-deck vehicles occurred during the later half of the nineteen nineties and the computer modelling and test track procedure had given trouble free products. This was important for the companies reputation and also for minimising warranty expenditure. A major structural issue built into a vehicle with a production run of several hundred would have serious consequences in both these regards.

By the end of 2000, Wrightbus Directors had decided to enter into the double-decker vehicle market. With no such design experience whatsoever, the development team proceeded with great caution! As usual, a finite element model was generated and any theoretical weaknesses designed out. The prototype vehicle was built in 2001 and delivered to Millbrook

Proving Ground. The stress gauge data was seen to be satisfactory. However, as this was a completely new project for Wrightbus, it was vital that we got it right first time; the vehicle remained at Millbrook and underwent five months of intense test track exposure. This accelerated endurance testing essentially put the same duty cycle into the vehicle that it would experience in 500,000 miles of normal in service use. On return to the factory, the bus was partly stripped for inspection and found to have no major issues. This was quite an achievement as the entire development programme was truncated into nine months. Mr Wright was impressed and with his well known sense of humour commented, "All that expensive Millbrook durability testing for nothing!"

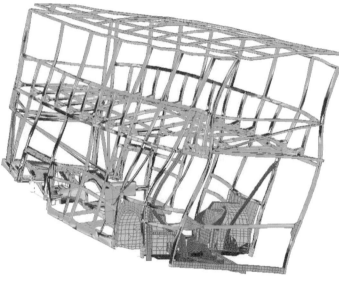

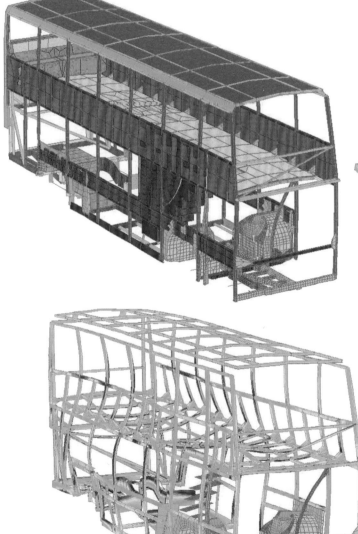

Above left: Wrightbus finite element model of Gemini body on B7TL Volvo chassis.

Above right: Finite element model results showing stress in body structure and exaggerated displacements due to cornering loads.

Left: Finite element model results showing stress in body structure and exaggerated displacements due to vertical loads.

Wrightbus Gemini body on Volvo B7TL chassis testing at Millbrook Proving Ground.

The Wrightbus Gemini double-deck body designed and engineered for Volvo and VDL chassis have indeed proven to be a great success with over 2000 plus to date.

An interesting derivative to the normal two-axle double-deckers are the three-axle vehicles developed for KMB in Hong Kong. This was undertaken in 2002 and 2004 on two different Volvo chassis (B10TL and B9TL).

The structural work was challenging, and again all due care and attention was applied to the structural design (computer predictions and stress measurements). The two main challenges with these vehicles were the minimization of the upper deck side sway and vehicle wrenching due to non-steer mid-axle tyre scrub on cornering.

A fully laden B10TL has a capacity of 120 persons, 53 of them upstairs. Including seat mass, upstairs mass is in the region of 4.5 tonnes. Also, there is half a tonne of airconditioning equipment. It soon became evident that a simple stretch of the UK decker would not have enough strength to deal with this upper deck sway as the bus negotiates corners. Therefore new heavy duty pillars and reinforced interfloor brackets were derived.

The tyre scrub phenomena gave severe chassis and lower body bending on cornering. The forces likely to be generated laterally on the mid axle were supplied by VBC and these were applied to and the effects studied using a finite element model of the proposed vehicle structure.

Underfloor structural and wheel-arch fibre-glass componentary were included in the finite element model in considerable detail, as it was feared (and rightly so) that these components would be exposed to large enforced displacements as the chassis flexes due to the mid-axle tyre scrub. The

KMB Volvo B10TL/ Wrightbus chassis testing at Millbrook Proving Ground loading and test equipment.

solution was to ensure that these Wrightbus components were mounted softly in the chassis. This allows a degree of chassis displacement and the components connections were designed to be flexible and thus isolate them to an extent. This 'floating floor' arrangement was carefully monitored at Millbrook where their steering pad with high friction surface was used to induce severe tyre scrub in the fully laden condition. Black tyre rubber marks on every cornering manoeuvre were testament to the sizes of the forced involved.

The new floating floor philosophy was found to be satisfactory and has been used for both tri-axle models supplied to KMB. In all 164 such vehicles were delivered between 2003 and 2005. The older vehicles have now covered over 300,000 miles with no structural issues.

A special relationship –
How Wrightbus helped First achieve its objectives

As I mentioned earlier, my first meeting with Moir Lockhead, whose position was then Managing Director of Grampian Regional Transport, was in early 1993. Robert Wright and Son, as the company was then known, had forwarded an offer to supply a number of 12m single-deck buses.

With the specifications for both contracts it was obvious to me that this was a company that appreciated its customers. The buses were to be to a high specification with high quality seating for both passengers and drivers, air conditioning, and pre-heating to ensure the passenger saloon was the most comfortable place on a warm summer day or cold winter morning in Aberdeen.

During the build of these buses I had various meetings with both Moir Lockhead and Gordon Mills, both of whom I hold in high regard and respect. Their vision of public transport is to provide their customers with a quality service. One only had to travel on a Grampian Regional Transport bus to see and feel the difference. Grampian and Wrights complemented each other, as the objective of Wrights was to provide operators with a superior bus that would incorporate innovative thinking.

In those early days Wrights learned a lot from listening to Moir Lockhead's vision of what he would like to introduce – and they are still listening and learning!

The merger of Grampian Regional Transport and the Badgerline Group, both very high profile companies, and the formation of FirstGroup on 16 June 1995 created the largest bus company in the United Kingdom.

Over the years, Wrights has received substantial volume orders from

FirstGroup and Wrightbus people during a visit to the factory by FirstGroup directors.

FirstGroup on Volvo and Scania chassis. With the expansion of First Bus, whose operating companies are based all over the UK, it was agreed that we would jointly carry out market research with the drivers and passengers to determine what their preferences were, so we built a bus with the interior spaced into four different segments using a range of different components including seats from different manufactures, trims, colours, floor coverings, lighting, etc. When the results of the research were revealed, it soon became obvious that with ladies making up the largest percentage of users, the results reflected their views, with lighting, design and colour of seating and interior trim being very high on their agenda.

With the introduction of the new Wright Pathfinder 320 low floor buses in London, and with no financial assistance from the Government initially, operators were reluctant to spend the additional money on buses that cost more whilst carrying fewer seated passengers. Not FirstGroup. Its management team was one of the first to see the many advantages, both to the operator and to the general public; easier access for passengers would increase passenger usage and would speed up journey times. Their first order for accessible buses from Wrights was delivered to Sheffield for First Mainline in 1995.

When the senior management of FirstGroup decided to brand their company products (buses and trains) with a totally new corporate livery, Wrights was instructed/entrusted to build two buses using the new interior colour/trims and to paint the buses in the new corporate livery. We did, however, have one major problem – both the suppliers and Wrights were instructed that no one (other than those we had been working with), including all the management of the operating companies and competitors, were to be advised of, or to view, the new FirstGroup livery.

Keeping this operation totally secret was a major problem. To build two 12m buses on the line incorporating the new interior trim was not too difficult. However, once they were painted in the new corporate livery they were difficult to hide. On many occasions the buses had to be hidden away whilst visitors, including senior members of FirstGroup companies, were on the premises. We achieved the impossible and delivered the buses to London during the night for the preview and press coverage without anyone being aware of the company's plans.

The meeting, which had been scheduled for early morning, adjourned for a mid morning break, and the management from all the operating companies went out to view the new bus, not knowing they were to view the new corporate livery. I understand from those who were there, that the new livery was very well received after they got over the initial shock. They would never have chosen the interior trim colours but, more importantly, the travelling public approved.

Martin Lord and Carol Batters, assisted by Shona Byrne (Marketing Manager) FirstGroup, had done an excellent job and today FirstGroup probably has one of the strongest brand images of all the transport operators in the United Kingdom.

The two companies have much in common. Moir Lockhead's key objective is to operate a successful/profitable company whilst providing both his staff and his customers with clean modern transportation at an affordable price. William Wright, like his father before him, has similar views, in that he aims to provide his customers with a modern stylish, high quality product, with class-leading after-sales service. He views working with the company's partners to provide futuristic, innovative products to meet those companies' needs, as vital to survival. And that is what Robert Wright and Son, and later Wrightbus, have achieved for FirstGroup and others.

This was no more apparent than in 1998, when Moir expressed an interest in operating articulated buses and as you'll have read in Chapter 20 he gave us less than five months to build one for him! This was virtually an impossible task for any company but with the co-operation of our partners and staff we did it and delivered the bus to London on schedule. Moir Lockhead had achieved his objective – FirstGroup was the first company in the United Kingdom to operate accessible low floor articulated buses built in the United Kingdom. I am certain that he had little doubt we *would* meet his target, which showed his trust in the company's abilities.

The lessons learned from operating accessible articulated buses in densely populated cities in 2000-04 has now prompted Moir Lockhead to develop a entirely new concept, the StreetCar and, again, Wrights and Volvo were his chosen partners. But more of this later!

The Renown bus, and all its derivatives using the Classic design, was now needing a face lift to both the exterior and interior. There were a number of innovative ideas that Wrightbus wanted to engineer into the new product that would greatly reduce the costs of vandalism and accident damage. To reduce accident damage costs and down time, the company had developed and tested the R3 rapid to repair or replace system of repairing a bus framework. These and other improvements were introduced into the new Millennium product.

A key objective, which Moir Lockhead wanted the company to prioritise, was to design the bus to be easier to clean and refurbish. That included the use of a range of new plastic and trim materials, which would assist those responsible for keeping the fleet in pristine condition.

After two years' intensive market research into new materials and assembly methods, the company's proposals for the bus of the future, including outline drawings illustrating bold, new styling over a range of products, were shown to, and approved by, Moir Lockhead and the senior project development team at First Bus. It was Wrightbus' intention that the new range would set new standards in the bus industry.

Volvo was developing the new B7L product range, a chassis that would provide operators and passengers with a totally flat floor with no steps in the saloon. Scania was offering the L94 that had two steps in the rear saloon. First Bus purchased both Volvo and Scania, so therefore we developed the new Millennium bus on both chassis and the first of the new Eclipse city buses were delivered to First Mainline and First Manchester in May 2001. The Solar on the Scania L94 was introduced shortly afterwards

Like the Renown before it, the Eclipse soon became the market leader in the United Kingdom.

We received input not just from FirstGroup so it would be remiss of me not to pay tribute to all the engineering and operational managers from the company's key account customers, who all contributed and assisted Wrightbus in the development of the new Millennium city bus.

Whilst we were very successful in engineering, developing, and marketing the midi, single-deck and articulated range of products, UK operators were asking in ever increasing numbers when they could expect the company to be able to supply all of their operating requirements, including double-deck products.

After considerable research, it soon became clear that although they were dissatisfied with the products available, they did not want to pay more. We knew that if we were to build a new double-decker, incorporating all of the operator benefits that we had encompassed in the Eclipse single-decker, the costs would rise.

The costs of the infrastructure changes in the plant to allow the building of double-deck products, and the cost of development of the bus, would be substantial. The management had a major decision to make. The sales potential for double-deck buses was there. The questions we had to address were the cost of manufacture and the selling price. Would our customers, including First Bus, pay the additional cost for a better product from a manufacturer who had no experience in building double-deckers? Drawings for both the 10.2m and the 10.6m models were prepared in both single door and twin door format. These were presented to the board and after serious discussion it was agreed to fund the development of the Eclipse Gemini double-deck project with the one proviso that the initial orders would be for a two-door 10.2m bus to London Bus specification.

First Glasgow 32594 is typical of the Geminis delivered to FirstGroup companies. *(Will Hughes)*

Sir Moir Lockhead and William Wright shake hands on an order from FirstGroup. Also present are Nicola Shaw (FirstGroup), Steve Dewhurst (Volvo Bus) and Mark Nodder (Group Managing Director, The Wright Group)

First Bus engineers, having been involved in the market research and the development of the product, were enthusiastic about it and would have liked a 10.6 model but Wrightbus management made the decision that this model would follow the 10.2m model and be developed later. First Bus took delivery of the first of many Eclipse Gemini double-deck city buses in September 2003 with 43 going to London, 43 to Leeds and a further 18 going to Sheffield.

First Bus now had Wrightbus products, including service support across all of the range, supplied on a choice of chassis manufacturer, an offering that no other bus manufacturer in all of Europe could provide.

Moir Lockhead is a man with immense experience, a man with a vision for public transport. His key objectives are to ensure that FirstGroup is a successful company, delivering a quality, competitively priced service to meet his customers' needs and expectations and it was no surprise when he was knighted in the 2008 Birthday Honours.

William Wright has developed Wrightbus by listening to what his customers want, designing and developing a range of innovative, quality products to meet the customer's requirements – ideal partners in this tough and very competitive world of public transport.

The combination of the talents and enthusiasm of the aforementioned gentlemen was to lead to one of the most exciting developments in the history of either company, and possibly British public transport, the StreetCar ...

Streetcar
Transport for the 21st Century

In 2004, Moir Lockhead, in consultation with Mark Nodder (then Vice President – Business Development), introduced a totally new concept of public transport – a Rapid Transit vehicle, designed on similar lines to a tram, but based on an articulated bus chassis, initially driven by a conventional diesel power line but having the option of hybrid diesel electric power. Trams, although a fast transport system, have proven to be very expensive to introduce. They require major changes, all extremely costly, to the city's infrastructure, including the road network, to accommodate them and that, of course, comes with major cost implications. Equally important was the amount of cash needed from central and local government funds to support the systems.

Moir wanted concept drawings of the Streetcar so that FirstGroup could put forward proposals for developing a more affordable alternative to LRT that would cause less disruption, but would offer the passengers a similar service at much less cost to government. To ensure that the transport system proposed could compete with the tram it was necessary to have some infrastructure in place to ensure that the Streetcar would speed up the journey times.

Moir Lockhead's lobbying of government transport ministers was successful. First Bus was offering to develop a transport system that would reduce traffic congestion whilst providing reliable, safe and comfortable public transport.

Having had approval from the respective Boards, Wrightbus and FirstGroup set up specialist teams, to examine European Rapid Transport Systems and Passenger and Operator information systems, including how they play a vital role in controlling and monitoring the transport system. Methods of payment and fare collection, to speed up journey times by reducing dwell time at stops, were also part of the team's remit.

Detailed research was also undertaken on passenger seating, evaluating standee capacity versus seating capacity, and how best to accommodate the elderly and those with disabilities, taking all these into consideration and coming up with proposals that would meet the company's key objectives of providing a fast efficient public transport system.

Drivers of Rapid Transport Systems were consulted on their likes and dislikes with a view to developing a product with features that would assist the driver to operate the vehicle. The safety of the passengers is totally dependent on the driver and it is vital that he/she has good all round vision, including the interior of the passenger saloon

Another Product Development Team was tasked with developing the new chassis for this project with Volvo Bus. This was to be no easy task in the timescale agreed for the development. Wrightbus requested a number of fairly major changes/product improvements to the conventional Volvo chassis. These included repositioning the driver, the instrumentation and improvements to the suspension to provide the passengers with a smoother ride. Volvo was also introducing other product improvements including a range of new cleaner engines to meet Euro 4 legislation.

First Bus also nominated a team, under the leadership of Ian Davies (Divisional Director) and Barbara Bedford, to assist both Wrightbus and Volvo in developing the Streetcar to meet its operational requirements. Other key tasks were to select the operational territory and route, then examine and determine what changes were needed to the operational infrastructure, both on the route and in garages to accommodate Streetcar.

It was determined that changes to the operational infrastructure, similar to that provided to trams, would be required if the Streetcar was to be successful. Barbara Bedford (then ftr Project Director) was tasked with the difficult role of negotiating with the local Passenger Transport Authorities to ensure that the necessary changes to the route infrastructure to reduce dwell times and speed up journey times were completed prior to the new service being introduced. Sadly, in my opinion, the ideal infrastructure required to achieve the objective of speeding up the journey times has not yet been delivered. The cities carried out the minimum changes.

Whilst awaiting the Volvo chassis which would have all the necessary modifications required for the Streetcar project, a full scale mock up of the front of the Streetcar was built, including the driver's seating, instrumentation, exterior mirrors etc. To reduce dwell time, which would greatly reduce journey times, a major change had to take place in the way the public paid their fares. On entering the vehicle, passengers would proceed to a pay station. The pay station must accept cash but with the introduction of a Smartcard, First Bus aimed to achieve 85-90% payment by the card system, including free travel pass, with approximately 10% paying by cash. To achieve these targets, they realised that they had a major task in educating the general public to use the new technology. In this, it has to be said, we both failed, as the Streetcars in York had to be operated with a conductor on board.

From my limited experience, I would also be critical of the local authorities that had made promises about the changes required to the infrastructure in the cities. They were to provide a modern infrastructure, similar to that used by an inner city tram. This would have made all the difference; the dwell times would have been dramatically reduced, and the journey times would have greatly reduced. All too often it is those involved in transport

at local government level who fail to support the operators, whilst at every opportunity, many would criticise public transport for not performing.

Styling was vitally important both to the exterior and the interior of the product if both companies were to market the Streetcar as a totally new concept of passenger transport.

The 'Wow Factor' was important if First were to succeed in attracting the car driver and his passengers to travel in the new fast, ultramodern passenger transport system. The Wrightbus design engineer, Paul Blair, had overall responsibility for developing the styling and design that has had acclaim from all involved in public transport and set new standards of European design.

The new Volvo chassis arrived and build of the Streetcar commenced; unlike other projects the engineering, development and testing of the

Streetcar interior

prototype model was a much longer process. The first of the Streetcars was delivered to FirstGroup on 24 October 2005 for staff appraisal, including driver and staff training. This Streetcar was also to be used by other companies within the group to identify other potential locations for this new passenger transport system. It was also to be used at the locations where the first of the Streetcars were to be introduced, to advise the general public on the new transport system where they would not be in contact with the driver, the various methods for payments on and off board, all of which was vitally important to the success of the Streetcar.

The Streetcar was then presented to the trade press, Passenger Transport Executives and other transport officials who had been waiting patiently to view this new revolutionary form of passenger transport at a product launch on the 10 March 2006. Streetcar went into service in York on 8 May 2006 after extensive road tests at Millbrook Research Centre.

Like all buses, the Streetcar had to pass the mandatory tilt test.

Ted Hesketh, Mark Nodder and William Wright show the Streetcar to Dr John Lynch, Chairman of Coras Iompair Eireann.

William Wright and Moir Lockhead in discussion with Alastair Darling, then Transport Secretary.

The Streetcar, or 'ftr' in First-speak, on a modified Volvo B7LA chassis, was launched in 2005. The first vehicle was launched at Greenwich, where this photograph was taken.

Paul Blair, *Design Engineer*

Paul Blair is Wrights expert in industrial design and styling. After studying for his Masters in Automotive design at Coventry University, he joined Warner Brothers as a Conceptual Modelmaker. Paul joined Wrights in June 1997, taking over the reins from Trevor Erskine in 2000, so he had big boots to fill! Paul has since been the author of styling advances such as the double-deckers for the UK and Hong Kong, the StreetCar and new cabs and interiors. Recognising that style is important, he has looked at the Millennium family and ensured that new products come from the same stable. Paul's pride and joy is the StreetCar, an idea which came about during a break in the design schedule following the work on the Hong Kong double-decker. It was a designer's dream – a clean sheet, no parameters, a free project. And the opportunity to really design in the WOW! Factor. The primary force was the look – StreetCar had to be an alternative to light rail and bus, a tram on tyres concept, if you like. But lest it should be forgotten, the idea for StreetCar came first from the Design Team at Wrights!

Left: The first Streetcars entered service at York in May 2006.

Below: The StreetCar RTVs for Southern Nevada RTC, while looking very similar to the FirstGroup ftrs, were completely different machines, being built on a modified Hess trolleybus chassis with a hybrid driveline powered by a 10 litre Cummins engine. The first example was photographed in Belfast's Titanic Quarter, an area undergoing huge re-development from its shipyard origins.

Ivan Stewart

Ivan Stewart is the Principal Mechanical Engineer with the Hybrid Electric Vehicle team. He joined the Company in August 1983, immediately on leaving school and has progressed through the ranks. His attitude to resolving problems has made him popular with the engineering representatives of the chassis manufacturers. Ivan played a significant role in the development of the Volvo B6LE midibus chassis and the VDL SB120/SB200 midibus by preparing concept drawings of these products. His knowledge of chassis componentry and the appropriate legislation has been invaluable. A perfect example of this was when Ivan prepared the initial concept drawings for the Streetcar, including one where the engine was fitted to the nearside in the front saloon with the drive to the mid axle. When Volvo (Sweden) saw Ivan's work, the engineers were astounded. We learned much later that they were developing a similar product for a Swedish company and the drawing we had tabled was virtually the same!

Las Vegas orders Hybrid powered Street Car

The StreetCar (or ftr in First speak) had gained a global profile and led to a number of enquiries from overseas. One of the first of these was from Las Vegas, the fastest growing city in the United States. Transit in Las Vegas is bold. They already had tried hybrid electric with 12 Civis on a trial route and proved the concept. Fifty new vehicles were now required and tenders were sought. At this stage, without a US partner, Wrights couldn't quote, so passed on this opportunity.

As it happened, Las Vegas didn't award the tender and, as the revised tender was funded locally rather than federally, the 'Buy America' policy didn't apply. Against strong international competition, Wrights won through with an order for 50 vehicles based on the StreetCar, with an option for a further 100, for new routes presently under construction.

Although the US vehicles may look like StreetCar, underneath it is substantially different. It is constructed on a Hess special purpose trolleybus chassis, modified to meet the StreetCar configuration and is 18.6m long. A new hybrid driveline to Wrightbus design, powered by a 10 litre Cummins engine, has been developed in conjunction with Siemens ISE. The drive train features new, high output Siemens motors, very special performance and low fuel consumption, even with powerful air conditioning to meet all humidity and temperature reduction requirements.

The first vehicles were certified roadworthy and began their long journey to the United States in 2008. After leaving Southampton, the vehicles spend five weeks at sea, crossing the Atlantic, then passing through the Panama Canal before being off-loaded near Los Angeles (as there's nowhere in that port that they can be off-loaded – and it's about the size of the city of Belfast!) They'll then be driven to ISE at San Diego for commissioning before a 4-5 hour drive on to Las Vegas. Once there, driver and engineer training will commence prior to service operation commencing in March 2010.

Since the announcement of the Las Vegas order, enquiries have been received from Europe and the Middle East.

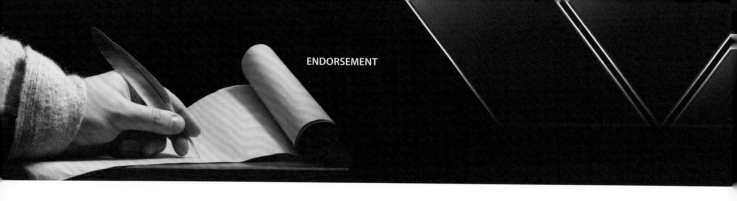

Bill Burrows
(International Sales Manager)
Lazzerini (Italy) Bus & Coach
Seating

My first encounter with Wrightbus was a chance meeting on Brussels Midi station whilst returning to UK from the Busworld fair. I remember changing trains to return to the airport and whilst checking the timetable a hand suddenly gripped my shoulder and a strong but friendly voice gently boomed "You must be Bill Burrows from Lazzerini". I turned to face my new acquaintance only to be greeted by an unknown but friendly face that I felt I ought to know. "Yes", I said, "I'm Bill Burrows and you must be … ?"

"Yes", he said, "I'm Jack Kernohan from Wrightbus" and so our acquaintance blossomed and an enduring personal friendship began and this was my introduction to Robert Wright and Son, Coachbuilders.

In 1999, when I entered the bus market, Wrightbus was significant but still one of the smaller bus builders producing around 350 single deck vehicles a year. Under the watchful eye of William Wright the company developed it's first double deck bus and it was his foresight that enabled the catalyst for growth and market share acquisition that sees the Wrightbus of 2010 with annual production of 1000 buses and new markets in North America and Dubai. This affirms a great lifetime achievement for William Wright and augers well for the future of this long established local family business now with a significant international market presence.

It was in 2002/03 that Lazzerini, in cooperation with Kowloon Motor Bus, assisted Wrightbus in developing the well known 'City' passenger seat for the new Wright Eclipse Gemini tri-axle double-decker and, with this vehicle Wrightbus entered the Hong Kong market in it's first venture into Asia. This heralded a much closer association between the two companies and subsequent orders for FirstGroup, Lothian, National Express (Travel London and Travel West Midlands) and Translink and many others

Lazzerini, back in private ownership since 2007, has long experience and a wealth of technical expertise and seating 'know how' and prides itself on it's creativity and innovation in developing modern, light weight seating platforms using latest technology material and 'know how'. It is therefore a real pleasure to cooperate with like minded professionals in today's challenging global market where the key to success is to stay ahead of the game with ideas and products that really respond to the market requirements of the bus of the future.

The Wrightbus of today is well organised, demanding but professional and a long way ahead of my first encounter almost 10 years ago. A big thank you to Jack Kernohan for that fateful hand on the shoulder back in 1999 and congratulations to William Wright for the invaluable history written for his company and the successful highway paved for its future.

Bill Burrows

Bill Burrows

Retirement

It was at this point that I retired from the Company after fifty years' service. I am proud to say that I have played a part in making Wrightbus/The Wright Group the successful business that it is today. I am in no doubt that it can do more, and the people are there to make it happen.

From my position as an interested observer of all things Wright, we'll take a brief look at some of the products which have been produced since I retired in 2005 and others which are yet to come. I'm extremely grateful to those employees who took the time to assist me with these pieces, especially Ivan Stewart for his insight into the development of hybrid technology, David Johnson for information on the development of double-deck products for both the home and export markets, Sam McCartney for detail on the Streetcar, Adrian Robinson for his piece on stress engineering and Charlie Murray for his assistance with the section on midibus development.

I am also pleased to highlight the loyalty which staff have shown to the Company, by including a list of those individuals, past and present, who have achieved twenty-five years' service. William Wright will tell you that the success of the Company has been as much down to the staff as it was to him and in my role in Sales I got to know all of these employees personally. A finer band of men and women, dedicated to serving the company, it would have been difficult to find. If I have missed anyone, I can assure you that it was not intentional. I will finish with this saying:

Loyalty can be rewarded but can never be bought

Jack Kernohan, 2010

Jack Kernohan (left) on his retirement day in 2005, with William Wright.

Employees with 25+ years' service to the Company

Michael Cathcart	Vincent Magee	Steven McMaster	Trevor Topping
David Purdy	Nat Dickey	Edward Murphy	Sam McCartney
Robert Alexander	Samuel Wright	Nicholas Boyle	Susan Eaton
James Smyth	Alistair Campbell	Ian French	Rodney Mark
Steven Dickey	John Boland	Sammy Currie	Ian Hutchison
George Knowles	John Smith	Amanda Knowles	David Millar

There are others who have left or retired from the Company, with 25+ years service, who contributed to the success of the company.

Muriel Finlay	Wylie Alexander	Tommy Orr	William Rock (Junior)
William Finlay	Ray Martin	Mary Rock	Sidney Adams
Albert Hanna	Billy McCullough	Eddie Law	
Trevor Erskine	Bertie Megaw	John Fleming	
Gordon Frew	Johnnie Steele	George Richards	

Employees who served the Company for 25+ years who are now deceased.

James Scullion	Frank McKendry	Samuel Robinson
Josh Spence	Hughie Rock	Jack McAllister
William McDowell	William Rock (Senior)	Johnnie Leach

Above: Alastair Campbell, Jimmy Smyth (with presentation plaque marking his fifty years service) and Nat Dickey

Below, left to right: Nat Dickey, Alistair Campbell, Jimmy Smyth, Mrs Susan Eaton, Sam McCartney, Nicky Boyle, Rodney Mark, Trevor Topping, Sammy Currie, Stephen Dickey, Ian Hutchinson, Eddie Murphy, Mrs Mandy Knowles, Robert Alexander, Stephen McMaster, Ian French, John Bolan, John Smith, Michael Cathcart, George Knowles and Davy Purdy.

Photo shows those with 25 years or more unbroken service still working within the company.

Unavailable for photo on the day were Vincent Magee, Damian McGarry, Davy Millar and Sammy Wright.

Reminiscences on 60 years of coachbuilding in Ballymena

The Future

When Ted Hesketh asked me to write my reminiscences of sixty years of Wrightbus I thought, "This is going to be fun!" And at times it has been fun; other times it has been extremely frustrating. Searching out the origins – the roots from which one draws strength to forge the future – should have been easy, but was it? Well, not really. Many of you will know that Wrightbus is possibly the largest family owned bus manufacturer in Europe, and is recognised as a world leader in the manufacture of city buses but where was the documentation to support its history? The answer is there was none, or at least very little. And why? The reason is simple. William Wright was always (and still is) an innovator, looking for ways to improve the company's existing products, whilst developing new ones to meet customers' future needs. See, so simple, he looked to the future not the past. The story of Wrightbus, in paper form at least, just doesn't exist – until now!

The point, though, is that Wrightbus is a company which is always looking ahead, not back. Because tomorrow is invented today, it is the company's key objective to dedicate its boundless imagination to future innovations. Everyone is a potential passenger, so Wrightbus has placed people at the very heart of its designs. This approach allows the company to create the most advanced designs both for passenger and driver wellbeing – comfort and ergonomics. And because there is no success without sharing, Wrightbus acts as a genuine partner for all its customers, their passengers and for the chosen chassis manufacturers.

Wrightbus believes in the future of public transport so that means committing the resources and the dedication to make it all possible. And in these days when we are more concerned about what is going on in the world around us there will be no future if we do not respect our environment. All of the Wrightbus range of buses is assembled from aluminium extrusions, which are 100% recyclable. In addition many steps have been taken to reduce emissions during manufacture, while the more fuel efficient engines reduce CO_2 emissions.

And so, here is an overview of how Wrightbus is developing cleaner, greener technology for the public transport sector. I must particularly thank Ivan Stewart, Principal Mechanical Engineer with the Hybrid Electric Vehicles team, David White, lead engineer responsible for the team developing the Wrightbus Hydrogen Powered Fuel Cell Bus, and Rodney Kernohan, Business Development Manager, for their assistance with this section. The story is rounded off with a look at some of the other products the company has developed since I retired in August 2005.

The Lightweight Bus Challenge

Surprisingly, though, modern citybuses use more fuel than their 1980s counterparts. Perhaps this is because modern design means vehicles are much heavier so recently the company was challenged by Moir Lockhead of FirstGroup, to reduce the unladen weight of the company's product range. After all, a London Routemaster bus, built in the 1960s, seats 64 passengers and weighs in at around 7.5 tons. An Eclipse Gemini to London specification also seats around 64 passengers and comes in at a whopping 13.5 tons!

International Development

I'm pleased to note that the management team is still very keen to explore new international business opportunities, gaining orders such as those from Singapore Bus Services and Regional Transportation Commission of Southern Nevada. But where next? Having looked around the globe, the Indian sub-continent was chosen, partly for the following for three reasons: 1. The National Highways Authority was constructing many new roads; 2. there is an enormous demand for public transport; and 3. demand for new buses will outstrip supply. And so a team of three – Damian McGarry, David Johnson and Rodney Kernohan – were despatched to investigate. Their first call was at BusWorld India where they were greeted with a hoarding on which was displayed a Wrightbus Solar in the familiar blue and white of Translink, albeit in left-hand drive form. Obviously the organisers weren't expecting anyone from Wrightbus to be attending!

Having great experience in supplying bus kits in completely knocked down (ckd) format, it was decided this was the way to go, certainly for that part of the world, to ensure Wrightbus' widely-renowned quality would

Rodney Kernohan

David Johnson and Damian McGarry at the 'BusWorld India' Exhibition in Mumbai.

be maintained, and still provide employment in Ballymena, I'm pleased to say. Research showed that some of the country's many bus builders were already using aluminium so with the right partner India could provide the Company with an amazing opportunity and good contacts have already been made. I wish the Company every success with this venture.

Wrightbus is well placed to continue the production of high quality, environmentally friendly buses. The company's international dimension and leadership in the field of public transport, gives it a unique perspective on the needs of its customers and the challenges of the future. I firmly believe that Wrightbus will lead and others will follow. And I hope that when this

A typical Mumbai bus.

volume is updated for the company's centenary in 2046, for I believe it will still be around, the reader will learn of more tremendous leaps forward in bus design, and will still recognise that faith that Bob Wright had back in 1946 when asked to build a van – "If I cannot build better than you are currently receiving I will close the doors" – and that the vision of his son William will be perpetuated in the product range.

Wrightbus has been at the forefront of eco-friendly technology for many years, engineering and developing sustainable solutions to limit energy consumption, reduce carbon emissions whilst preserving the quality of the air we breathe – an increasing vital and urgent necessity. Today the company is the United Kingdom market leader in the development of the Diesel-Hybrid Power Train. But what of other technologies? Well, it hasn't got a hydrogen fuel cell bus in service yet (but a prototype is under currently under test in America). The hybrid StreetCars for Regional Transportation Commission of Southern Nevada are built on a modified trolleybus chassis so could we see a full electric bus? Anything is possible, I suppose, and Wrightbus has the people there to do whatever is required. The future will not happen without the right people.

Developing Hybrid Technology

In December 2005, just four months after my retirement, the first production Electrocity was delivered to Go-Ahead London. However, the hybrid story began eight years earlier.

Around 1997 William Wright saw that the political will was beginning to change in favour of 'greener' modes of transport and that the ever tightening emissions standards would eventually promote electric and hybrid electric buses to the status of being a viable alternative for those in the passenger transport industry and so was born the 'Pulse' department.

The original objective was to design and build as light a vehicle as possible which produced zero emissions and when built, to hone the design and test its viability for the city bus market. After investigating possible driveline suppliers Wavedriver, an English company who had the backing of Powergen, was invited to collaborate on the initial project. Wavedriver was chosen because its driveline package was a zero emissions solution. This meant that the vehicle was completely electrically powered and produced no harmful exhaust emissions at all.

In late 1997 conceptual work and development began on a prototype 10m midibus capable of seating 35 passengers. Numerous methods were used to help keep the weight of the body to a minimum including sourcing ultra light weight seating from Australia.

The chosen chassis, a Dennis Dart SLF (Super Low Floor), had to be

This battery powered bus, based on a Dennis Dart chassis, with Wright Crusader body was operated experimentally as a joint Wright/Ulsterbus project in Ballymena during September 2000. *(Raymond Bell)*

highly modified, the standard Cummins engine and Allison AT545 gearbox being replaced with a GKN ADF132 drive motor and GKN 1.4:1 ratio gear reduction unit combination. The chassis frame behind the rear axle was modified to accept the Wavedriver system but even more radical at this time was the removal of the original chassis frame between the front and rear axles and replacing it with a single wedge shaped longitudinal which ran down the centre line of the chassis and contributed to supporting the floor. Two substantial traction battery packs were located under the floor on both sides of the bus.

Wrights built a Crusader body on this chassis, it being known as the Crusader ELF (Electric Low Floor). It became apparent during testing, though, that the range of the vehicle between charges and the duration of each charge would be unacceptable if the bus were ever to make it into fare paying operation. These initial problems were not seen as setbacks, though, but rather as experience gained from experimentation at a practical level – and all was not lost!

The two main types of Hybrid electric bus are Parallel hybrid and Series hybrid, and each has its own advantages and disadvantages. A Parallel system maintains a direct mechanical link between the engine and the drive axle and is well suited to occasions of prolonged high speed as found for example on inter-urban routes. A Series system has an opposing design ethos where the traction battery pack is usually larger and the engine usually smaller. A bus with this type of driveline is well suited to urban work where routes consist of multiple stops and low speeds which give ample opportunity for the traction batteries to be charged. Both types of bus can be universally capable in their own right if the driveline components are specified correctly. As the Wrightbus objective was to develop and build a city bus it was decided to

Electrocity Midibus chassis.

The Cadet-based Electrocity prototype featured a diesel-powered Capstone turbine linked to an Enova drive motor. Ulsterbus used it on local town routes in the Ballymena area.

seek out a new Series system supplier and this came all the way from Los Angeles.

Enova Inc. was an experienced driveline supplier which utilised Korean built motors in trucks and buses in both the USA and in Europe. The on board charging unit would also be provided by Capstone, a manufacturer of small, extremely efficient turbines, also based in Los Angeles. These two companies had worked together previously and their pedigree was not in question.

The decision to build a second prototype was a logical progression towards a marketable product. Wrightbus' standard midibus chassis was by this time the DAF SB120LF, so it would make commercial sense to use this Dutch chassis.

The new prototype was designated 'Electrocity'. Its design brief was singular in nature. This was that the integration of the hybrid driveline was to have a minimal effect upon the outward appearance of the bus when compared to its conventionally powered equivalent. At 10.2m it was slightly longer than the first prototype and this time a middle exit door was specified, which limited passenger seating to 31.

The driveline was compacted into the engine bay including a fuel tank that wasn't required previously with the Wavedriver system. The area behind the rear five seats was panelled off providing a much needed compartment to accommodate an overflow of electronic components upwards. Access to this was from the exterior via a converted hinged emergency rear window. The exhaust tail pipe protruding upward through the roof and the loss of the rear window were the only major aesthetic differences apart from livery between the Electrocity and the SB120LF-based Cadet.

In January 2002 conversion work started on the original prototype to bring it up to the current specification. The opportunity was also taken to experiment with the traction battery pack. The Crusader ELF prototype was renamed as an Electrocity and received a make-over by way of a brand new livery similar to its sibling to advertise its green credentials. An official launch in January of 2002 made it to the front covers of the trade press, whilst performance and operational testing commenced with both vehicles in and around Ballymena.

The next step was to have the vehicles certified roadworthy to facilitate demonstrations. David Miller, the UK Chief Certifying Officer of VOSA

(Vehicle and Operator Services Agency) who was stationed at Grantham was invited to do the honours. Armed with encyclopaedic legislative knowledge he was extremely thorough. Even to the point of requesting the entrance and exit door closing forces and he definitely put the Pulse team through their paces. The Electrocity was successfully certified in September 2002, with a passenger capacity of 31 seated and 22 standing. It could have accommodated slightly more but a further secondary emergency exit would have been required if the payload of 53 were to be exceeded.

The original ELF, having been modified to a similar specification as the Electrocity, was sent to the Millbrook proving ground in November 2003 for a week to undergo emissions testing funded by the Energy Savings Trust. These tests were conducted using London's 159 route data.

The turbine fitted to this vehicle was an efficient (not to be confused with economical) burner of fuel. Hydrocarbons, nitrous-oxides, particulates, carbon-monoxide and carbon-dioxide are the components which constitute the emissions produced whenever diesel combusts and, with the exception of the last, these were all measured at very low levels. With carbon-dioxide politically being the greenhouse gas of choice to eliminate so the end was in sight for the turbine generator set. However, despite this Wrightbus' pioneering Electrocity buses in this guise did see quite a bit of action and were demonstrated in Bristol, Bath, Swansea, York, London, Sheffield, Aberdeen, Worthing, in Bradford twice and one also went on loan to the local Translink depot in Ballymena.

A small internal combustion engine powered generator set was now determined as the best way forward.

The engine chosen was the latest 'Stage 4' common rail diesel from the General Motors stable and utilised exhaust gas regeneration (EGR) to meet its emissions standards. and A new generator also had to be sourced. This naturally enough came from Enova. A new generation of battery module was also specified. These upgrades were to be realised in the Pulse team's first contract. The vehicles themselves were to London specification, with a mid powered exit door.

When the first bus of the Go-Ahead contract was made operational, it underwent a few days road testing in Ballymena

Peter Hendy (TfL), Ken Livingstone (then Mayor of London) and William Wright at the launch of Electrocity.

and then was sent to Millbrook proving ground in Bedfordshire for testing proper. These were all passed with flying colours and Go Ahead took delivery of their first Electrocity in December 2005. Go-Ahead reported positively to the trade press after one year of running the Electrocitys and should at this point be thanked for their co-operation and patience.

The Pulse team was not to rest on its laurels. Conceptual work began on a very important project for the company – the design and development of a hybrid electric powered double decked city bus.

The concept started to become a reality at the beginning of 2006 when the donor vehicle was delivered from the main Wrightbus factory into the Pulse team's workshop. The chassis was a VDL DB250, with a partially completed Pulsar Gemini body. The 10.3m bus was to Arriva London's specification with a mid exit door and a driver's air conditioning system. It was designed to accommodate 64 seats but a bit of work had to be done to keep standing passenger numbers competitive.

Siemens Automotive was chosen to supply and commission its proven ELFA system. To move the bus there were two drive motors mated to a gear box to which the chassis prop shaft was attached. A generator was coupled to the General Motors engine to charge the batteries and an auxiliary drive motor was supplied to drive other essential systems.

Bill Frame, a highly qualified acoustics engineer, was contracted to perform extensive testing and following his advice even the hollow Aluminique body pillars were filled to prevent noise emanating from the engine bay to the upper deck. The vehicle would go on to easily pass legislative noise requirements and those stipulated by Transport for London (TfL).

On completion of the build the vehicle weighed in at 12641kgs and, amazingly, the all important rear axle weight was only 4kgs more than what had been predicted eight months previously!

The Gemini HEV was delivered to Millbrook in October 2006 for the usual certification testing but was on the move after only two weeks as arrangements had been made for Ken Livingstone, the then Mayor of London, to officially launch the product prior to it being unveiled at the 2006 Bus and Coach exhibition in Birmingham, where it was unveiled amid great fanfare as the world's first series hybrid electric double-decker bus.

Arriva London finally got its hands on the vehicle for long term evaluation purposes at the Wood Green depot in February 2007.

In April 2007 the efforts of the Pulse team were recognised as Wrightbus won the 'Large company' category of the Carbon Trust Innovation Awards for both their Electrocity and Gemini HEV products. The Gemini HEV however was always going to be the 'jewel in the crown' for the Pulse team and became even more so when Wrightbus won the coveted Renishaw award for innovation on the strength of its design at the UK Manufacturing

Impressive design together – London's City Hall and our Gemini. This was the HEV, the world's first series hybrid double-decker bus.

Excellence awards in London in June of the same year.

The Pulse team then progressed to a contract of five Electrocity midi buses for Travel London. A commercial directive was made to site the radiators on the roof to improve cooling and keep the radiators themselves cleaner. The engine on the generator set was also to change. The Ford ZSD424 2.4 litre TDCi Puma engine was now in favour. It was envisaged that better durability could be achieved from an engine that was tested to van and truck standards. Delivery commenced in November 2007.

Three of the Electrocity buses delivered to London General for service around Greenwich are seen by the O2 Arena.

The alterations did improve reliability, but the enhancements didn't stop there. A contract of one was next, destined for London General and was to be the first Electrocity to be fitted with lithium-ion battery packs.

As for the Gemini HEV, it was already the beginning of the end! Production of the DB250 chassis was to cease. The last two came to Ballymena, were fitted with the Ford engine and sold to Arriva London and Dublin Bus. The initial feed-back from Dublin bus was mainly positive. There was, however, a request to limit the vehicle's performance. Apparently the acceleration was throwing standing passengers off balance. This was easily sorted with a few parameter changes to the bus's programming.

Present at the handover of the Gemini HEV to Dublin Bus were Dr John Lynch, Chairman of CIÉ, William Wright, Noel Dempsey, TD, Minister for Transport and Joe Meagher, Chief Executive of Dublin Bus.

One issue that was mildly amusing which was more a case of "Not seeing the wood for the trees" was that the vehicle's mobile Sim card was a UK one. This meant that when the bus was dialled for data gathering by Dublin Bus they were being charged foreign phone call rates. And worse still, the bus was also being charged for receiving the call! The same applied if the bus was dialled from Ballymena because the UK Sim was being relayed through an Irish service provider!

The demise of the DB250 chassis heralded yet more development work. Its successor was the Wrightbus DB300, which would become an integral part of the Gemini 2 diesel and HEV variants.

The Gemini 2 was longer than its predecessor (10.4m) but its rear overhang was shorter, by 160mm. To compound this problem, the rear of the bus was rounded as well, so the rear corners offered less space again. Integrating the hybrid driveline was not going to be easy but despite this, hope sprang eternal because this chassis promised longevity and stability to the new hybrid driveline. Quite a few improvements were also designed in.

Initially, 10 Gemini 2 HEVs were built – five for First London and five for Arriva London. One, from the Arriva London build, was allocated to be tested at Millbrook proving ground and all had to undergo 1000 miles of road testing to prove reliability prior to delivery.

The new product was unveiled at the November 2008 Bus and Coach exhibition held in the NEC Birmingham. The same bus was at the official launch and handover to FirstGroup on 22 December 2008 at Horse Guards parade ground in London.

The Pulse team has come a long way since late 1997 and gained a fortune of experience in the process. I'm sure, too, that it has applied, and will continue to apply, that experience to design and build products which can more than hold their own in the market place.

The future is looking pretty bright indeed.

Tomorrow's World
Hydrogen Technology using Fuel Cell Power

We're told the fuel of the future is hydrogen so I'm pleased to learn that, having pioneered hybrid (diesel electric) powered passenger transport in the United Kingdom, Wrightbus is moving forward in line with technological developments and a hydrogen powered city bus is currently being developed on a (heavily modified) SB200 from VDL, a well proven unit with which the company is very familiar. The diesel engine has been replaced with a Fuel Cell Hybrid with a sophisticated drive system. This model will offer major benefits in terms of resource conservation and a major reduction of emissions associated with producing the required hydrogen. The hydrogen-powered Fuel Cell Bus will emit absolutely no pollutants whilst in motion, and when running on the streets of your cities will be virtually silent. This makes this new product ideal for use in highly congested inner cities operational routes.

David White, the lead engineer responsible for the team developing the Wrightbus Hydrogen Powered Fuel Cell Bus, has been able to call upon the company's immense expertise and knowledge in the field of hybrid powered diesel / electric alternative drive systems. The Fuel Cell bus draws from the experience gained from the other hybrid projects. Since its drive system technology is a completely new development, the Project Development Engineers first had to source suppliers for a hydrogen powered fuel cell drive line, one that would meet the future needs of the company. The power will be supplied by a 75kW Ballard fuel cell with the hydrogen fuel (46.5kg) stored in tanks mounted on the roof. Energy storage for the system will be by the ISE Ultra Capacitor System which is also roof mounted. The electric propulsion drive system is the well proven Siemens ELFA System incorporating two drive motors, ELFA II Invertors, high voltage Inductor and Brake Resistor.

David White

The first bus underwent extensive monitoring of its performance in normal operations, including tests on the Hydrogen powered Fuel Cell drive line, in San Diego before returning back to base for final inspection. Structural and tilt testing etc will follow, prior to being placed in service.

The first Wrightbus hydrogen powered fuel cell buses are being purchased by Transport for London and will be operated by FirstGroup. A new garage, incorporating all the facilities to provide the necessary servicing for these new buses, will be commissioned prior to them going into service. The first buses will be delivered to London in the first quarter of 2010 after extensive road testing. The initial delivery will be used for driver training and considerable time will also be spent ensuring that maintenance staff are fully up to speed with the new technology and associated processes, thereby ensuring that the introduction of these buses to London will be a success.

The prototype Wrightbus fuel cell vehicle is seen here when undergoing extensive testing in San Diego, USA.

The hydrogen fuel is carried in tanks on the bus roof. This engineering drawing shows a possible layout and how the tanks, etc will be shielded from public view, at least from street level.

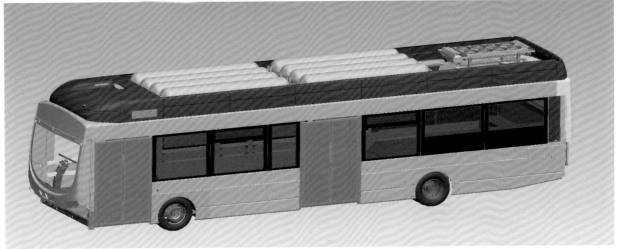

Alistair Campbell

Alistair Campbell joined the Company in July 1974 and is now one of the Company's 'old hands' having completed thirty-five years' service. Having progressed through most, if not all, of the production departments he now works on the production line making the new fuel cell city bus for London. Alistair is just one of those people who is always willing to help and on many occasions, Albert Hanna, then in charge of Production, praised Alistair for taking the initiative, resolving problems and by doing so ensuring that buses were delivered to customers on time.

New Models

The Meridian – a new level of quality

The Wrightbus Meridian is based on the MAN A22 chassis and will provide operators with a high quality, full low floor city bus incorporating all the attributes synonymous with two of Europe's leading bus marques.

The MAN chassis is powered by the well proven 10.6 litre D2066 diesel engine, developing 270bhp. The power from the engine is matched to a ZF6 speed automatic gearbox incorporating an integral retarder. The high chassis specification includes electronically controlled air suspension, electronic braking system including (ABS and ASR).

The new Meridian body incorporates a heavy duty tubular steel dash rail built into the front module to provide enhanced driver protection in the event of a frontal impact while the driver's station provides him with a

The first Meridian-bodied MAN out of a test run from the factory.

spacious cab offering excellent vision all around. The Meridian is available in both single and twin door configuration.

The first of the new Meridian city buses was sold to one of Wrightbus's most valued customers – Whitelaw's, based in Stonehouse in Lanarkshire. At the product launch at Millbrook on 26 September 2007, Sandra Whitelaw commented, "The combination of the MAN and Wrightbus product, who is our preferred coachbuilder, made the Meridian very attractive to our company and a very attractive addition to our fleet. We are excited about the new product and delighted to see it start its working life in Whitelaw's livery. We believe it will prove to be a high quality city bus that is easy to maintain, fuel efficient and will offer low running costs."

New Products for Ulsterbus

Wrightbus has always had a good working relationship with its local operator, Translink (Citybus/Ulsterbus/Northern Ireland Railways). And when new vehicles were required for specific purposes in 2006, and again in 2008, Wrightbus was able to engineer a vehicle which met the operator's specific tender requirements.

Wrightbus develops safer school transport

Ulsterbus operates the greatest percentage of schools transport journeys in Northern Ireland and had traditionally ordered vehicles with 49/53 seats which saw use on all types of work. (Approximately 110,000 pupils travel to school by bus each day - 65% by Translink, 27% by the Education and Library Boards and 8% by private contractors.) The number of seats on a low floor bus, between 40 and 45, some of those on tip-up or side-facing seats, was less than operators were used to. That led to problems for Ulsterbus as children had to stand on their journeys to and from school. The school children usually gathered in the area designated for the mothers with baby buggies and wheelchairs and should the driver have needed to brake suddenly this was an accident waiting to happen.

A number of high profile accidents involving vehicles on school transport in the GB and the Republic of Ireland led politicians and parents to demand increased standards of safety on school buses. Ulsterbus management was well aware of the problem and, being very proactive to customers' needs, in 2005 they approached Wrightbus with proposals for the development of a bus specifically designed to transport children.

The remit was to provide a vehicle which:

• Met all current legislation;

• Was suitable for children from different age groups;

• Would have all seats fitted with three-point belts;

- Had overhead racking for the storage of the children's bags and sports kit;

- Would be fully accessible; and

- Where all wheelchair passengers would be secured with approved equipment.

To meet their requirements for a high seating capacity (to ensure that no child had to stand), Ulsterbus chose the straight-framed Volvo B7R chassis, fitted with the well proven seven-litre Euro 4 specification engine driving through a ZF automatic gearbox. Wrightbus then developed a high floor version of the well established Eclipse to meet Ulsterbus' demands, with various seating/wheelchair capacities, in 3+2 seating configuration – 66 with removable seats for one wheelchair space, 62 plus one dedicated wheelchair space, or 63 with removable seats for four wheelchairs, if the need arises. One bus was designed to carry up to 20 wheelchairs. This was good forward thinking by the management of Ulsterbus. The first vehicles were delivered in May 2006 and after driver training, particularly on the side mounted wheelchair lift and the correct securing procedures for wheelchairs, the first of 160 SchoolRuns, as the model had been named, took up service at the start of the new school year in September 2006.

Mark Nodder, then Vice President of Business Development, commented, "This was a very significant order for Wrightbus and showed that in partnership with Volvo we can provide safe, modern and well engineered school buses that are economical and viable" while Northern's Ireland's Transport Minister, Conor Murphy, MP, MLA, welcomed the introduction of the fleet of new buses saying, "The safety of our children to and from school is of paramount importance to us all, and with the introduction of these impressive new vehicles for school services will add greater safety and help to protect our young people."

Mark Nodder
(Wright Group),
Philip O'Neill
(Translink) and Mike
Ball (Volvo Bus).

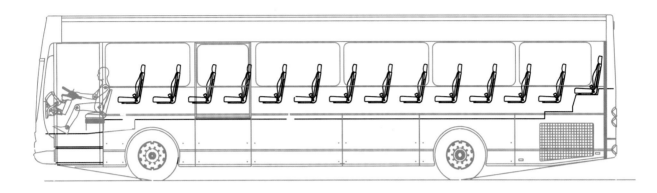

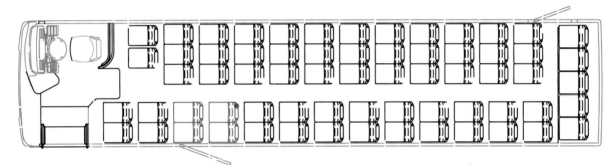

Seating layout for the Eclipse SchoolRun.
Up to 66 seats can be accommodated in
the bodywork. The seats shown in red
are removable to permit the carriage of a
wheelchair-bound passenger.

The Eclipse SchoolRun is built on the Volvo B7R chassis and although higher built features
many components common across the range. With a stepped entrance, wheelchair access
is by lift, which is located behind the front axle. Seating is provided for up to 66 passengers
in 3+2 seating and deep luggage racks are provided for the safe stowage of school bags and
sports kit. All seats are fitted with three-point belts for safety. *(Paul Savage)*

Children from our local primary school test the new Eclipse SchoolRun

Towards the end of 2009 and into 2010, Ulsterbus took delivery of a further 60 Eclipse-bodied Volvo B7R high capacity buses. These feature 3+2 seating for 62 passengers and a side mounted lift for wheelchair access. No 364 is allocated to Londonderry depot and was photographed in the snows of January 2010. *(John Durey)*

Ulsterbus sets new standards for passengers in rural Ulster

Looking much like a normal Solar, the Rural, built on the Scania K230 chassis, features a shorter front overhang, greater ground clearance and wheelchair access via a second door situated just behind the front axle. Built to Ulsterbus' specification, this batch of 45 vehicles seats 55 passengers in a mix of 2+2 and 3+2 seating. *(Paul Savage)*

Having received the order for 160 SchoolRun vehicles, Ulsterbus then turned its attention to providing a high capacity, low floor vehicle for use on its rural and inter-urban routes.

While the standard Renown and Solar low floor buses are a boon, particularly to the elderly, Ulsterbus' operational managers determined that there was a need for a bus that would provide the ease of access of a low floor bus, with priority seating for mothers with prams, the elderly and wheelchair

passengers yet providing a higher seating capacity than that then on offer. Thus was born the Solar Rural, for which Ulsterbus chose the Scania K230 chassis with the DC9 16 230hp engine. The first five were built to Euro 5 specification, with the remaining 40 supplied to Euro 4. All 45 were equipped with the ZF automatic gearbox.

The Solar Rural bus was supplied with 55 high back seats from two manufacturers, Lazzerini and Rowan Telmac, in a mix of 2+2 and 3+2 configuration. To allow extra space in the saloon area and provide increased seating capacity, the front overhang was reduced, wheelchair access being via an additional door behind the front axle. A manual pull out ramp, designed by Wrightbus and Compak is fitted in the doorway, providing easy access for all passengers using wheelchairs. Wheelchair-bound passengers then travel facing forward, secured with a Q-Straint system.

The first of the Solar Rural buses was delivered in May 2008 and they are well liked by Ulsterbus management which finds the 55-seat capacity extremely useful; the standard Solar city bus seats 43 so there is an operational benefit for the company. Forty-eight similar vehicles were delivered in the Spring of 2010.

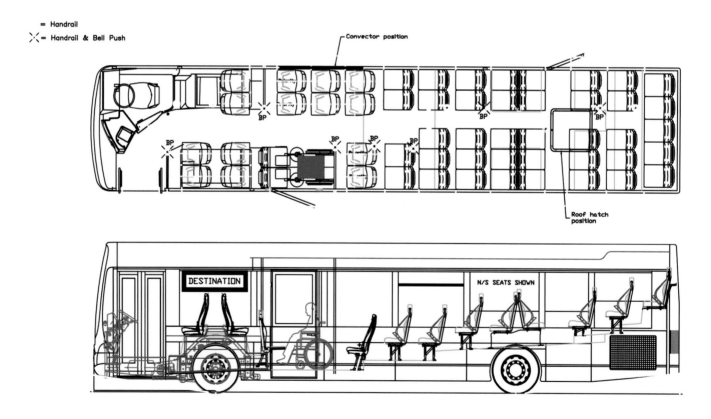

Gemini 2 –
The Future of Double-deckers

The Gemini 2, a complete Wrightbus product which can be powered by both Euro 5/EEV diesel (DL) and hybrid-electric (HEV) drivelines, was unveiled at Euro Bus Expo in November 2008. It has been designed as a modular concept and is fully compliant with both Transport for London and provincial specifications.

The diesel (DL) version is powered by a 6.7 litre Cummins engine while the series hybrid electric model is provided with a 2.4 litre Ford Puma diesel engine and Siemens traction components, both variants being offered with the choice of ZF or Voith automatic transmission. The hybrid electric version has been developed following extensive in-service evaluation with Arriva London.

The Wrightbus Gemini 2 undergoes tilt testing at Millbrook. *(Millbrook)*

The low height version of the integral Gemini 2 double-decker was launched in October 2009. Demonstrating one of the benefits of being 170mm lower than the standard Gemini is the first example, for Arriva Yorkshire.

Wrightbus Product Manager David McCaughey hands over the first vehicle to Arriva Yorkshire Managing Director Phil Cummins.

Optimising weight to deliver excellent fuel economy was a key objective for the product development team and in an independent test cycle at Millbrook the Gemini 2 HEV achieved the best results for fuel consumption (10 mpg) and CO2 emissions ever recorded there for a double-deck vehicle. The team had worked closely with chassis partner VDL on chassis weight and layout and also on reducing noise with the fitting new radiator design. The company was also able to use its expertise in Light Resin Transfer Moulding to extend the use of automotive quality panels on this vehicle and reduce weight further. A new driver's area was also created.

The first production Gemini 2 HEV was handed over to FirstGroup on 6 November 2008 and entered service in the capital as part of a TfL-supported evaluation trial. February 2009 saw Arriva order 57 Wrightbus Gemini 2 DL models to TfL specification. The VDL chassis platform features the Euro 5 Cummins engine, Voith D854.5 gearbox and ZF rear axle.

The Eclipse Gemini had been designed with maximum headroom in the passenger saloons. This resulted in an overall height of 14'5", taller than our competitors' vehicles. While this height was acceptable in cities, on rural and some interurban routes, it could be a problem, especially when many double-deckers had previously been built to 13'8" to cope with low bridges. The product development team had been considering an appropriate solution for some time, to give operators greater flexibility in the allocation of vehicles. And so, following an approach from Arriva, in October 2009, Wrightbus launched a low height version of its integral Gemini 2 double-decker, which uses VDL-built DB300 chassis modules. The low height Gemini 2 is around 7 inches/170mm lower than the standard Gemini 2 yet shares 85% of parts with it. The first have already been delivered to Arriva Yorkshire, while Arriva North East has placed an order for 15. "These specially developed vehicles have all the advantages we'd expect from a Wrightbus double-deck in terms of quality, style and comfort," commented Arriva Yorkshire's Engineering Director, Phil Cummins. "It provides a solution and gives us the flexibility to switch buses between routes, including routes where we previously couldn't deploy double-deck buses because of height restrictions."

2010 and a new product - StreetLite
Wrightbus develops a range of compact integrated midibuses

The Wrightbus offering to the midibus sector is presently the Cadet, on VDL units, but, although a successful product, the management was aware that it was not as competitively priced as similar products from other manufacturers. There were two main reasons for this –

1. the chassis had to be transported from the Netherlands and
2. the recent strength of the Euro/weakness of the Pound. As our competitors both produced their chassis in-house in the United Kingdom they had none of these additional costs.

Over recent years, a number of new and enhanced products have raised the bar in the midibus sector and, with this formidable opposition, the Company was losing out and had to respond. So 2010 will see the launch of StreetLite, a range of midibuses incorporating all of the features with which the Company has become synonymous.

This project started back in 2005 when the Company first started looking at this product to determine the (case for) savings of designing and engineering an integral midibus. Market research with our customers established that there was a demand for a range of stylish, highly manoeuvrable, durable, reliable and economical midibuses from Wrightbus. Top of our customers' wish-list was manoeuvrability, simply because of the locations where most midibuses operated. They wanted reduced turning circles coupled with reduced vehicle width. The market research also clearly showed that customers did not want a long wheelbase vehicle.

Having seen what was wanted from the Company, Product Development Director, Damian McGarry, began the engineering process by searching out a professional chassis design engineer. Charlie Murray was appointed and the Product Development Team began looking at options.

The team initially looked at an all-welded stainless steel body structure but, having evaluated the lower costs of steel against the longer life Aluminique construction, it was agreed that, although slightly more expensive, the many benefits gained would in the long term benefit the customer. The Aluminique fully integrated StreetLite will have a mild steel chassis. The integrated chassis and body combination are designed to work with each other and produce a structure that offers greater structural strength is lightweight and has the added benefit that it suits the current production system much better and offers the engineers greater flexibility to meet changing market demands.

As a full vehicle, StreetLite will bring many changes to Wrightbus, with a lot of new systems that are normally the responsibility of Wrightbus' chassis partners. The reason for designing the whole vehicle is simply that there isn't an existing, economically viable chassis available to act as a platform for this range of buses. The chassis elements don't just mean a change in the design group but right through the Company – purchasing, manufacture, quality – and for the end user. There will also be an additional role for Customcare.

A very clear target right from the start was to use proprietary units and the industry was scoured for the range of components required.

Each supplier was evaluated on quality, warranty, after sales support and product costings. Another factor was choosing products with which customers' engineering staff would already be familiar. However, it was quickly realised that to achieve the required performance (particularly driver/passenger interface) we would have to develop some bespoke units.

Further key tasks were to maximise the seating capacity, while enhancing manoeuvrability and the Product Development Team soon established that if they were to achieve these objectives, and comply with the new European Directive, there was a need for two models, each in two lengths. The 8.8m and the 9.5m vehicles would have the entrance door to the rear of the front axle, which eliminates front wheel-arch intrusion, provides a totally flat floor, maximises passenger capacities and makes it even more accessible for the elderly or those with disabilities while the 10.2m and the 10.8m vehicles would have the door in the standard position ahead of the front axle, thus reducing the wheel base and ensuring the manoeuvrability of the midibus would meet the customers' expectations. The overall width of the bus would be reduced by 60mm to 2440mm; this reduction would be greatly appreciated by drivers as midibuses tend to spend most of their operating life in very tight traffic corridors, such as housing estates where it is often difficult to operate.

The StreetLite range will feature independent front suspension (the front and rear suspension includes some novel features for a city bus), these units were developed in-house based around components that are not only well proven but are well known and easily serviced in the industry, with full air suspension on both axles to enhance ride quality. The Voith D823.3E fully automatic gearbox with integrated hydrodynamic retarder will be offered with a choice of highly efficient TDI diesel engines, which combine exceptional economy, impressive pulling power and smooth running while producing emissions that meet the latest Euro 5 legislation. A number of driveline options will be available including:-

- Cummins 160b iSBe 4 Cylinder Turbo Diesel
- Cummins 180b iSBe 4 cylinder Turbo Diesel Engine;
- Cummins 225b iSBe 6 cylinder Turbo Diesel Engine; and
- Hybrid Drive System, will be available later to meet the operators' future needs

Another feature which should please the operators' engineering staff is that the engine, gearbox and exhaust system will all be mounted on a quick-release demountable skid, to reduce service costs and downtime when a major overall of the driveline is required. Dual circuit disc brakes will be fitted all round and a centralised, fully multiplexed, 24 volt electrical system will make fault finding much easier via a lap-top based diagnostic programme. Faults can be found, and rectified, within a few minutes.

As already noted, the new StreetLite range of midibuses will be manufactured from the well-proven Aluminique system, with all the major benefits that have been developed to reduce component costs and downtime while the bus is off the road being repaired. *Dinol* anti-rust protection treatment, including the wax injection of all tubular steel sections, will be applied to the exposed framework. The Aluminique framework also enhances side impact protection offering improved safety for all those seated in the lower part of the saloon. The buses have also been designed to offer greater protection for the driver in the event of a frontal collision. Permanent daytime running lights, along with high mounted rear brake lights as an added safety feature, are fitted as standard.

The passenger saloon features a thermostatically controlled, roof mounted, forced air heating/ventilation system, while a three-speed, forced-air heating and demist system ensures the driver's comfort and safety. The cab has been designed to comply with Driver Ergonomics ISO 16121 and incorporates a soft feel VDO Driver's workplace. The Wrightbus trademark top mounted windscreen wipers will further improve what is excellent driver visibility while the windscreen itself has been designed to reduce reflections to a minimum, providing the driver with improved visibility of the road ahead, particularly at night.

StreetLite has been designed and engineered to comply with the new European Whole Vehicle Type Approval which has applied to all vehicles since October 2009. One factor of these regulations that has to be taken into consideration, and which could affect the seating/standee capacity in some of the competitors products is that passengers are now rated at 68kg, an increase of 3kg per person, and this will have significant effect (subject to model and customer specification) on some of the lightweight products currently on the market.

Economy, a principal operator requirement, has been a particular goal and while the team can mix and match engines, gearboxes and axles, the main influence the Company can have on fuel efficiency is to minimise weight but that has to be done without sacrificing the traditional virtues of the Wrightbus product.

Wrightbus is not renowned for offering a cheap product. Instead it has always striven to provide customers with a quality product using tried and tested components that professional engineers recognise offer a longer life cycle in what is today a very tough operational environment. I have every reason to believe that the StreetLite range of fully integrated midibuses will set new standards in the bus industry for styling, durability, manoeuvrability, reliability, passenger and driver comfort including the most important feature of all, safety. My one regret is that I wish I had had StreetLite to offer to our customers when I first starting marketing the Company and its products in the United Kingdom!

Wrightbus to design and build New Bus for London

On 23 December 2009, at the end of a difficult year, Wrightbus received an early Christmas present with the announcement by Transport for London (TfL) that the Company had been selected as the preferred manufacturer for the design and build of the New Bus for London. In the press statement, David Brown, Transport for London's Managing Director of Surface Transport, noted that, at the end of a very competitive international tendering process, TfL was delighted to select Wrightbus as the preferred manufacturer to take this project forward adding that it was expected that the first example of the New Bus for London should be on the road in 2011.

The New Bus, based on the iconic Routemaster, a small number of which are still in service in the capital, will feature an open platform at the rear, to allow the reinstatement of a hop on/hop off service; it will be possible to close off the open platform area as and when required, for example in the late evenings. The design will feature three doors and two staircases, to reduce dwell time at stops, and carry approx. 87 passengers. The New Bus will also be easily accessible for mothers with buggies and passengers using wheelchairs.

Wrightbus supplied the world's first hybrid power double-decker to London in 2007 which has given the Company great experience of operating in that tough environment. The New Bus, however, will be even greener, incorporating the latest hybrid technology, being 40% more fuel efficient than conventional diesel bus and 15% more fuel efficient than current London hybrid buses.

Boris Johnson, Mayor of London, commented "Londoners have waited with stoic patience as work has continued to select the manufacturer to make the 21st century Routemaster a reality. The decision has now been made and we can now look forward to a new icon of London that not only returns to the capital the joy of having an open platform, but also utilises the latest state-of-the art green technology, slashing pollution and fuel consumption"

For Wrightbus, Mark Nodder (Group Managing Director) stated "We are delighted to have been chosen by TfL to be the preferred manufacturer on the New Bus for London project. Wrightbus is proud to be chosen as a partner to develop a new transport icon for London. It is a privilege and a wonderful opportunity for everyone within the Wright Group, to design a vehicle that will doubtless become recognisable the world over". Dr William Wright, on being advised on the success of the company's proposals, stated that he was delighted. "This news will provide great encouragement and motivation to the entire workforce for 2010." He added that the Company has a proud history of product development and innovation, including pioneering low floor fully accessible buses in the United Kingdom with London Transport.

Just as we were about to close for press, computer-generated images of the New Bus for London became available. The design makes use of lightweight materials, with glass highlighting key features. An impressive glass 'swoop' at the rear and offside pick out the two staircases. Design partner Heatherwick Studio has taken the lead on the styling of the bus to support Wrightbus in the design and development process. *(Transport for London)*

Wright Composites proving to be an ideal fit

Wright Composites, a wholly owned subsidiary of the Wright Group, is poised for further growth to meet the growing demand for its GRP products, which now includes customers from a variety of industry sectors.

The specialist producer of fibreglass components was set up in November 2005, with the assistance of Invest Northern Ireland, to secure the supply of vital components for the Wright Group. Continued growth in demand from both in-house and from external customers has led to a further expansion of production capacity at Wright Composites.

Composites now has a world-class production facility in a 4,800m² building, immediately adjacent to the Wrightbus factory at Galgorm, near Ballymena. With turnover in the financial year to September 2010 forecast to be in excess of £5m, an additional 60 staff have now been recruited for the operation which, in total, now numbers 130 employees and represents an investment of £1.8m for the Wright Group.

According to General Manager Andy Colhoun, the establishment of a dedicated Composites operation was a logical step for the Wright Group. "With production of all vehicles now nearing 1,000 a year and with every double-deck bus requiring up to 100 panels in a variety of shapes and forms, the need to secure both the quantity and the quality of this vital component was becoming increasingly obvious. With the valuable assistance of INI, we have been able to make the necessary strategic investment in this important new facility."

The design of modern day buses relies heavily on the use of GRP panels, and the fit and finish of the these components has a significant impact not only in appearance, but also in the level of vibration and overall aerodynamics of a vehicle, which in turn can have a significant impact on fuel efficiency and therefore whole life operating costs.

Wright Composites is already supplying around 50% of the production requirements at the Ballymena bus facility, with plans to further increase this to around 70% by the end of the year. The Group will also continue to work with existing suppliers of GRP components to ensure continuity of supply going forward.

As well as an immediate need to supply in-house production requirements, there is also a growing demand to supply OEM quality panels through the Wright Group's Customcare aftermarket organisation. "We work very closely with our colleagues in Customcare to ensure that a supply of panels from every model in the Wrightbus product range is readily available. Quality and availability is such that GRP panels for non-Wrightbus products are now also increasingly in demand."

Wrights Composites is able to undertake the development of new fibreglass components, including the construction of moulds and tools for production. According to Andy Colhoun, the companies extensive "closed mould" capabilities delivers consistent dimensional accuracy and a surface finish level of automotive quality, has proved to be a particularly significant investment for the business..

Rodney Kernohan, David McAleese, Andy Colhoun and Moira Parke

"The reputation of Wright Composites now goes way beyond just the bus industry and we are in active discussions with manufacturers in sectors such as aerospace and marine applications, where quality and conformance to exacting specifications are a paramount."

In the near future, Rodney Kernohan, Business Development Manager, sees great potential for further expansion of Wright Composites. "The business has made great strides in a relatively short period of time and has already established itself as a centre of excellence for GRP mouldings in Northern Ireland. What began as a move to safeguard a strategically important part of our production supply chain, has quickly developed into a significant stand alone business with a growing customer base".

He added, "The first half of next year will see an additional 20-30% Composite manufacturing capacity coming on stream with a further extension to the Ballymena facility and we also have ambitions to develop our capability in the structural composites sector."

The Wright People

The Third Generation of the Wright Family

William Wright's children – Amanda, Jeff and Lorraine – followed in their father's footsteps, assisting him in the development of the Company. Like their father and grandfather before them, they all promote a very high Christian ethos, which they practice daily in their workplace whilst, outside working hours, they try to assist those less fortunate or who are finding life difficult. The family was educated at Cambridge House School in Ballymena, noted for its high educational standards.

The Wright Family –
Back row: Dr William
Wright, Dr Lorraine
Rock, Jeff Wright
Front row: Mrs Ruby
Wright and Mrs
Mandy Knowles

Group Board

Jeff Wright, *Chairman*

One of Jeff's earliest childhood memories is of his grandfather getting him into a wheelbarrow and taking him on a tour of the factory. He says, "I had no idea then, the part it would play in the lives of all of our family," Jeff wanted to follow in his father's footsteps, although he acknowledges that there was never any pressure put on him to do so. During the school holidays, he would spend some of his time in the workshop assisting the men assemble the framework of buses and, when he eventually left college on a Friday, he commenced his career in the company on the following Monday morning!

William Wright agreed a management training programme for his son's career advancement in the company. Jeff would spend time in each department to gain knowledge of the products, the processes involved, the men and management team.

He started in the chassis shop and followed the various products through all the build processes and, like every other apprentice, although he was the boss's son, he would be sent to the stores for the 'Long Stand', 'Skyhooks' or be asked to locate the silencer for the grinder from another of the teams who would direct him around the workshops – all part of the fun of working with and being accepted by your work colleagues.

While in the Stores Department he soon realised that efficiencies could be made and, with the help of the team, changes were implemented that were to improve the supply of the components to the assembly lines. In those early days, many of the components were manufactured in-house, and that was Jeff's next move, to assist in parts manufacture, improve quality and to ensure that those components were available to Production on time.

Having gained valuable knowledge in the production environment Jeff then moved to the various offices involved, from Marketing/Sales Administration/Design/Drawing/Preproduction/Purchasing/Quality Control and Accounts.

After time in the various offices, Jeff's next move, at the age of 24, was to the new production facility at Galgorm to take charge of production. With sales/customers demanding more, his biggest task was to increase production from one to six buses per week.

I think Jeff was of the impression that all the problems in production were caused by sales but, after spending time in Sales Administration, meeting customers and the management of the various chassis suppliers, he was soon to learn that the customer is King. He also learned much from listening to their thoughts on the Company's products. This was to lead to Jeff taking a more active role in new Product Developments. Today Jeff would tell you that the period he spent in developing new concepts of public transport was the time he enjoyed most.

Despite the time taken by his successful business career, it was not a case of 'all work and no play'. Jeff always enjoyed his football and played at Senior League level with Ballymena United and Coleraine, winning an Irish Cup Winner's medal with the former.

Away from business, Jeff started to translate his Christian upbringing and beliefs into practical action. He was the visionary and founder of The Wash Basin, an unusual but memorable name for an inter-denominational outreach centre based in the village of Ahoghill. (This little village has gone from anti-social behaviour and vandalism on a Saturday night, to winning the Calor Village of the Year 2009 Award, the judges noting that the village is a thriving, caring and innovative rural community with an exceptional level of community involvement, including the key role that businesses play in village life.) The Wash Basin's mission is to serve the people of Ahoghill for the sake of Christ, and it has been a cornerstone in the village's accomplishment. Ahoghill itself, and the work carried out by the Wash Basin, is regarded by the Police Service of NI as a major achievement.

As time went by, Jeff's increasing devotion to the business of saving souls led him to set up Green Pastures – the Peoples Church, conveniently situated close by the Wrightbus factory at Galgorm. In setting up this Church, it is evident that Jeff has brought his managerial and organisational skills, honed in the world of industry, and applied them to this major religious enterprise.

Almost inevitably, Jeff's commitment as Senior Pastor at Green Pastures has meant a scaling back of his involvement with the bus business and in 2006 he succeeded his father as Chairman. He has no doubt that his toughest challenge has been this move from Chief Executive to become Chairman of the Group and he readily acknowledges the effect it had on the entire business. He adds that it is fantastic to see the other Directors rising to the challenge and all working together successfully to take the business forward.

While recognising that his father had been the driving force in the Company for many years, the challenge is now to retain and maintain the ability to read the market, listen to the customers and establish the future needs of the industry, then to apply engineering know-how and technological advancements – identifying ideas before they become a reality.

This is a major challenge for any business today, and both he and the other Directors realise that the legacy of the previous generation of Directors will be hard to better.

Although there are many people who have helped Jeff progress through the Company, he has paid particular tribute was Charles Stewart, a Director in the late 1990s. Charles had the time to listen to his problems and advise him what actions he might take and so influenced his career greatly at that time. I, too, would like to put on record my appreciation of the assistance Charles was to me, a wonderful man who made a big impression on everyone he came in contact with and one who had an immense knowledge in sales and customer relations.

Jeff also admires Moir Lockhead saying, "I learned a lot from listening to a man with a vision of the quality of public transport he wanted to provide to all of FirstGroup's passengers"

Dr Lorraine Rock, *Managing Director – Wrightbus Ltd*

Lorraine Rock went to university to study Pharmacy, graduating with a BSc in 1979 and obtaining her PhD in Pharmaceutical Microbiology in 1983. After almost twenty years in this field, Lorraine then joined her father, William, her sister, Amanda and her brother, Jeff, in the Company in August 2002. This was a complete change of direction and Lorraine will freely admit that she struggled. If she had to do it all again, she would have ensured there was a better induction programme so that she would have had a clearer overall picture of the Company, its objectives, its products, customers and a better understanding of each department's problems. She now knows the problems anyone coming into the company from an entirely different background encounters and believes everyone who needs to be fully conversant with the company's products should spend not less than one year on the workshop floor.

After a spell as Materials Director, Lorraine became Managing Director in 2007, a role which brought new challenges. However, the single biggest problem she has encountered was the year that the chassis manufacturers introduced the new Euro 4 engines/drivelines. This was a problem over which she had no control. All chassis, across all production lines, had major changes and engineers and product development teams simply couldn't cope with the work load. Again, Albert Hanna was asked to assist and Lorraine will be forever grateful for his assistance.

And what of the future? Perhaps surprisingly Lorraine thinks one of the biggest problems the company will face won't be technological but simply finding a suitable replacement for her father! His shoes will be hard to fill, and she sees no one man fulfilling that role but rather three or four people who know the industry, the key decision makers, the chassis manufacturers and above all, someone with the drive and enthusiasm, someone prepared to take risks to make and retain the Company as a global name in the manufacture of high quality passenger transit systems.

Lorraine says, "The fact that we frequently do the unexpected and come up with an entirely new product maintains the Company's lead over our competitors. Not all of this is down to my father, although he does play a major part. A lot of the Company's success is down to the individuals we employ – their sheer drive and inspiration at all levels within the company. It really comes down to everyone focusing their attention on the needs of our customers and improvements in both products and service. Innovation is one of the company's core values. Many of our past innovations have inspired loyalty and trust in our customers. We value that loyalty."

Amanda (Mandy) Knowles, *Group H.R. Director*

Amanda Knowles joined the Company's management team in September 1977, having gained valuable experience with the Department of the Environment (Roads Service).

Beginning her career in the company's finance department, she moved to Sales Administration, where she was involved in all of the day-to-day activities of a busy office. Whilst there, assisted by Aveline Finlay, she set up the company's sales and marketing records. (The records from that period were of great assistance to me in preparing the information for this book.)

That initial market research covered welfare/school buses and the Public Service Vehicles and highlighted the business potential in those segments. The detail of the research was to prove invaluable when the sales team targeted key account customers in Great Britain.

Amanda's next move was to Human Resources, where she has played an important role and one which she has thoroughly enjoyed. Reasons cited include:

- It is vitally important that you ensure that the right people with the right skill are available to do the right job at the right time for Wrightbus.
- That you provide adequate training to enable them to do the job properly.
- The welfare of the staff – they know they have someone at Director level with whom they can discuss any problem in total privacy.

She was appointed to the position of Director of Human Resources in 1995 and is considered by many as one of the workers, who likes meeting people, who takes time to listen and has a sympathetic ear to the many problems that young families can encounter today. She is very proud of how the staff welfare system has developed; it is progressive, forward thinking and goes beyond the onus of an employer in helping their employees, both in social and working needs.

For Amanda, the one memory stands out above all others. On the afternoon I came back from London with a major order from London Transport for 116 midibuses, Amanda was then working in Sales and Marketing. She knew then that the company had made a significant step forward in being recognised in the PSV market so I asked her where she would like to see the company positioned in ten years time. She replied that she would like to think that Wrights would be recognised as being among the world's leading bus manufacturers, having played a significant role in developing public transport, building buses with significantly reduced emissions and much more fuel efficient. And wasn't she right? Like her sister, Amanda is very proud of what her father (and grandfather before him) has achieved and is grateful for the assistance and guidance she has had from him during her career. And given what has been said in this paragraph I think some of the vision that Bob and William had has rubbed off on her!

Dr William Wright OBE, *Director*

Having been involved in the business almost from the very start, William Wright stepped down as Chairman in 2001. He still, though, maintains an interest in the Company and, importantly, in its people. With his many contacts throughout the industry, William now plays an important ambassadorial role with key customers.

Mark Nodder, *Group Managing Director*

Mark joined The Wright Group in 1998 to develop export sales, the Customcare aftersales division and in recent years the UK Bus Sales and Marketing activities of the Company. Since December 2006, he has taken the position of Group Managing Director with overall responsibility for all the Company's business units, which include Wrightbus, Customcare, Expotech, Hybrid Vehicles and Wright Composites.

A lawyer by training, with over 25 years experience of business development, project management, sales and marketing, he worked for the National Audit Office, the Saudi Ministry of Defence and Aviation and Shorts Missile Systems before joining The Wright Group.

James Nicholl, *Group Finance Director*

James Nicholl is the Group Finance Director. In this role, James is responsible for all aspects of Group Finances and plays an active role in setting the strategic direction for the Company. He joined Dale Farm Dairies Ltd in 1997 as graduate trainee and participated in their parent company's UK Graduate Intake Scheme and quickly moved through ranks to hold Financial Controller position. He joined Wrightbus Ltd in 2003 as Finance Director and after a successful two years of improving financial controls and systems was promoted to the Wright Group Board as Group Finance Director in October 2005.

Maurice Perl, *Non-Executive Director*

Born and educated in London, Maurice Perl worked in and advised the automotive and transport industry prior to becoming associated with the Wright family in the late 1980s. He was invited to review the then existing business and identify possible alternative markets for the obvious skills and expertise inherent in the company. This was the start of its major growth in public transport provision. He was appointed a non executive Director of the company in the 1990s and has enjoyed an unbroken association of over twenty years during which time the company has grown ten fold.

Ted Hesketh, CBE, *Non-Executive Director*

Like the vast majority of Wrights people, Ted Hesketh is a Co Antrim man. On leaving university he joined Shorts, the aircraft and missile manufacturer before moving, in 1971, to the bus industry, with Ulsterbus, where he initially followed a financial career. This later broadened into general management, becoming Managing Director of Ulsterbus and Citybus in 1988. In 1995, he was also appointed Managing Director of Northern Ireland Railways, leading the integration with the bus companies to form Translink. He retired in 2003 and joined the Board of The Wright Group. He continues to serve as Chairman of the Transport Training Board, which promotes training for those wishing to pursue a career in the transport industry.

Alan Barr, *Non-Executive Director*

Born and brought up in Aghadowey, a few miles north of Wrights factory, Alan went to university in Wales and married Bronwen. He qualified as a lawyer in the City of London and now lives in Bristol where he is a senior partner of Burges Salmon LLP specialising in corporate law. His working career has involved over twenty years experience acting for clients in the public transport sector. He enjoys the opportunity Wrights has given him to combine those interests with a welcome "return to his roots", particularly as a director of a world class, innovative, manufacturing company which is so committed to providing employment in Northern Ireland and enhancing the Northern Irish economy.

Wrightbus Board

Mark Nodder, *Group Managing Director*

Dr Lorraine Rock, *Managing Director – Wrightbus Ltd*

Amanda (Mandy) Knowles, *Group H.R. Director*

James Nicholl, *Group Finance Director*

Dr Paul Dykes, *Quality and Business Improvement Director*

Paul has spent much of his career in the automotive industry, starting as a Graduate Engineer with Land Rover in 1986 where he progressed to senior project management on Range Rover. After spells as Technical Director of The Tempered Spring Company Ltd and as General Manager of TK-ECC Ltd, he joined Wrightbus in 2004 as Business Improvement Executive but left in 2006 to join the Survitec Group as Group Quality Director. He returned to The Wright Group fold in 2008 and is currently responsible for quality assurance/control, quality systems and supplier quality assurance where his main objective is to improve the business by developing the working systems/procedures in order to manufacture better products, increase customer satisfaction and decrease defects. He established the ISO 9001 system from scratch, and is currently in the process of establishing an ISO 14001 Environmental Management System to meet the "green" needs of the business along with environmental legislation.

Stephen Francey, *Production Director*

Stephen Francey began his career with Wrightbus twenty-three years ago, in October 1986, when he joined the company as an apprentice coachbuilder. During that time, Stephen has progressed through the various stages of management, becoming Production Director in October 2007. He was in charge of the initial set up of Wright Composites production and generated £4m turnover in two years. He is now responsible for the smooth operation of all production lines and has 600+ employees under his charge. As well as the general day to day running of the production lines, Stephen also has an input into new designs and the upgrading of products and so has regular communication with the various design teams and other section heads.

Martin Graham, *IT & Logistics Director*

As the IT & Logistics Director of Wrightbus Ltd, Martin is responsible for the Purchasing and Stores Teams in Wrightbus, delivery of material to the production line just in time, and also manages the IT function for Wrights Group. After spells with Bombardier, the Local Enterprise Development Unit and Invest Northern Ireland, Martin joined Wrightbus as IT Manager in 2003 becoming IT Director in 2007, with the additional responsibility of Logistics later in the same year.

Brian Maybin, *Engineering Director*

Brian Maybin came to Wrights in September 1995 from Nissan, becoming Wrights first professionally qualified engineer. Having spent a year in design, he became Production Engineering Manager, then Production Co-ordinator, Engineering Manager until he was appointed Engineering Director in 1999. Brian's roles within the company have included new material development, reliability engineering (validating design, problem solving, setting Wrightbus engineering standards), development of the Aluminique construction system, multiplex electrical system (introduced in 1999 and the first in the UK), anti-corrision systems and advances in electronically controlled heating systems. The Gemini is a product Brian is particularly proud of, and although it eliminated many of the problems with competitors' double-deckers, he believes Wrights can still do better.

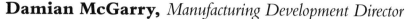

Damian McGarry, *Manufacturing Development Director*

Damian McGarry is a perfect example of just what working at Wrights can do for your career! Damian joined the company in 1984 after obtaining Mechanical and Technical qualifications at Ballymena Technical College. He was interviewed for the role of Parts Manager and was successful. In 1986, he moved to the Drawing Office, planning and engineering buses from specification to completion, and later became Drawing Office Manager. A move to Materials and Development saw him involved in a global sourcing exercise for an alternative system when the designs for Alusuisse expired in the United Kingdom in 1997/8. This resulted in the development of Aluminique, with Wrights designed/patented features. Damian also played a part in new product development – primary concept vehicles- and was eventually persuaded to move across to Production as Production Director (Designate) under Albert Hanna, with whom he had an eighteen month handover. He has been Manufacturing Development Director since 2006. Company career highlights include leading the manufacturing growth strategy from 300 units pa to 1000 pa, successfully bringing to market the Euro 4 product range and new Gemini complete product and reducing and maintaining net manufacturing cost via new product introduction in conjunction with an improved supply chain strategy.

Sam McLaren, *Commercial Director*

Having worked in various roles the bus industry for many years, Sam McLaren joined The Wright Group in 1997 as Aftersales Manager, to set up the newly created Customcare Aftersales Division. He was promoted to Customcare General Manager in 1999 with responsibility for increasing and creating additional Customcare Support Dealers covering the Great Britain and Ireland. His success saw him promoted to his current role as Commercial Director (Wrightbus). He is responsible for four National Account Managers. In addition to this, Sam also has responsibility for the sales administration team based in Ballymena and is responsible for programming chassis deliveries to meet production requirements. Sam McLaren is acknowledged by the management as having played an integral part in this progression and has helped establish Wrightbus as the leading manufacturer of buses in the UK.

Geoff Potter, *Customcare Director*

As Customcare Director, Geoff has full profit and loss responsibility for Customcare, our Aftersales division, and is responsible for the strategic development and daily operation of all aftersales activities including parts sales, parts logistics and technical support. During his tenure, Customcare has undergone a period of extensive expansion and the business has been restructured to deliver significant quality improvements.

Geoff started his career with National Freight Consortium and on completion of NFC's Graduate Management Training programme assumed commercial and operational responsibility for various activities including contract maintenance, truck rental and contract distribution. After a period with DAF Trucks he joined Wrightbus ten years ago. He holds a postgraduate diploma in Accounting & Finance (DipAF), is a Member of the Institute of Road Transport Engineers and a Chartered member of the Institute of Logistics & Transport.

Jonathan Poynton, *Business Development Director*

Jonathan has been with the Group since 2001 when he was appointed Export Director, a position he held for four years. During 2005/6 he assumed the role of Product Development and Innovation Director becoming Business Development Director in 2006. In his present role he is responsible for all business development activities within Wright Group, ongoing development of current product range and development of new vehicle concepts for international markets. He cites the development of single deck vehicle for the Netherlands and new double deck vehicle for Hong Kong as Group career highlights.

The Next Generation

William and Ruby Wright (centre) with their children, grandchildren and great-grandchildren. Looks like the Wright name will be around the bus building business for a long time to come!

Awards

The innovation and product excellence for which The Wright Group has so rightly become renowned throughout the industry has been recognised with numerous awards and presentations. Space precludes the inclusion of a complete list but below is a selection of awards the company has received over recent years.

2006

The Worshipful Company of Carmen Viva Shield

The Wright Group, together with FirstGroup plc and Volvo Bus Limited, was awarded the Viva Shield by the Worship Company of Carmen, one of the original Guilds of the City of London, with a history dating back to 1517, for the joint development of the StreetCar product. The Viva Shield is awarded for transport innovation and development in Europe.

The Renishaw Award for Product Innovation

This award was presented to Wrightbus, at the Manufacturing Excellence Awards, for its submission centred on the development of the StreetCar for FirstGroup plc, the introduction of the hybrid 'Electrocity' and the combination of technology from both these products in the development of the Hybrid Electric Streetcar RTV project for Las Vegas.

2007

The Carbon Trust/Daily Telegraph Innovation Awards

These awards recognise individuals, and public and private sector bodies that are pioneering innovative technologies or energy efficiency measures that help reduce the United Kingdom's carbon emissions. The Wright Group won the 'Larger Companies' category ward for its development of the world's first hybrid electric double-decker which uses innovative battery technology and a two-litre car engine, reducing fuel consumption by 34% and carbon emissions by 31%.

The Renishaw Award for Product Innovation

The Wright Group won this award for the second year running, this time for its development of the Wrightbus Gemini HEV hybrid electric double-deck bus. The Wrightbus Gemini HEV was the first vehicle of its kind to enter service in London earlier in 2007.

2008
UK Government's BERR Award for Manufacturing Excellence

The Wright Group was named winner in three out of the 13 categories at the Manufacturing Excellence Awards – including the prized overall Award for Manufacturing Excellence, which involved rigorous assessment of the entire company practices across 11 categories. The Group also won the Autodesk Award for Product Innovation for the combination of technologies in the form of the Streetcar RTV for Las Vegas. The third award, the National B2B Centre Award for Integrated e-Business, was for the Group's total IT infrastructure which supports the entire business function.

2009
ISO 9001 Certification

L-R: **Andy Colhoun** - *General Manager, Wright Composites*, **Dr Lorraine Rock** - *Managing Director, Wrightbus*, **Geoff Potter** - *Customcare Director*, **Ellen Davison** - *Account Manager, LRQA*, **Mark Nodder** - *Managing Director, The Wright Group*, **Dr Paul Dykes** - *Quality & Business Improvement Director, The Wright Group (accepting certificate on behalf of Wrightbus)*

The Wright Group has attained full ISO 9001- 2000 certification, part of the International Organization for Standardization's ISO 9000 family of standards concerning quality management. Highly regarded and much sought after by leading companies worldwide, the award of ISO9001 certification applies across all divisions of The Wright Group, from Wrightbus to Customcare and Composites.

2009
The Institution of Engineering and Technology Coales Medal for Achievement in Transport

This year saw Dr William Wright, OBE being recognised by the UK Institution of Engineering and Technology (IET) for his contribution to the transport sector. The IET is one of the world's leading professional societies for the engineering and technology community, with more than 150,000 members in 127 countries and awards its medals only to nominees who have made major and distinguished contributions in the various sectors of engineering and technology.

The IET panel looked for outstanding and sustained excellence in one or more activities before making its final decision and noted, "The Wright Group attracts engineers of all disciplines worldwide and has a strong relationship with universities to attract aspiring engineers. At the age of 82, Dr Wright shows no signs of slowing down. He is still involved in the business and is currently managing the next generation of hybrid electric buses."

Appendix
Product list from 1976

Wrights BUS PRODUCT RANGE FROM 1976 TO 2008				
Model Reference	Chassis Manufacturer	Type	O/length	Production Commenced
Welfare/School				
TX 202	Iveco-Ford 40.8	Welfare/School	6.50m	1989
TX 202	Iveco-Ford 49.10	Welfare/School	6.50m	1989
TS 202	Mercedes Benz 709D	Welfare/School	7.50m	1988
TS 202	Mercedes Benz 811D	Welfare/School	8.50m	1989
TS 202	Renault S56/75	Welfare/School	8.50m	1989
TT 202	Bedford VAS	Welfare/School	9.6m	1980
TT 202	Leyland Cub	Welfare/School	9.6m	1978
TT202	Bedford SB	School	10.6m	1983
TT202	Bedford YMQ	School	12.m	1976
TT202	Bedford YMT	School	12m	1976
Consort	Leyland Swift	School	10.6m	1988

Service Buses High Floor				
Nimbus	Mercedes 709D	Mini Bus	7.50m	1991
Nimbus	Mercedes 711D	Mini Bus	7.50m	1995
Nimbus	Mercedes 811D	Mini Bus	8.50m	1996
TC404	Mercedes 811D	Mini Coach	8.50m	1992
TS 303	Renault S76	Midi Bus	8.50m	1989
Royal	Leyland Leopard	Service Coach	11m	1982
Endeavour	Leyland Tiger	Service Coach	12m	1992
Endeavour	Scania K93	City Bus	12m	1993
Endurance	Volvo B10B	City Bus	12m	1993
Endurance	Scania N113	City Bus	12m	1991
City Ranger	Mercedes 0405	City Bus	12m	1992
Handy Bus	Dennis Dart	Midi Bus	9.4, 10.2, 10.6m	1990
Urban Ranger	Mercedes OH1416	City Bus	11.5m	1993
Contour Coaches				
Contour Coach	Bedford YNT	Luxury Coach	12m	1983
Contour Coach	Leyland Tiger	Luxury Coach	11, 12m	1984/5
Contour Coach	Ford R150	Luxury Coach	10m	1984
Contour Coach	Ace Puma	Luxury Coach	9m	1985
Contour Imperial	Volvo B10M	Luxury Coach	12m	1989
Accessible Buses 1993 / 2009				
Pathfinder 320	Dennis Lance SLF	City Bus	12m	1993
Axcess Ultra Low	Scania N113	City Bus	12m	1994
Crusader	Dennis Dart SLF	Midi Bus	8.8, 9.4, 10.2, 10.8m	1996

Crusader	Volvo B6LE	Midi Bus	10.8m	1999
Cadet	VDL SB 120 LF (Euro2)	Midi Bus	9.4, 10.2, 10.8m	2000
Cadet	VDL SB 180 LF (Euro3)	Midi Bus	10.3, 10.8m	2007
Cadet (L/H Drive)	VDL SB 120 LF (Euro2)	Midi Bus	10.2m	2001
Commander	VDL SB 200 LF	City Bus	11.8m	2000
Commander (L/H Drive)	VDL SB 200 LF	City Bus	11.8m	2001
Renown	Volvo B10BLE	City Bus	12m	1996
Liberator	Volvo B10L	City Bus	12m	1996
Eclipse Metro	Volvo B7L	City Bus	12m	2001
Eclipse Urban	Volvo B7RLE	City Bus	12m	2002
Eclipse SchoolRun	Volvo B7R	School Bus	12m	2007
Merit	Midi	Volvo/Daf SB120	Midi Bus	10.3 / 10.8m
Fusion	Volvo B10LA	City Bus (Articulated)	18m	1999
Eclipse Fusion	Volvo B7LA	City Bus (Articulated)	18m	2000
Axcess Floline	Scania L94UB	City Bus	12m	1997
Solar	Scania L94 UB	City Bus	12m	2001
Solar Fusion	Scania L94UA	City Bus (Articulated)	18m	2001
Solar (Euro 4)	Scania K230	City Bus	12m	2007
Solar (Rural)	Scania K230	City Bus	12m	2008
Eclipse Gemini	Volvo B7TL	City Bus(Double Deck)	10.2 , 10.6m	2001
Pulsar Gemini	VDL DB250	City Bus(Double Deck)	10.3m	2003
Opus (midi)	Chance (Optima) (America)	City Bus	30′, 34′	2001
Opus (midi)	Chance (Optima) (America) ISBe engine	City Bus	31′, 35′	2002
Electrocity (midi)	W / SB120 (Glider Chassis Frame)	Hybrid City Bus	10.3m	2002

Electrocity (midi)	W SB180 (Glider Chassis Frame)	Hybrid City Bus	10.3m	2007
Gemini HEV (D/Deck)	W / SB250 (mod)	Hybrid Double Deck	10.3m	2007
Gemini HEV MkII (D/Deck)	W / DB300 (mod)	Hybrid Double Deck	10.3m	2008
Commuter	Volvo BR7LE	Accessible Coach	12m	2004
Super Olympian	Volvo B10TL Tri Axle	Double Deck City Bus	12m	2003
Super Olympian	Volvo B9TL Tri Axle	Double Deck City Bus	12m	
StreetCar	Volvo B7LA	Mass Transit System	18.6m	2004
Meridian	MAN A22	City Bus	12m	2007
Pulsar	VDL SB200	City Bus	11.3m	2007
StreetCar RTV	Wright/Hess	Hybrid Drive	Mass Transit System	18.6m
Electrocity HPD	W /SB 220 powered by Hydrogen Fuel Cell	City Bus	11.8m	2009

Reminiscences on 60 years of coachbuilding in Ballymena

People

Reminiscences on 60 years of coachbuilding in Ballymena

Products